Giacomo Bevilacqua

THE SOUND OF THE WORLD BY HEART

WRITTEN AND ILLUSTRATED BY
GIACOMO BEVILACQUA

LOCALIZATION AND EDITING BY MIKE KENNEDY

THE SOUND OF THE WORLD BY HEART
2017. FIRST PRINTING
ISBN: 978-1-941302-38- 5

PUBLISHED AS PART OF
THE MAGNETIC COLLECTION
BY
THE LION FORGE, LLC
6600 MANCHESTER AVE.
ST. LOUIS, MO 63139

Names: Bevilacqua, Giacomo, 1983- author, illustrator. | Kennedy, Mike (Graphic novelist), editor.
Title: The sound of the world by heart / written and illustrated by Giacomo Bevilacqua ; localization and editing by Mike Kennedy.
Other Titles: Suono del mondo a memoria. English
Description: English language edition. | St. Louis, MO : The Lion Forge, LLC, 2017. | Translation of: Il suono del mondo a memoria. | "Published as part of the Magnetic Collection ... "--Title page verso.
Identifiers: ISBN 978-1-941302-38-5
Subjects: LCSH: Photojournalists--New York (State)--New York--Comic books, strips, etc. | Social isolation-- New York (State)--New York--Comic books, strips, etc. | Self-realization--Comic books, strips, etc. | Soul mates--Comic books, strips, etc. | New York (N.Y.)--Comic books, strips, etc. | LCGFT: Graphic novels.
Classification: LCC PN6767.B48 S8613 2017 | DDC 741.5973 [Fic]--dc23

WWW.LIONFORGE.COM

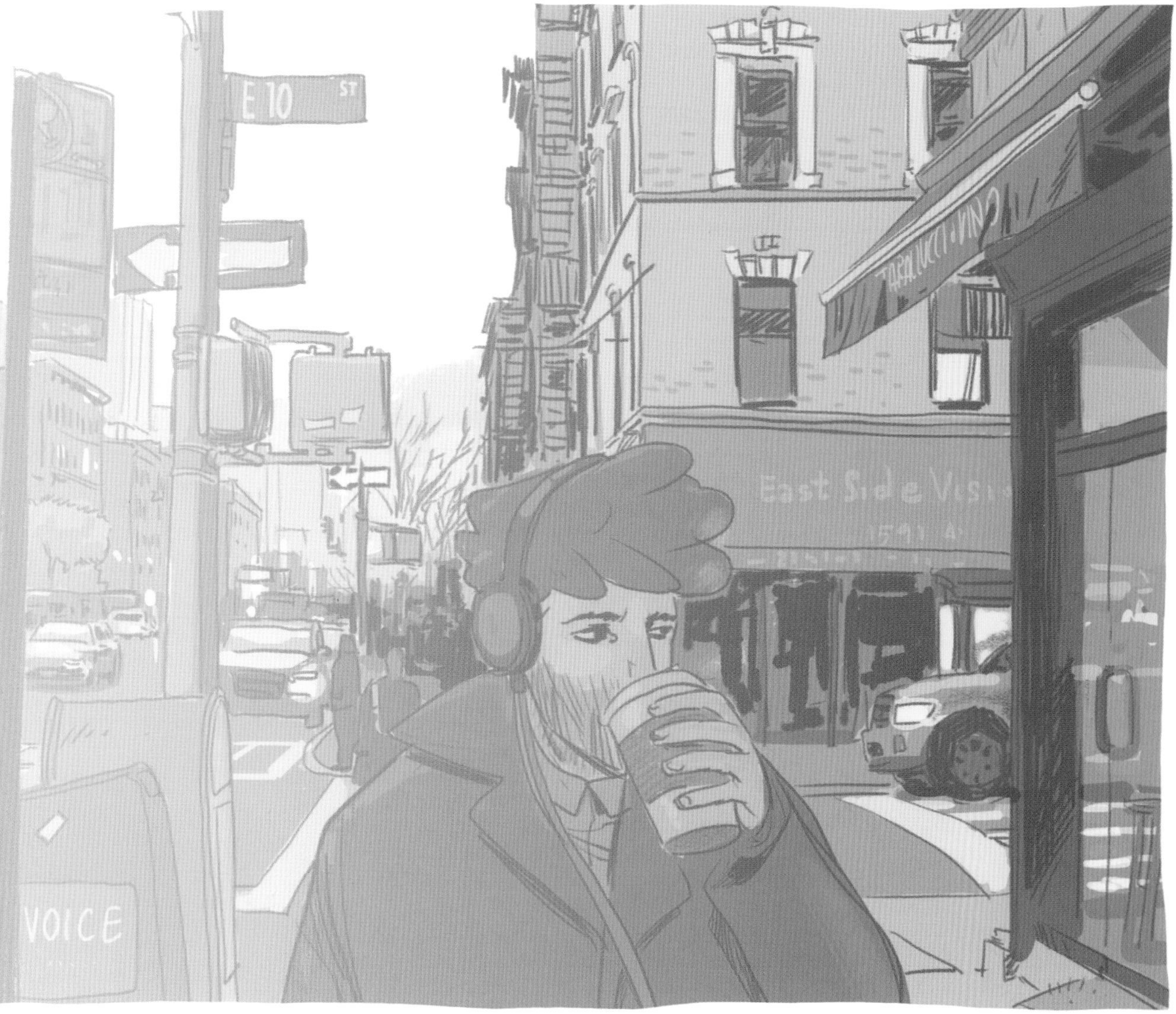
E 10 ST
TARALUCCI • VINO
VOICE

WITHOUT YOU
I WOULDN'T HAVE LIVED IN NEW YORK,
I WOULDN'T HAVE FOUND THE WORDS,
I WOULDN'T HAVE WRITTEN THIS BOOK,
I WOULDN'T HAVE STARTED STUDYING AGAIN,
I WOULDN'T HAVE DEFEATED MY FRUSTRATION,
I WOULDN'T HAVE DISCOVERED THE COLORS,
I WOULDN'T HAVE ASKED ANYONE
TO MARRY ME
AND NO ONE WOULD HAVE ANSWERED:

"YES! BUT LET'S KEEP IT OUR LITTLE SECRET, OKAY?
DON'T GO TELLING EVERYONE LIKE YOU ALWAYS DO."

SO THIS BOOK IS FOR YOU,
BECAUSE IF IT WEREN'T FOR YOU,
FROM MY WINDOW,
I WOULD STILL SEE THE WORLD IN BLACK AND WHITE.

MANHATTANHENGE
ASTOR PLACE
JULY 12TH, 2013
8:22 PM

NOVEMBER 15TH

NOVEMBER

MON	TUE	WED	THU	FRI	SAT	SUN
			1 ✕	2 ✕	3 ✕	4 ✕
5 ✕	6 ✕	7 ✕	8 ✕	9 ✕	10 ✕	11 ✕
12 ✕	13 ✕	14 ✕	15	16	17	18
19	20	21	22	23	24	25
26	27	28	29	30		

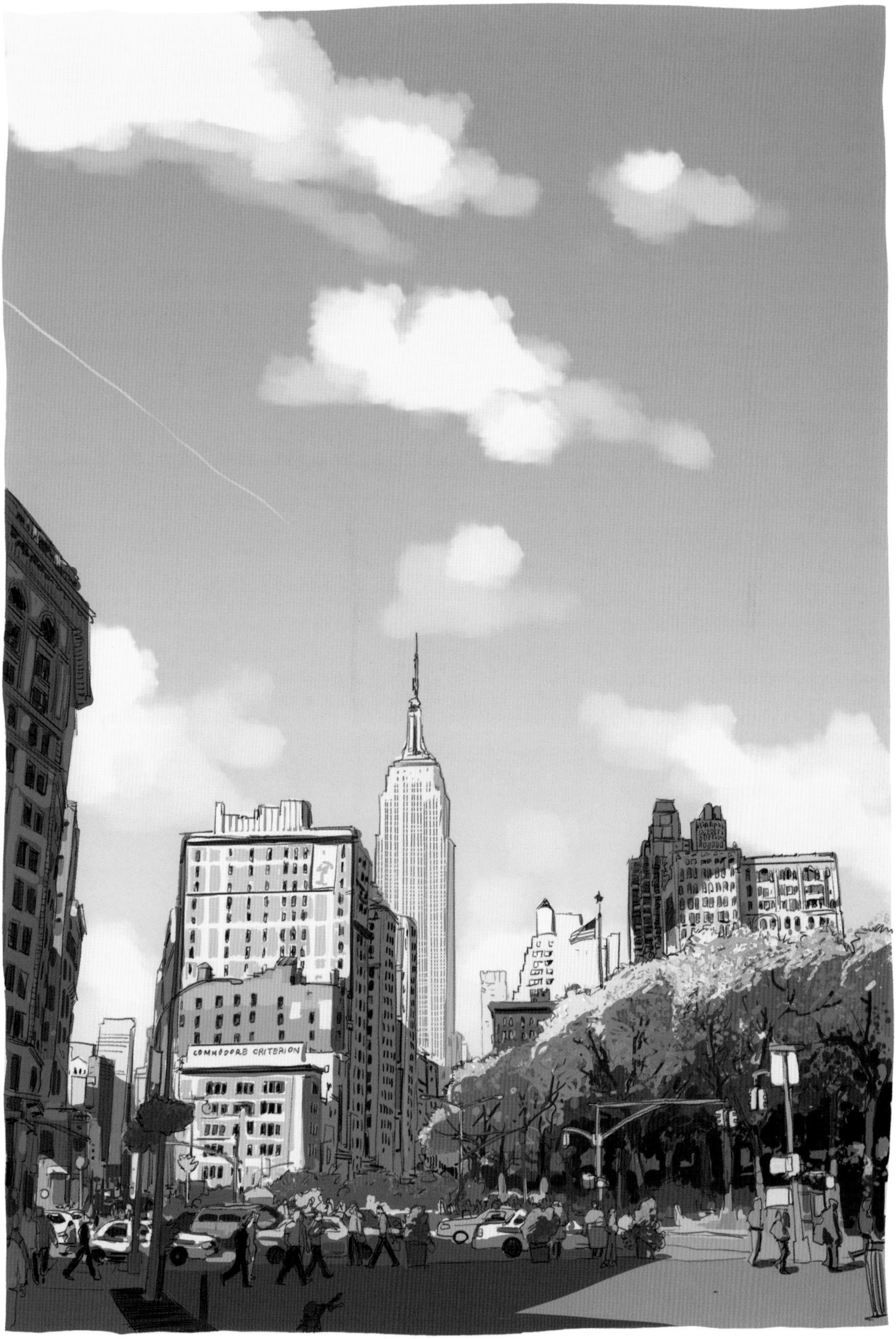
COMMODORE CRITERION

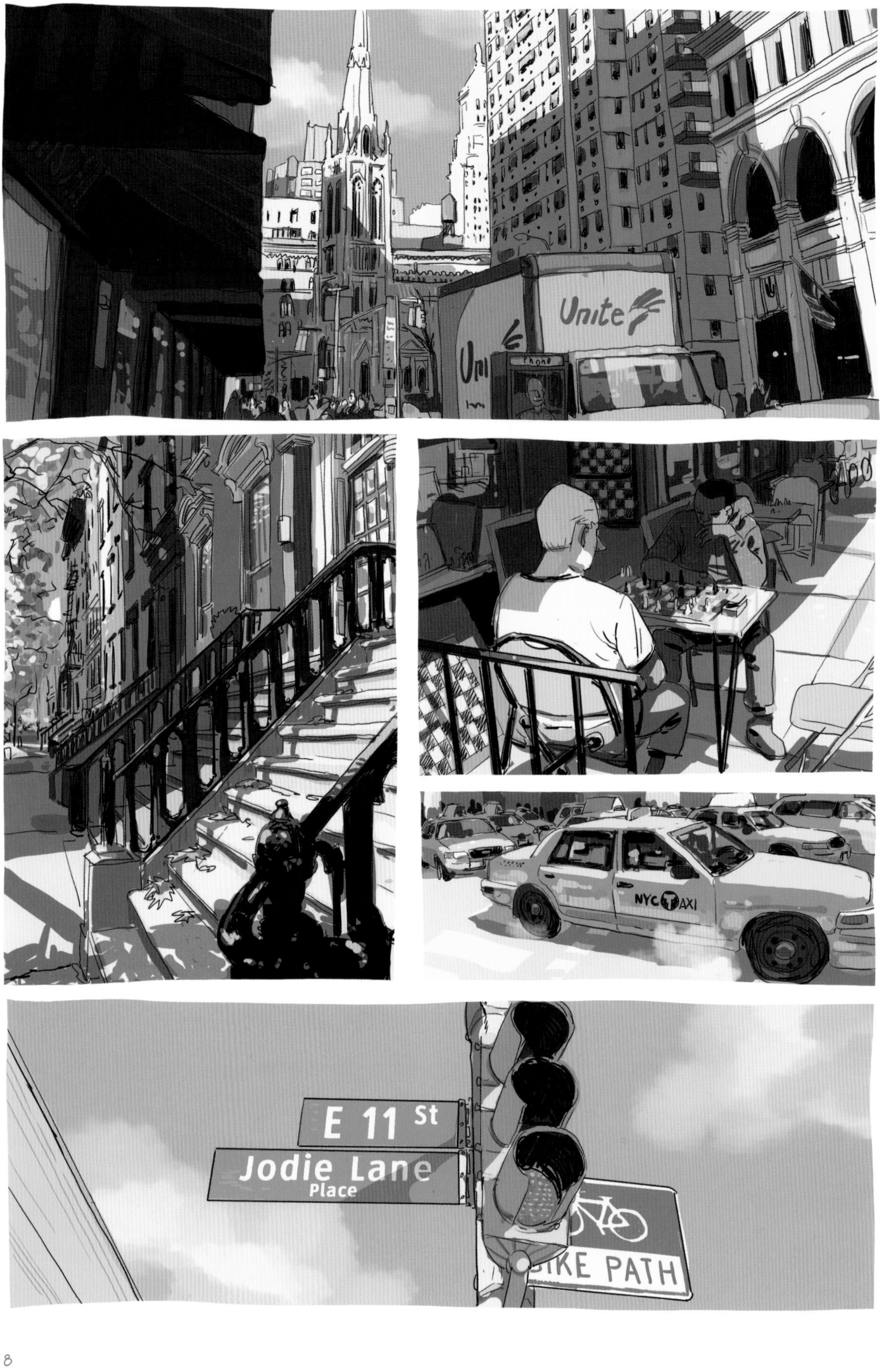
Unite
Phone
NYC TAXI
E 11 St
Jodie Lane
Place
BIKE PATH

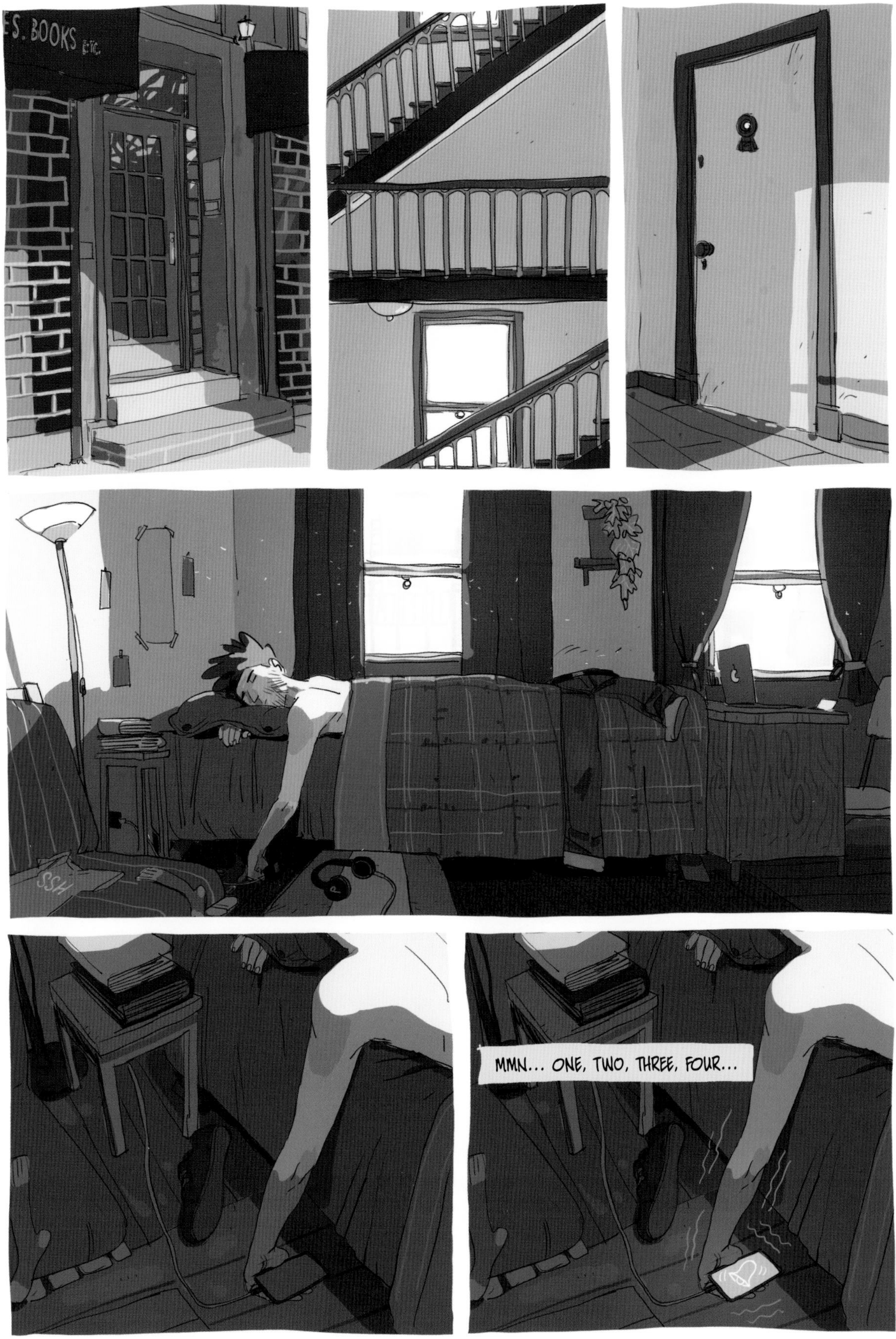

E S. BOOKS Etc.
SSH
MMN... ONE, TWO, THREE, FOUR...

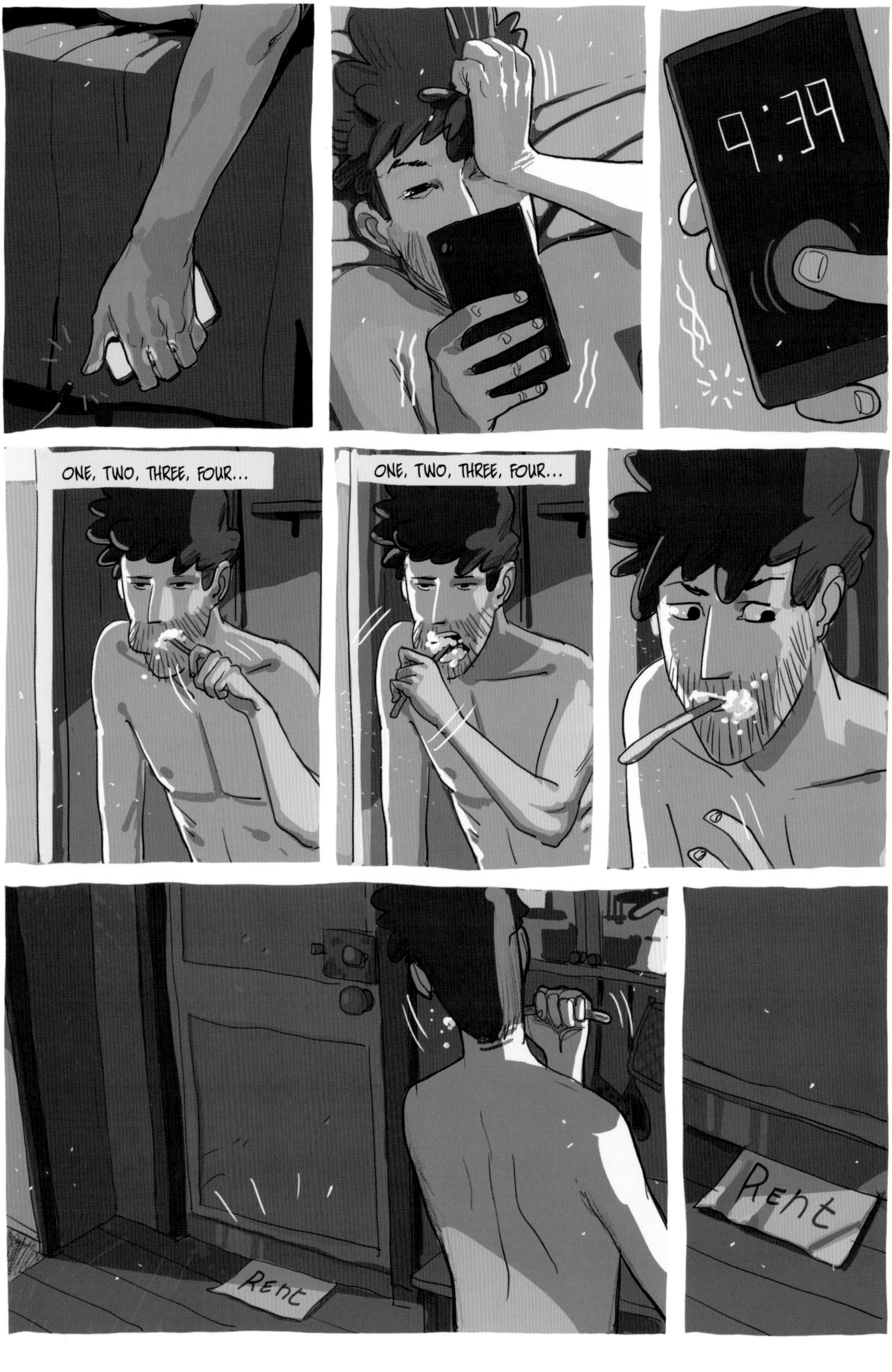
9:39
ONE, TWO, THREE, FOUR...
ONE, TWO, THREE, FOUR...
Rent
Rent

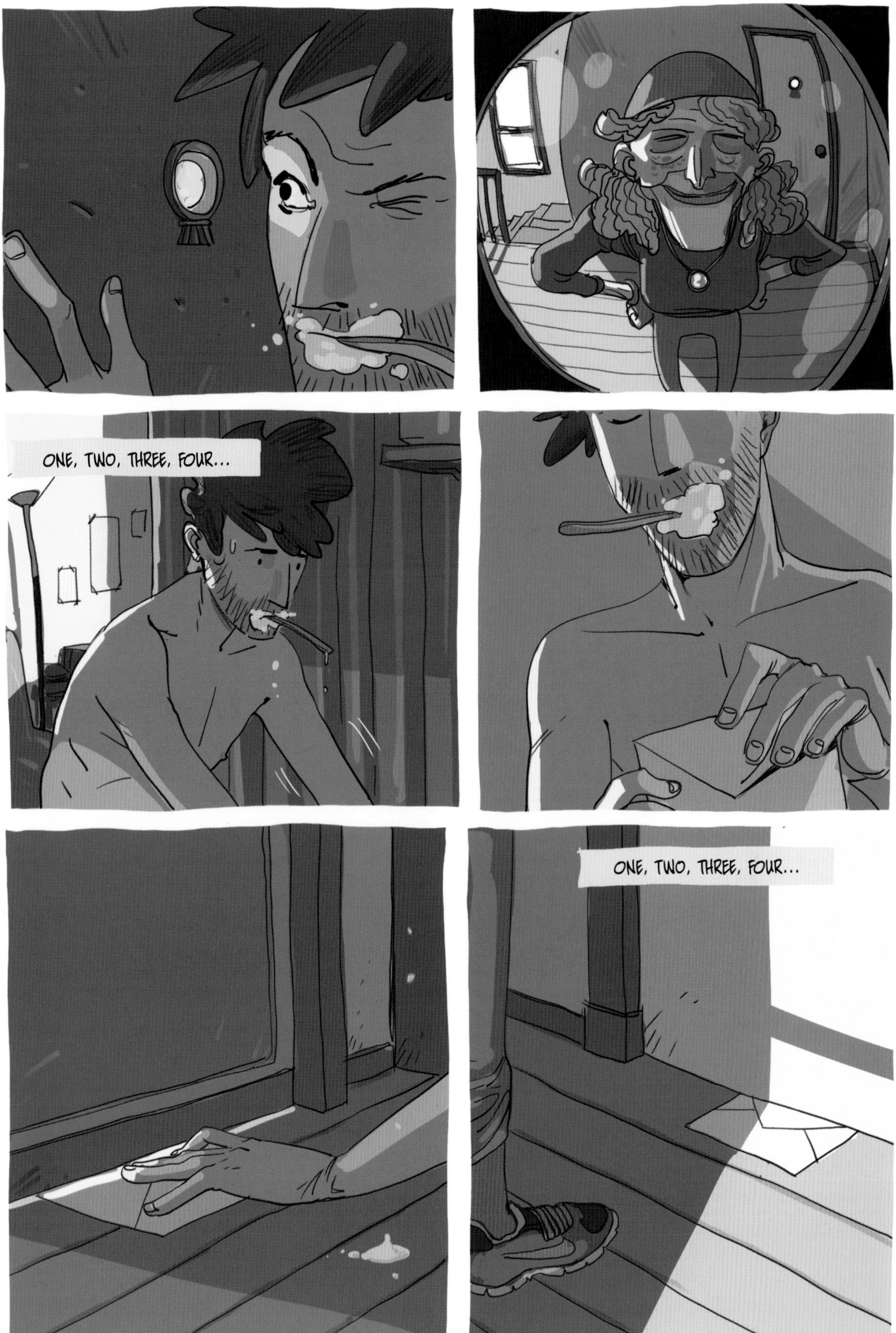
ONE, TWO, THREE, FOUR...
ONE, TWO, THREE, FOUR...

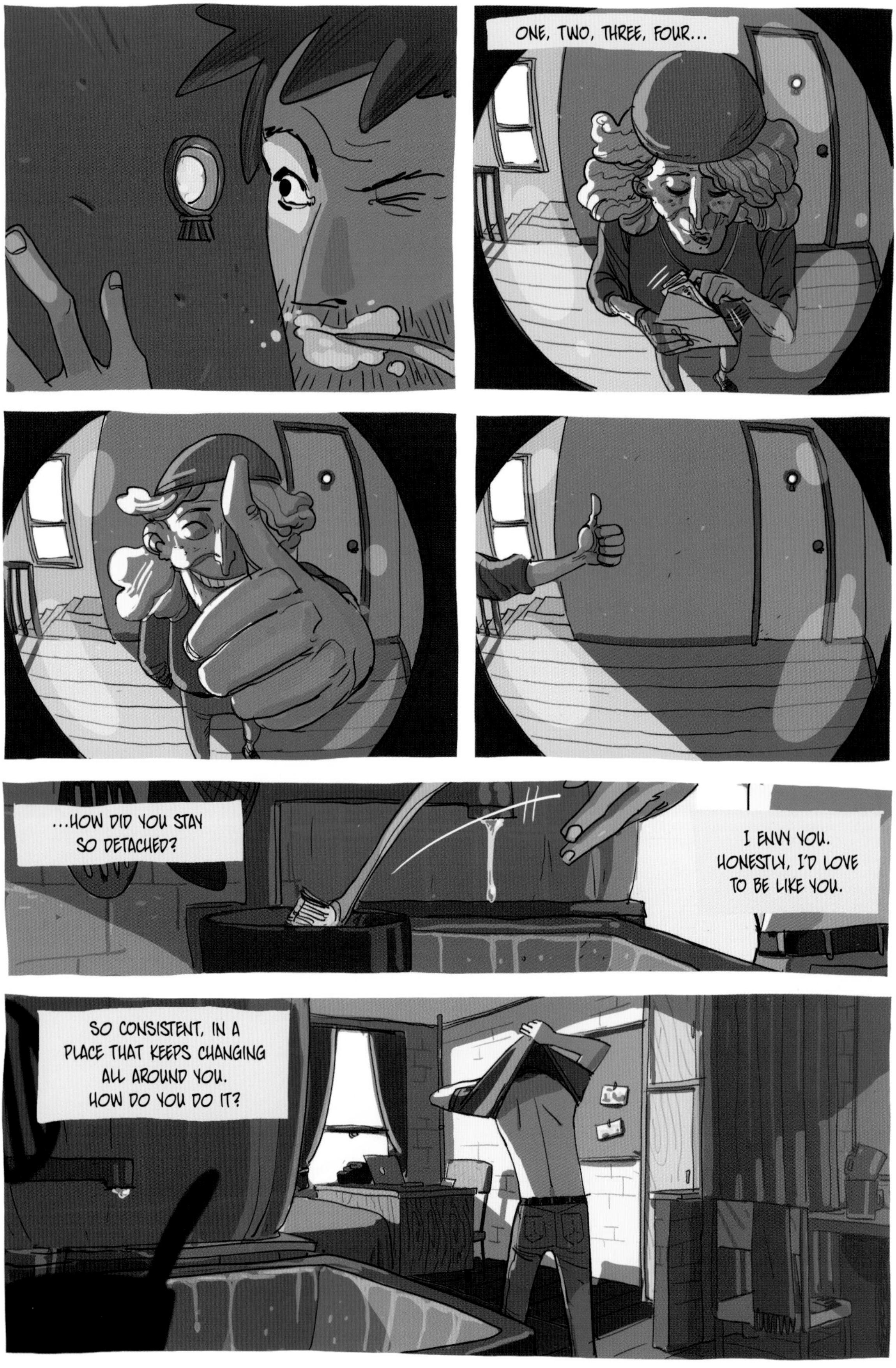
ONE, TWO, THREE, FOUR...
...HOW DID YOU STAY SO DETACHED?
I ENVY YOU. HONESTLY, I'D LOVE TO BE LIKE YOU.
SO CONSISTENT, IN A PLACE THAT KEEPS CHANGING ALL AROUND YOU. HOW DO YOU DO IT?

ONE DAY THEY TELL YOU THEY'RE GONNA FLIP THAT RENT-CONTROLLED SHIT-HOLE YOU'VE CALLED "HOME" FOR SO LONG...

...INTO A $6K PER MONTH LUXURY APARTMENT

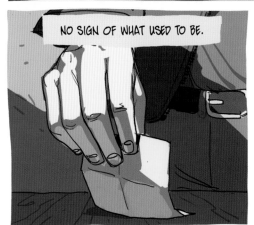

THEN YOU'LL GO TO YOUR FAVORITE RESTAURANT...

... AND IT WON'T BE THERE ANYMORE.

NO SIGN OF WHAT USED TO BE.

REPLACED BY SOMETHING NEWER, BIGGER...

"BETTER."

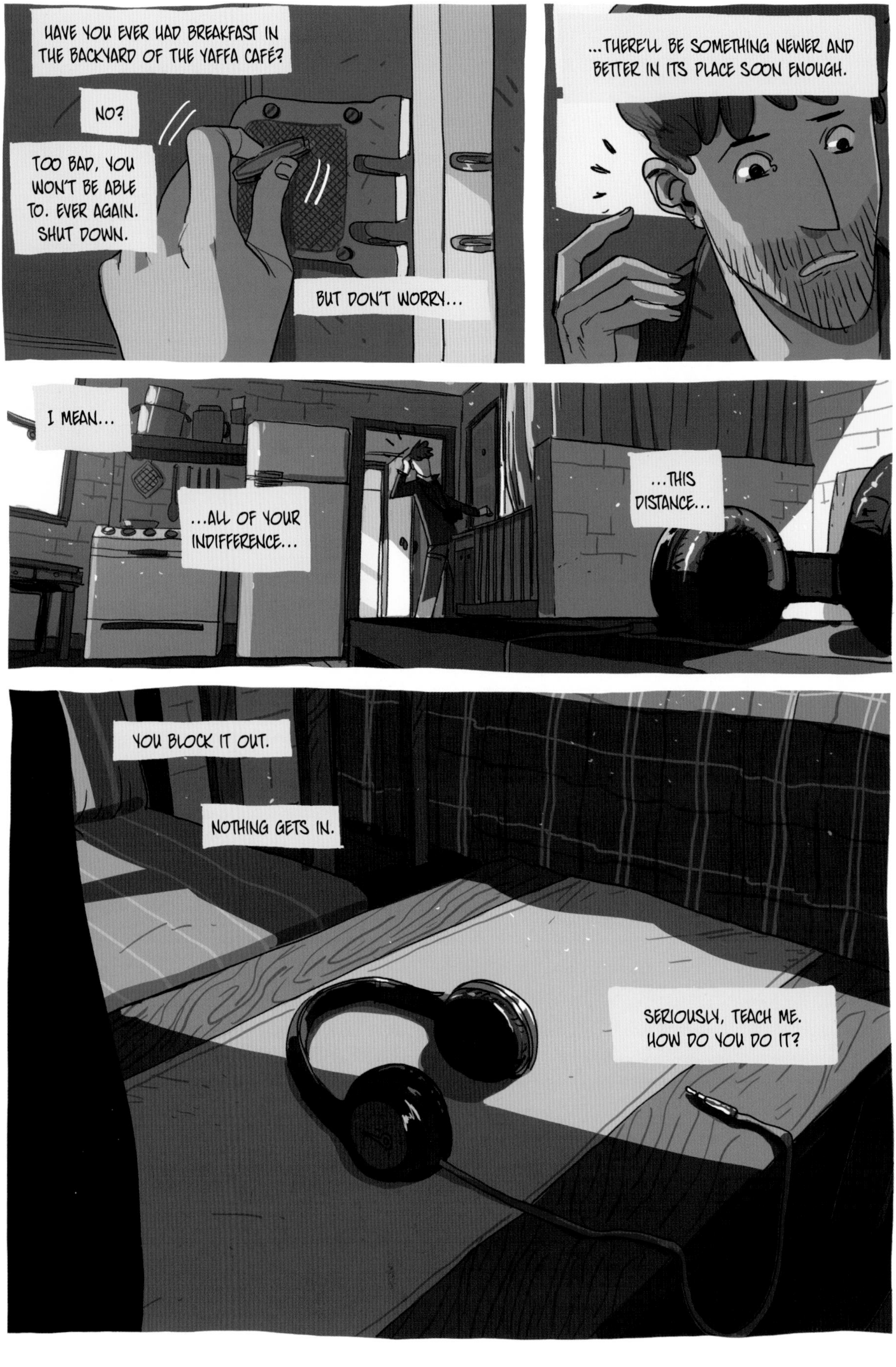
HAVE YOU EVER HAD BREAKFAST IN THE BACKYARD OF THE YAFFA CAFÉ?
NO?
TOO BAD, YOU WON'T BE ABLE TO. EVER AGAIN. SHUT DOWN.
BUT DON'T WORRY...
...THERE'LL BE SOMETHING NEWER AND BETTER IN ITS PLACE SOON ENOUGH.
I MEAN...
...ALL OF YOUR INDIFFERENCE...
...THIS DISTANCE...
YOU BLOCK IT OUT.
NOTHING GETS IN.
SERIOUSLY, TEACH ME. HOW DO YOU DO IT?

A COLD MASK.

ATTRACTIVE, EVEN.

BUT CLOSED OFF.

14° New York

THU	FRI	SAT	SUN	MON
14	14	13	12	11
10	10	9	9	8

NO ONE GETS IN.

THE ONLY ONES INSIDE ARE GHOSTS AND MEMORIES.

I'M CURIOUS --

-- WHAT'S YOUR EARLIEST MEMORY?

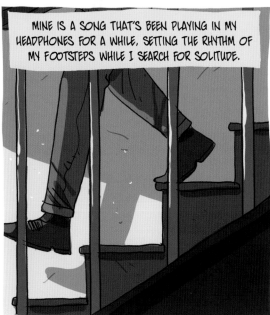

MINE IS A SONG THAT'S BEEN PLAYING IN MY HEADPHONES FOR A WHILE, SETTING THE RHYTHM OF MY FOOTSTEPS WHILE I SEARCH FOR SOLITUDE.

ONE, TWO, THREE, FOUR...

ONE, TWO, THREE, FOUR...

15

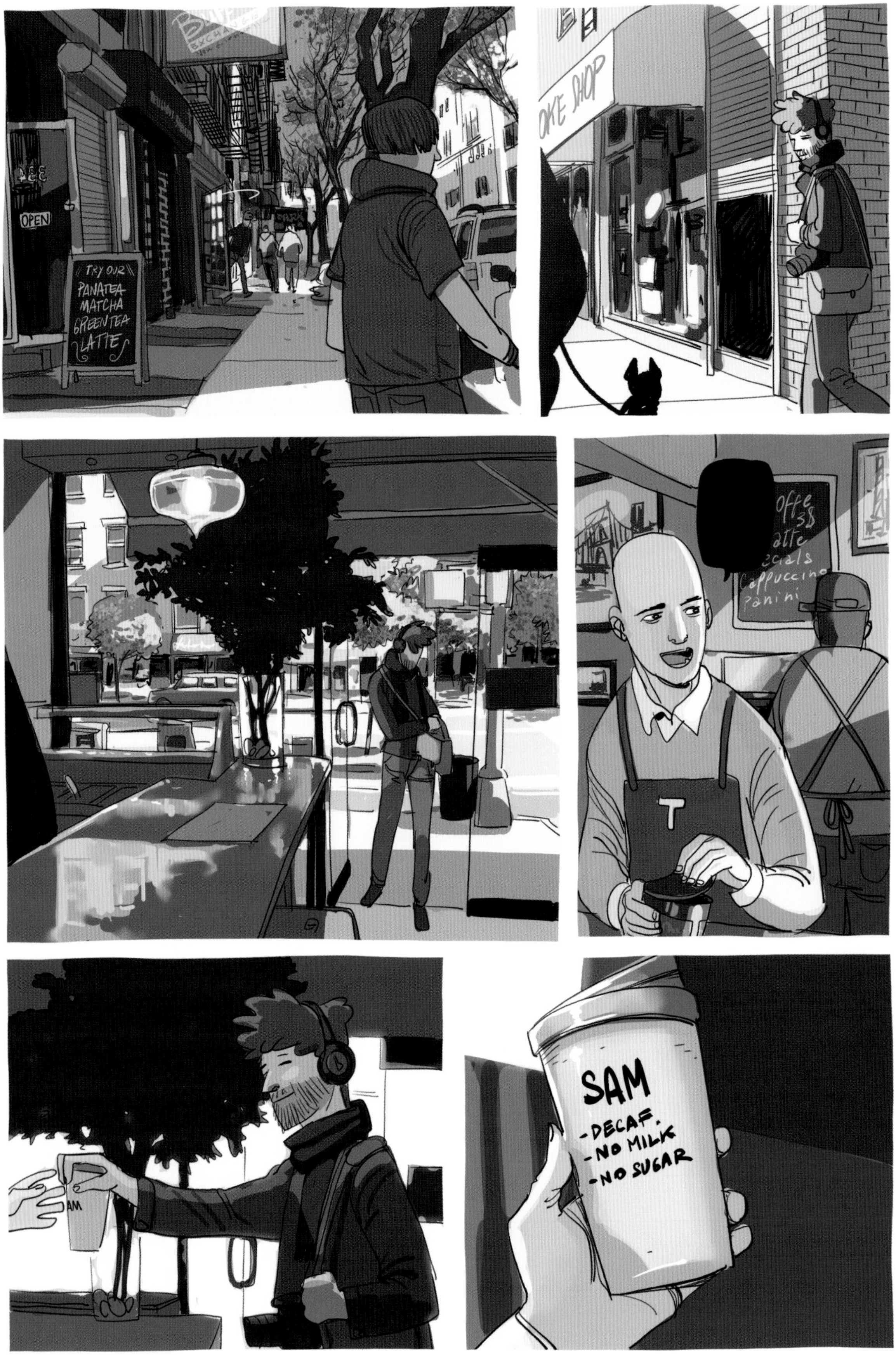
OPEN
TRY OUR
PANATEA
MATCHA
GREENTEA
LATTE
OKE SHOP
offe
atte
ecials
cappuccino
panini
SAM
SAM
-DECAF.
-NO MILK
-NO SUGAR

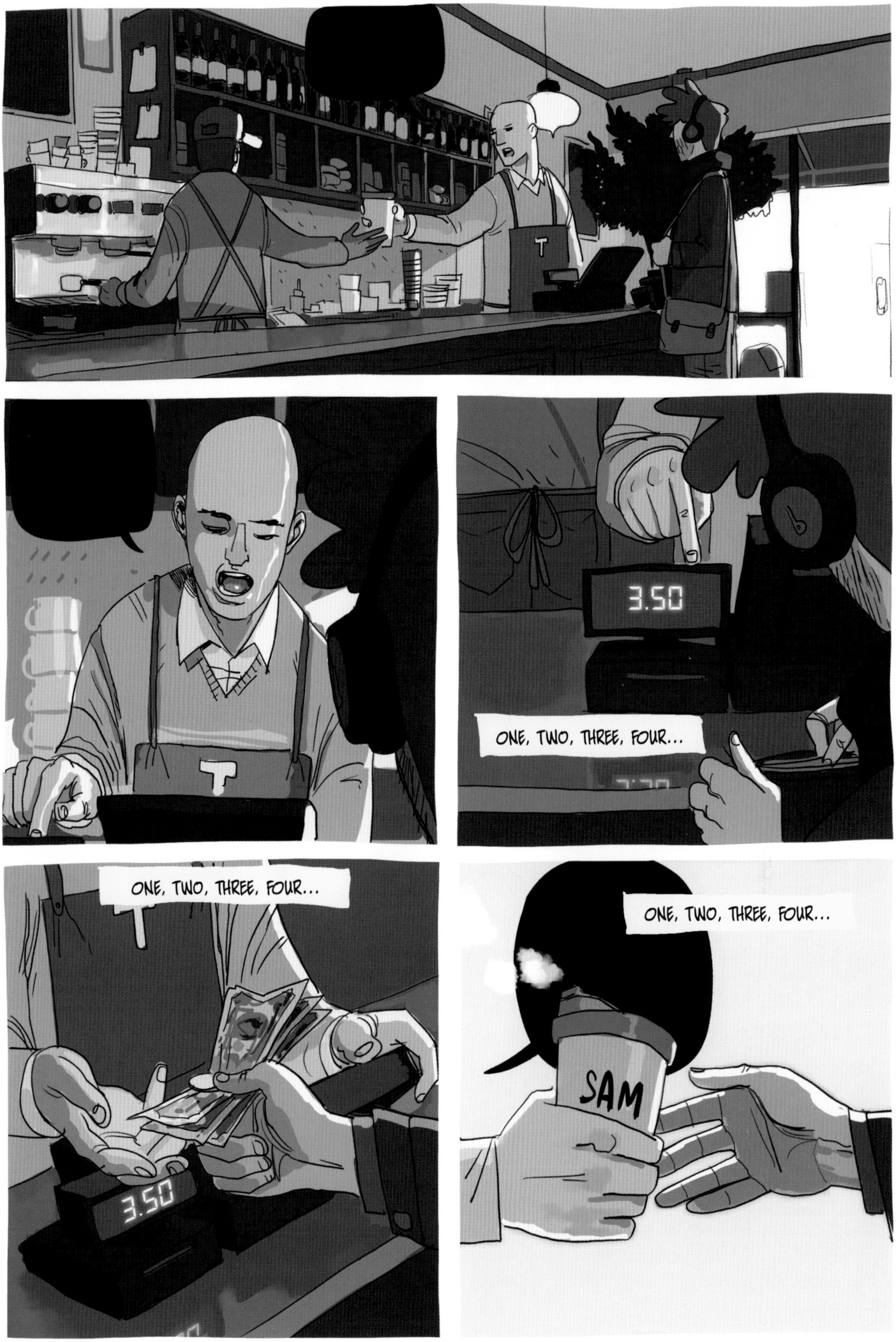
3.50
ONE, TWO, THREE, FOUR...
ONE, TWO, THREE, FOUR...
3.50
ONE, TWO, THREE, FOUR...
SAM

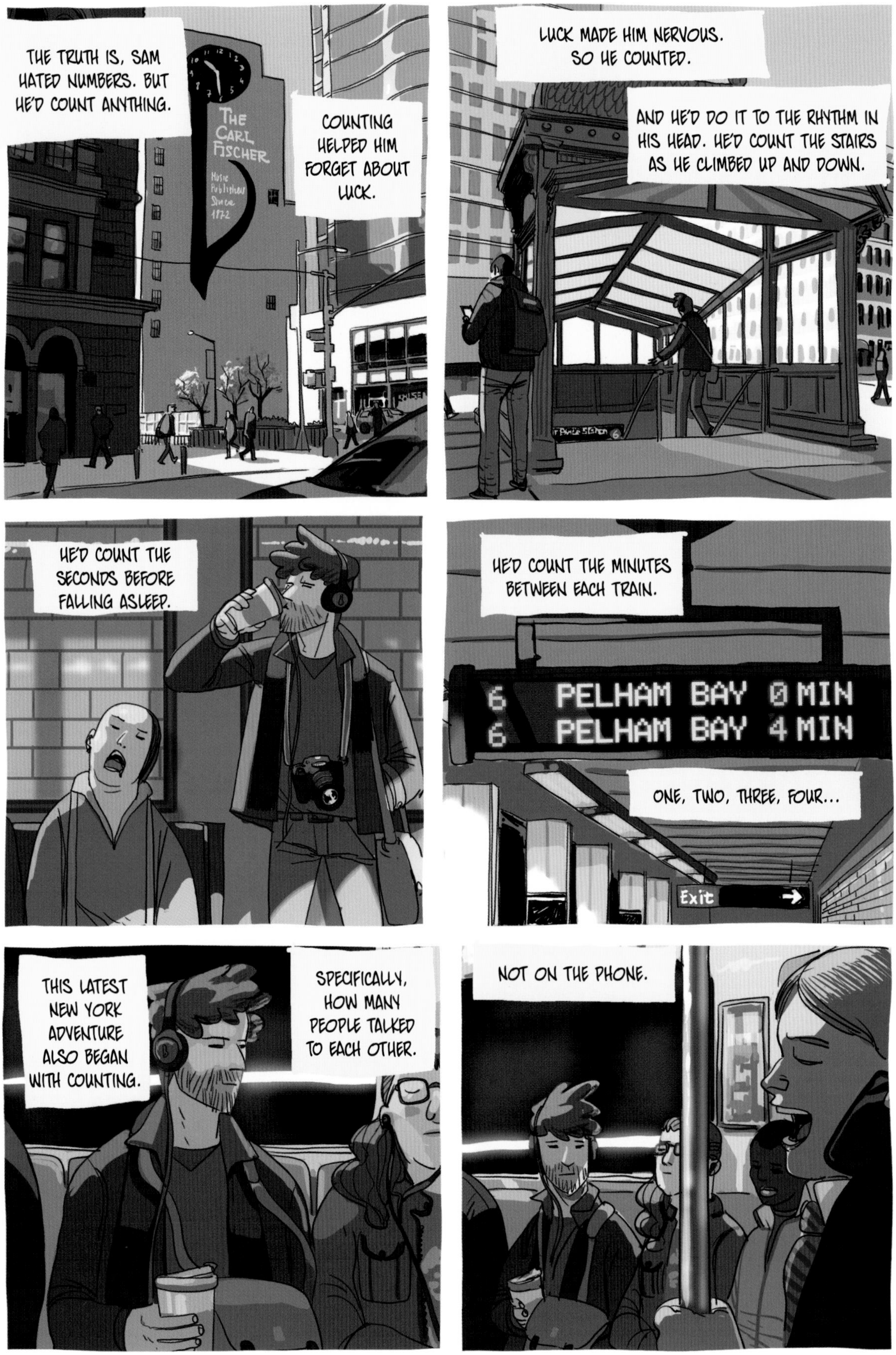
THE TRUTH IS, SAM HATED NUMBERS. BUT HE'D COUNT ANYTHING.
THE CARL FISCHER
COUNTING HELPED HIM FORGET ABOUT LUCK.
LUCK MADE HIM NERVOUS. SO HE COUNTED.
AND HE'D DO IT TO THE RHYTHM IN HIS HEAD. HE'D COUNT THE STAIRS AS HE CLIMBED UP AND DOWN.
HE'D COUNT THE SECONDS BEFORE FALLING ASLEEP.
HE'D COUNT THE MINUTES BETWEEN EACH TRAIN.
6 PELHAM BAY 0 MIN
6 PELHAM BAY 4 MIN
ONE, TWO, THREE, FOUR...
Exit
THIS LATEST NEW YORK ADVENTURE ALSO BEGAN WITH COUNTING.
SPECIFICALLY, HOW MANY PEOPLE TALKED TO EACH OTHER.
NOT ON THE PHONE.

NOT BY TEXT.

NOT BY EMAIL.

OR ANY OTHER SOCIAL NETWORK.

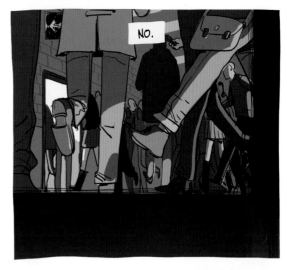

NO.

I MEAN, TALK TO EACH OTHER. ON THE STREET.

Union Square   Subway

IN CAFÉS.

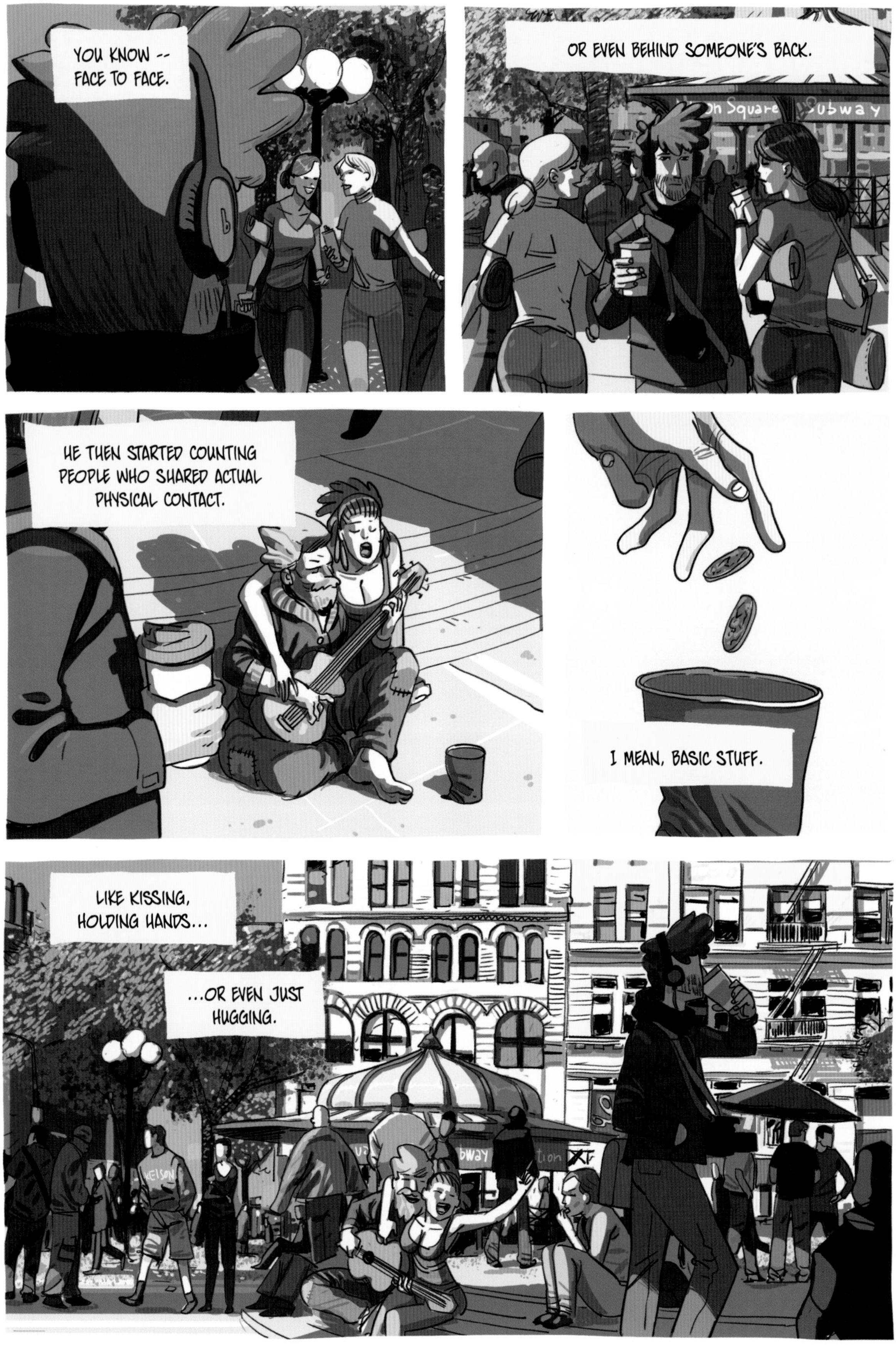
YOU KNOW --
FACE TO FACE.
OR EVEN BEHIND SOMEONE'S BACK.
HE THEN STARTED COUNTING
PEOPLE WHO SHARED ACTUAL
PHYSICAL CONTACT.
I MEAN, BASIC STUFF.
LIKE KISSING,
HOLDING HANDS...
...OR EVEN JUST
HUGGING.

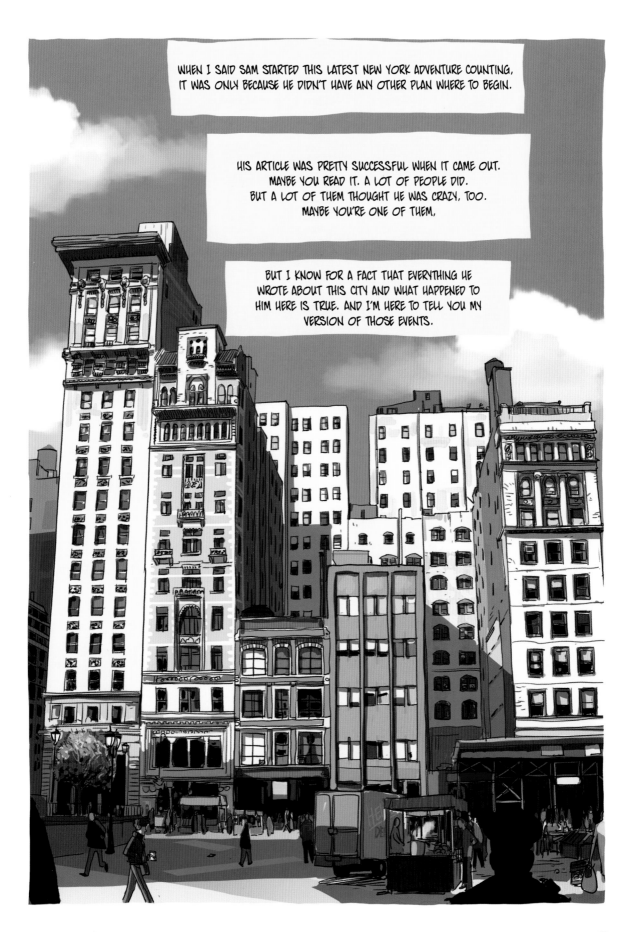

WHEN I SAID SAM STARTED THIS LATEST NEW YORK ADVENTURE COUNTING, IT WAS ONLY BECAUSE HE DIDN'T HAVE ANY OTHER PLAN WHERE TO BEGIN.

HIS ARTICLE WAS PRETTY SUCCESSFUL WHEN IT CAME OUT. MAYBE YOU READ IT. A LOT OF PEOPLE DID. BUT A LOT OF THEM THOUGHT HE WAS CRAZY, TOO. MAYBE YOU'RE ONE OF THEM,

BUT I KNOW FOR A FACT THAT EVERYTHING HE WROTE ABOUT THIS CITY AND WHAT HAPPENED TO HIM HERE IS TRUE. AND I'M HERE TO TELL YOU MY VERSION OF THOSE EVENTS.

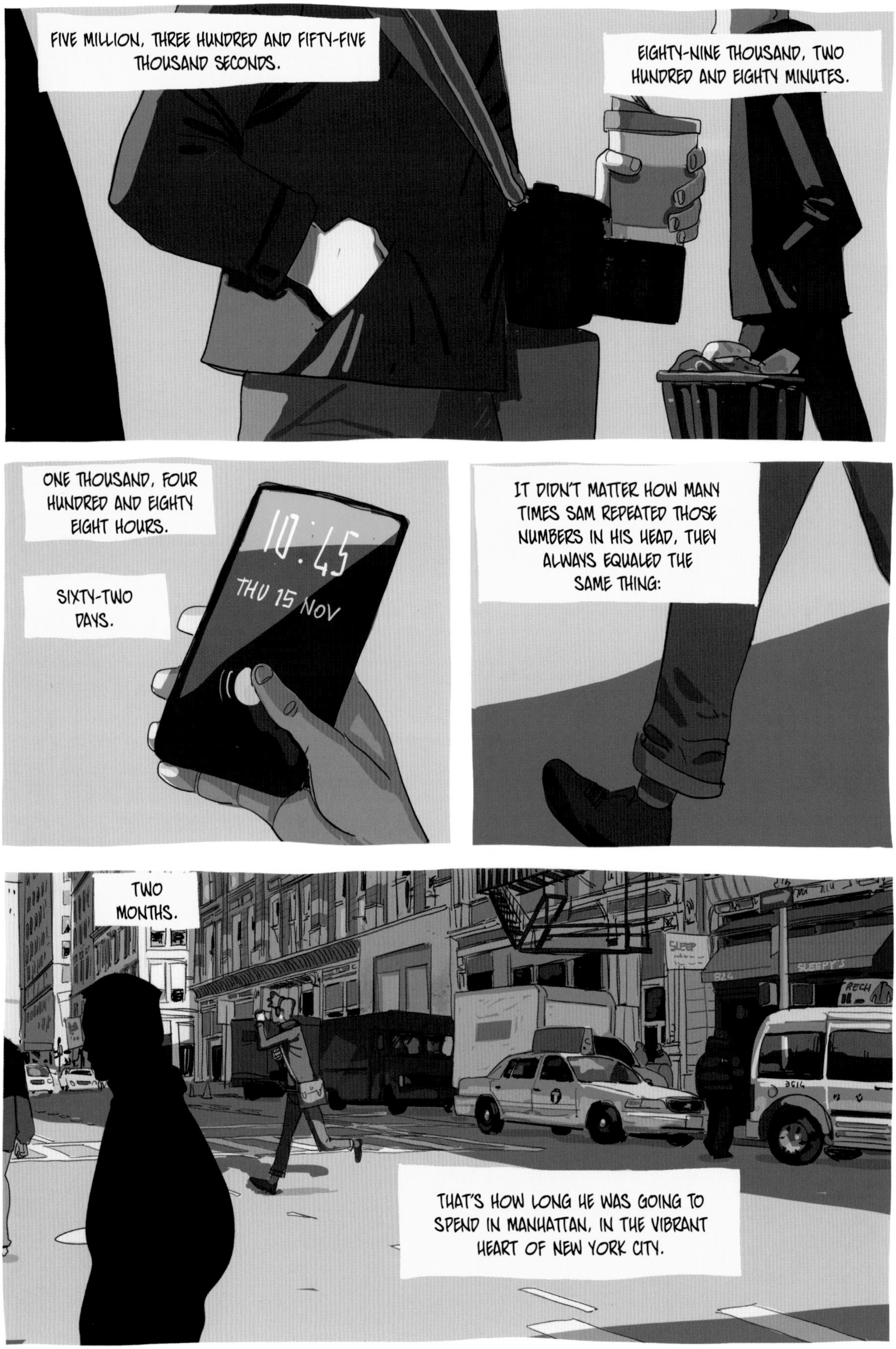
FIVE MILLION, THREE HUNDRED AND FIFTY-FIVE THOUSAND SECONDS.
EIGHTY-NINE THOUSAND, TWO HUNDRED AND EIGHTY MINUTES.
ONE THOUSAND, FOUR HUNDRED AND EIGHTY EIGHT HOURS.
10:45
THU 15 NOV
SIXTY-TWO DAYS.
IT DIDN'T MATTER HOW MANY TIMES SAM REPEATED THOSE NUMBERS IN HIS HEAD, THEY ALWAYS EQUALED THE SAME THING:
TWO MONTHS.
THAT'S HOW LONG HE WAS GOING TO SPEND IN MANHATTAN, IN THE VIBRANT HEART OF NEW YORK CITY.

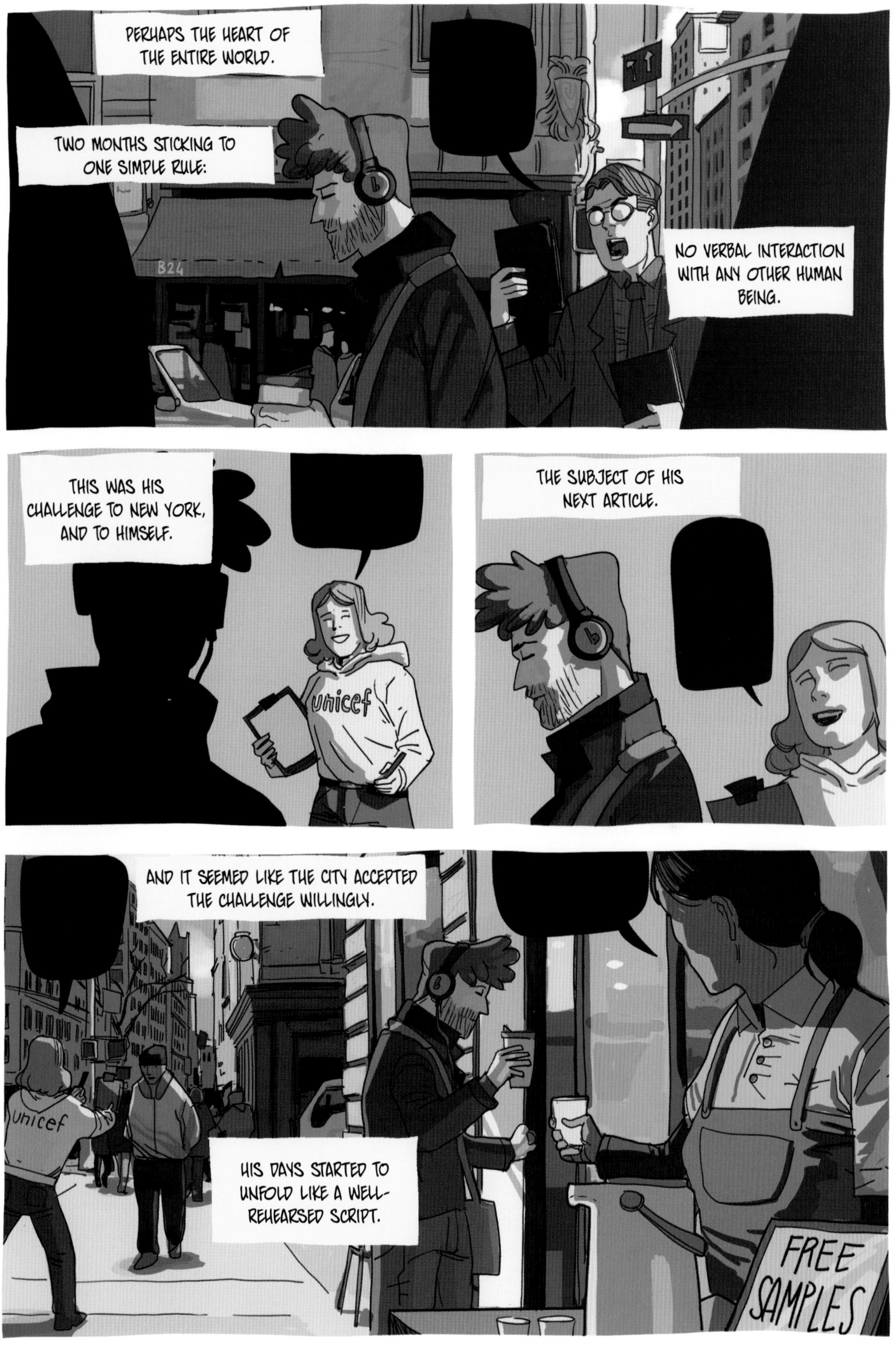
PERHAPS THE HEART OF THE ENTIRE WORLD.
TWO MONTHS STICKING TO ONE SIMPLE RULE:
NO VERBAL INTERACTION WITH ANY OTHER HUMAN BEING.
B24
THIS WAS HIS CHALLENGE TO NEW YORK, AND TO HIMSELF.
unicef
THE SUBJECT OF HIS NEXT ARTICLE.
AND IT SEEMED LIKE THE CITY ACCEPTED THE CHALLENGE WILLINGLY.
unicef
HIS DAYS STARTED TO UNFOLD LIKE A WELL-REHEARSED SCRIPT.
FREE SAMPLES

AT LEAST UNTIL
THURSDAY, NOVEMBER
15TH...

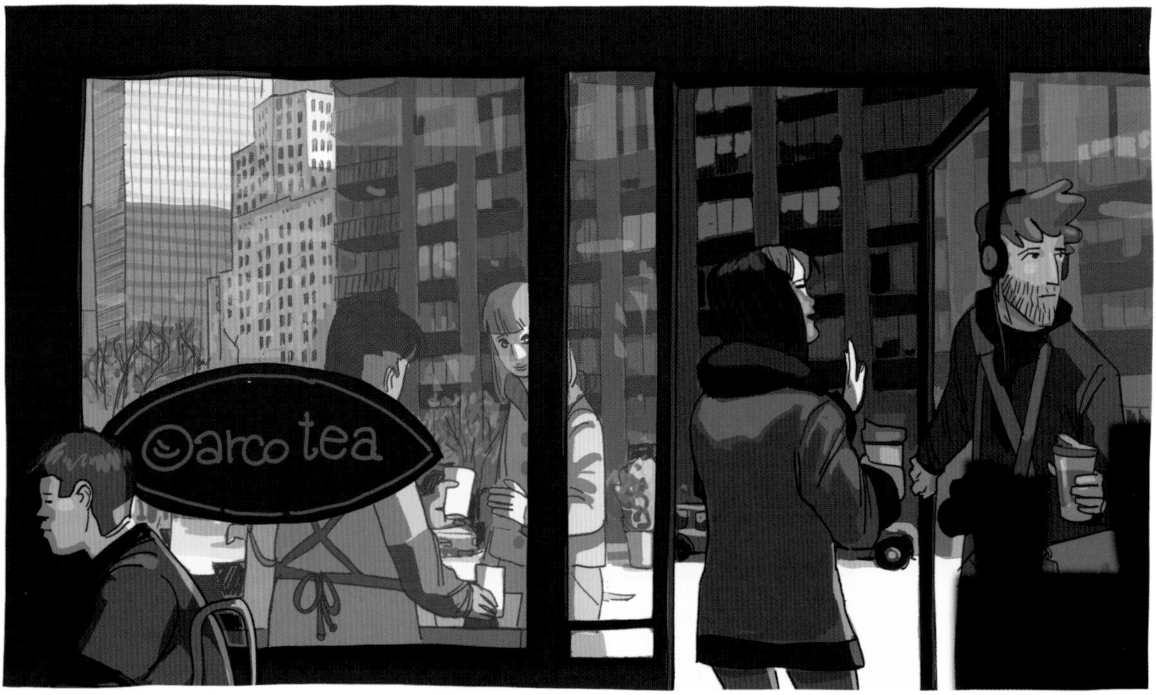
arco tea

...A MONTH AFTER HIS ARRIVAL,
AT WHICH POINT EVERYTHING CHANGED...

...BUT LET'S START FROM
THE TOP.

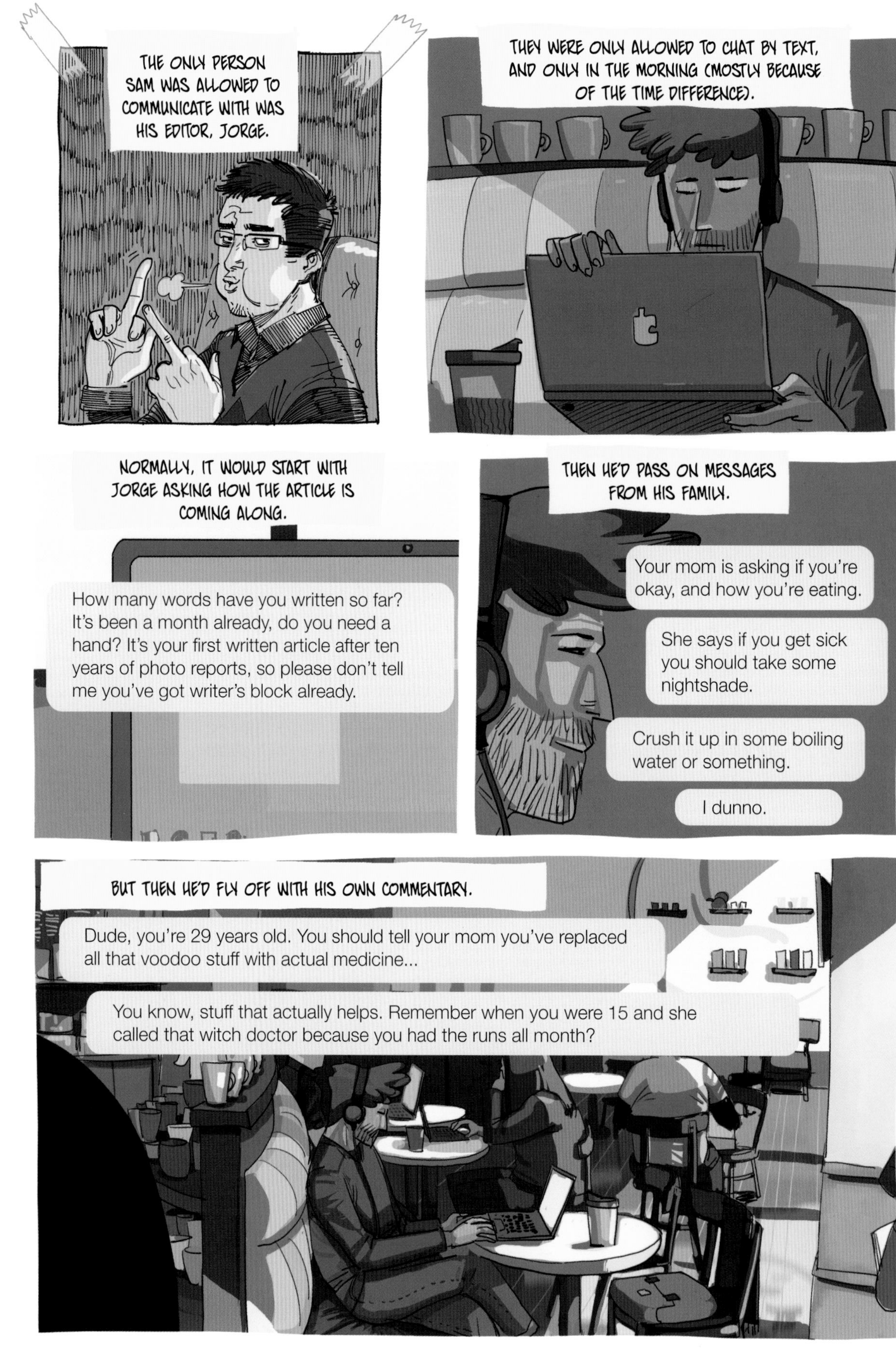
THE ONLY PERSON SAM WAS ALLOWED TO COMMUNICATE WITH WAS HIS EDITOR, JORGE.
THEY WERE ONLY ALLOWED TO CHAT BY TEXT, AND ONLY IN THE MORNING (MOSTLY BECAUSE OF THE TIME DIFFERENCE).
NORMALLY, IT WOULD START WITH JORGE ASKING HOW THE ARTICLE IS COMING ALONG.
How many words have you written so far? It's been a month already, do you need a hand? It's your first written article after ten years of photo reports, so please don't tell me you've got writer's block already.
THEN HE'D PASS ON MESSAGES FROM HIS FAMILY.
Your mom is asking if you're okay, and how you're eating.
She says if you get sick you should take some nightshade.
Crush it up in some boiling water or something.
I dunno.
BUT THEN HE'D FLY OFF WITH HIS OWN COMMENTARY.
Dude, you're 29 years old. You should tell your mom you've replaced all that voodoo stuff with actual medicine...
You know, stuff that actually helps. Remember when you were 15 and she called that witch doctor because you had the runs all month?

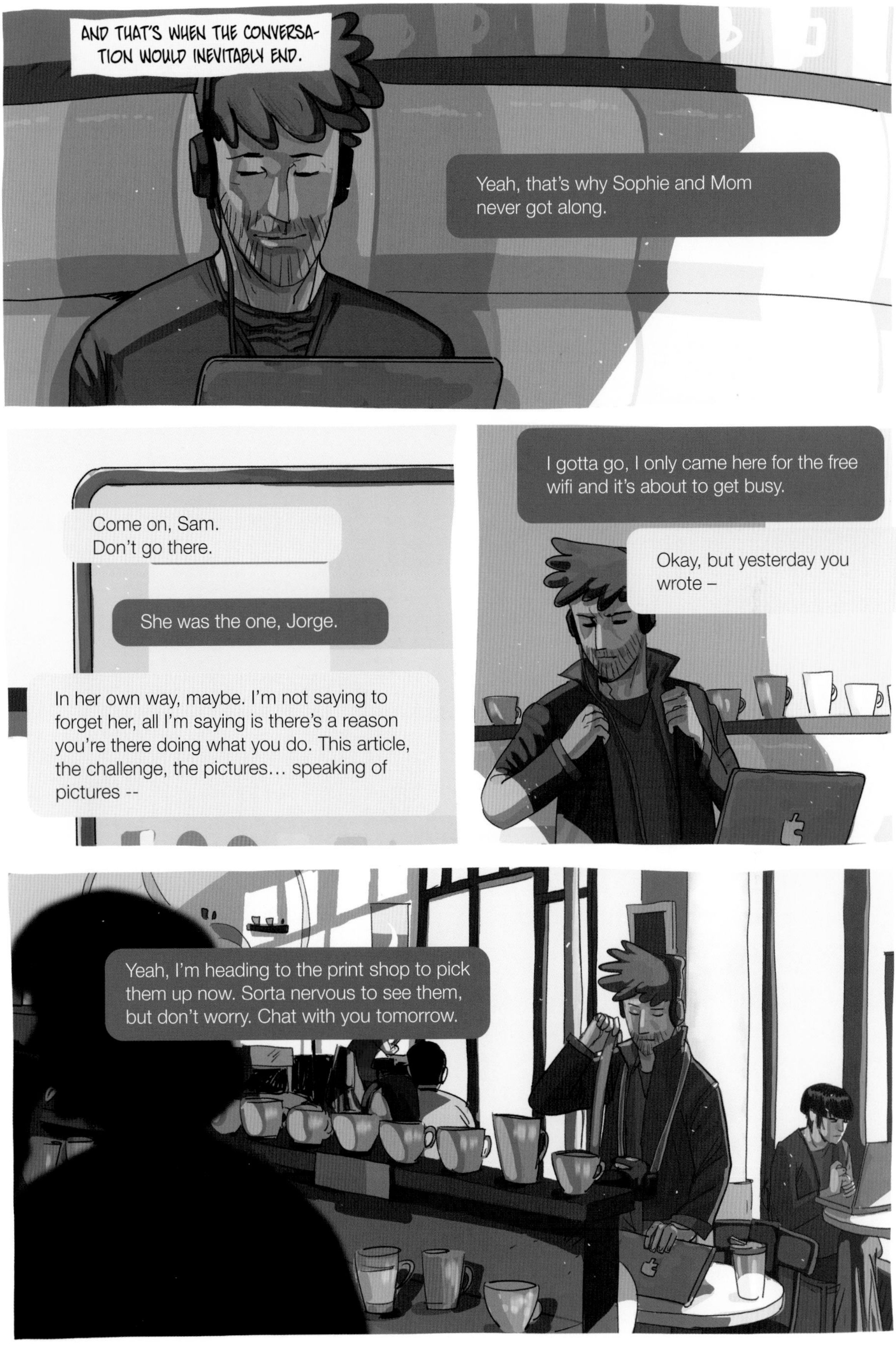
AND THAT'S WHEN THE CONVERSATION WOULD INEVITABLY END.
Yeah, that's why Sophie and Mom never got along.
Come on, Sam. Don't go there.
She was the one, Jorge.
In her own way, maybe. I'm not saying to forget her, all I'm saying is there's a reason you're there doing what you do. This article, the challenge, the pictures… speaking of pictures --
I gotta go, I only came here for the free wifi and it's about to get busy.
Okay, but yesterday you wrote –
Yeah, I'm heading to the print shop to pick them up now. Sorta nervous to see them, but don't worry. Chat with you tomorrow.

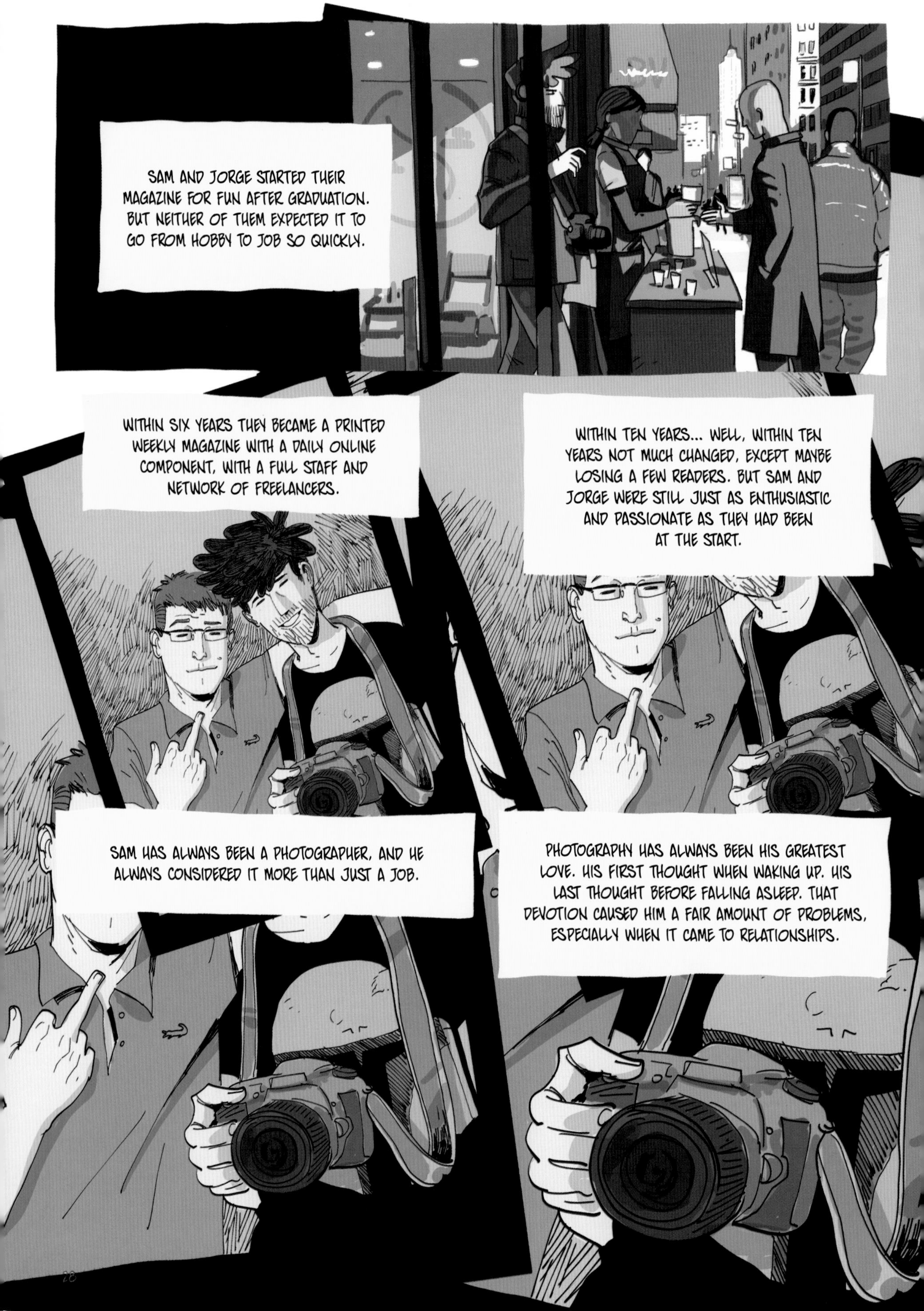
SAM AND JORGE STARTED THEIR MAGAZINE FOR FUN AFTER GRADUATION. BUT NEITHER OF THEM EXPECTED IT TO GO FROM HOBBY TO JOB SO QUICKLY.
WITHIN SIX YEARS THEY BECAME A PRINTED WEEKLY MAGAZINE WITH A DAILY ONLINE COMPONENT, WITH A FULL STAFF AND NETWORK OF FREELANCERS.
WITHIN TEN YEARS... WELL, WITHIN TEN YEARS NOT MUCH CHANGED, EXCEPT MAYBE LOSING A FEW READERS. BUT SAM AND JORGE WERE STILL JUST AS ENTHUSIASTIC AND PASSIONATE AS THEY HAD BEEN AT THE START.
SAM HAS ALWAYS BEEN A PHOTOGRAPHER, AND HE ALWAYS CONSIDERED IT MORE THAN JUST A JOB.
PHOTOGRAPHY HAS ALWAYS BEEN HIS GREATEST LOVE. HIS FIRST THOUGHT WHEN WAKING UP. HIS LAST THOUGHT BEFORE FALLING ASLEEP. THAT DEVOTION CAUSED HIM A FAIR AMOUNT OF PROBLEMS, ESPECIALLY WHEN IT CAME TO RELATIONSHIPS.

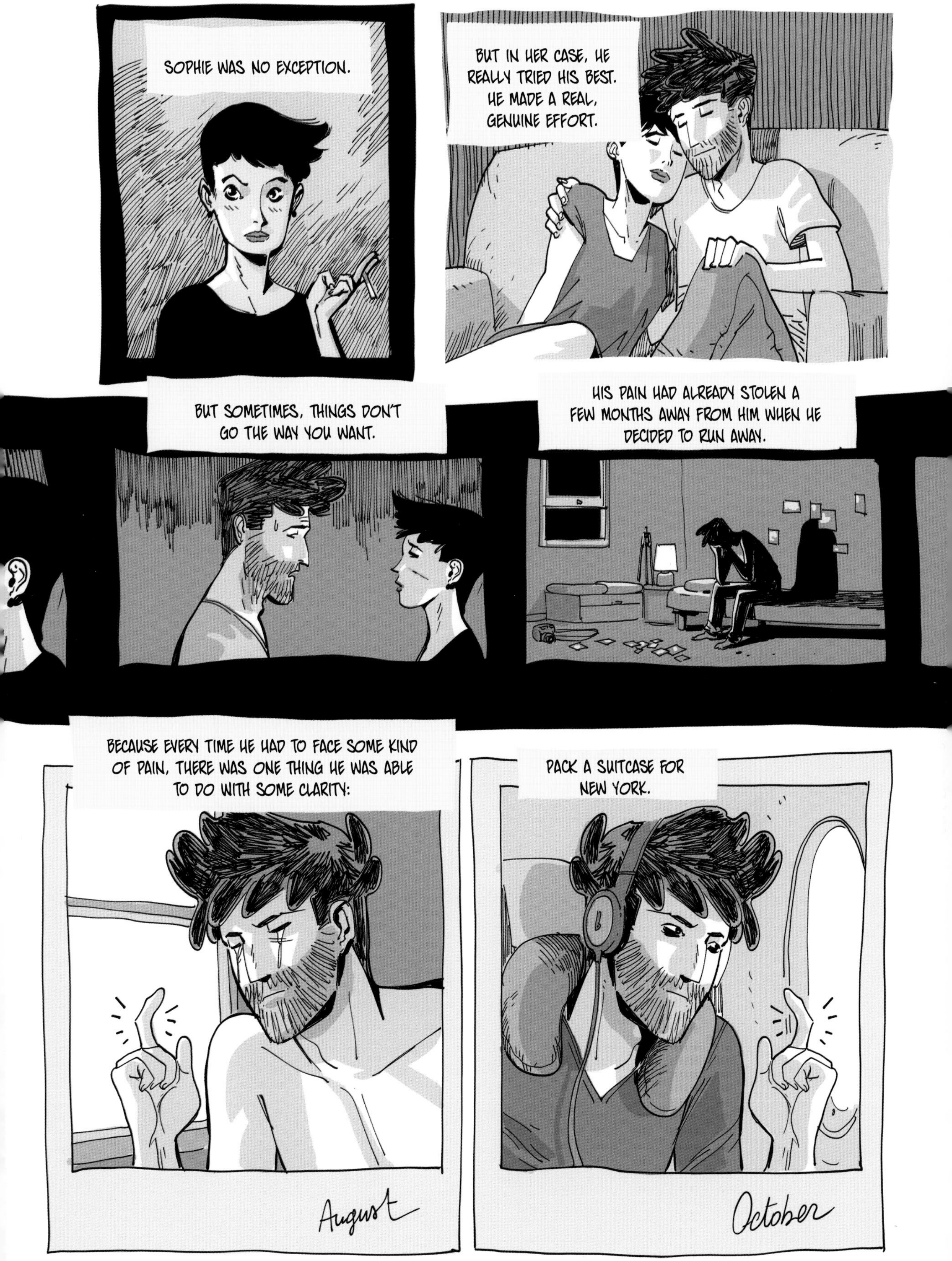
SOPHIE WAS NO EXCEPTION.
BUT IN HER CASE, HE REALLY TRIED HIS BEST. HE MADE A REAL, GENUINE EFFORT.
BUT SOMETIMES, THINGS DON'T GO THE WAY YOU WANT.
HIS PAIN HAD ALREADY STOLEN A FEW MONTHS AWAY FROM HIM WHEN HE DECIDED TO RUN AWAY.
BECAUSE EVERY TIME HE HAD TO FACE SOME KIND OF PAIN, THERE WAS ONE THING HE WAS ABLE TO DO WITH SOME CLARITY:
PACK A SUITCASE FOR NEW YORK.
August
October

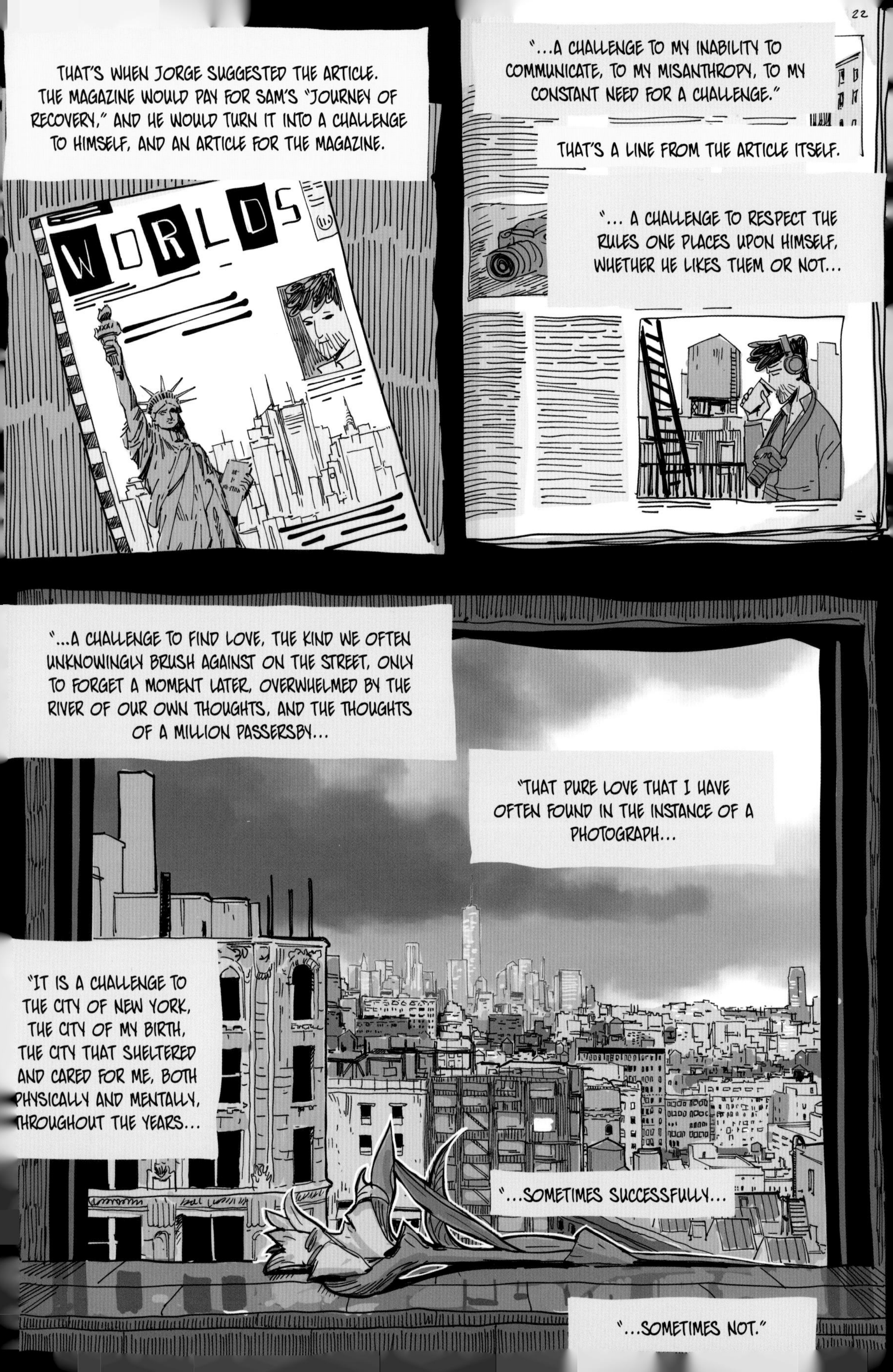
THAT'S WHEN JORGE SUGGESTED THE ARTICLE. THE MAGAZINE WOULD PAY FOR SAM'S "JOURNEY OF RECOVERY," AND HE WOULD TURN IT INTO A CHALLENGE TO HIMSELF, AND AN ARTICLE FOR THE MAGAZINE.
WORLDS
"...A CHALLENGE TO MY INABILITY TO COMMUNICATE, TO MY MISANTHROPY, TO MY CONSTANT NEED FOR A CHALLENGE."
THAT'S A LINE FROM THE ARTICLE ITSELF.
"... A CHALLENGE TO RESPECT THE RULES ONE PLACES UPON HIMSELF, WHETHER HE LIKES THEM OR NOT...
"...A CHALLENGE TO FIND LOVE, THE KIND WE OFTEN UNKNOWINGLY BRUSH AGAINST ON THE STREET, ONLY TO FORGET A MOMENT LATER, OVERWHELMED BY THE RIVER OF OUR OWN THOUGHTS, AND THE THOUGHTS OF A MILLION PASSERSBY...
"THAT PURE LOVE THAT I HAVE OFTEN FOUND IN THE INSTANCE OF A PHOTOGRAPH...
"IT IS A CHALLENGE TO THE CITY OF NEW YORK, THE CITY OF MY BIRTH, THE CITY THAT SHELTERED AND CARED FOR ME, BOTH PHYSICALLY AND MENTALLY, THROUGHOUT THE YEARS...
"...SOMETIMES SUCCESSFULLY...
"...SOMETIMES NOT."

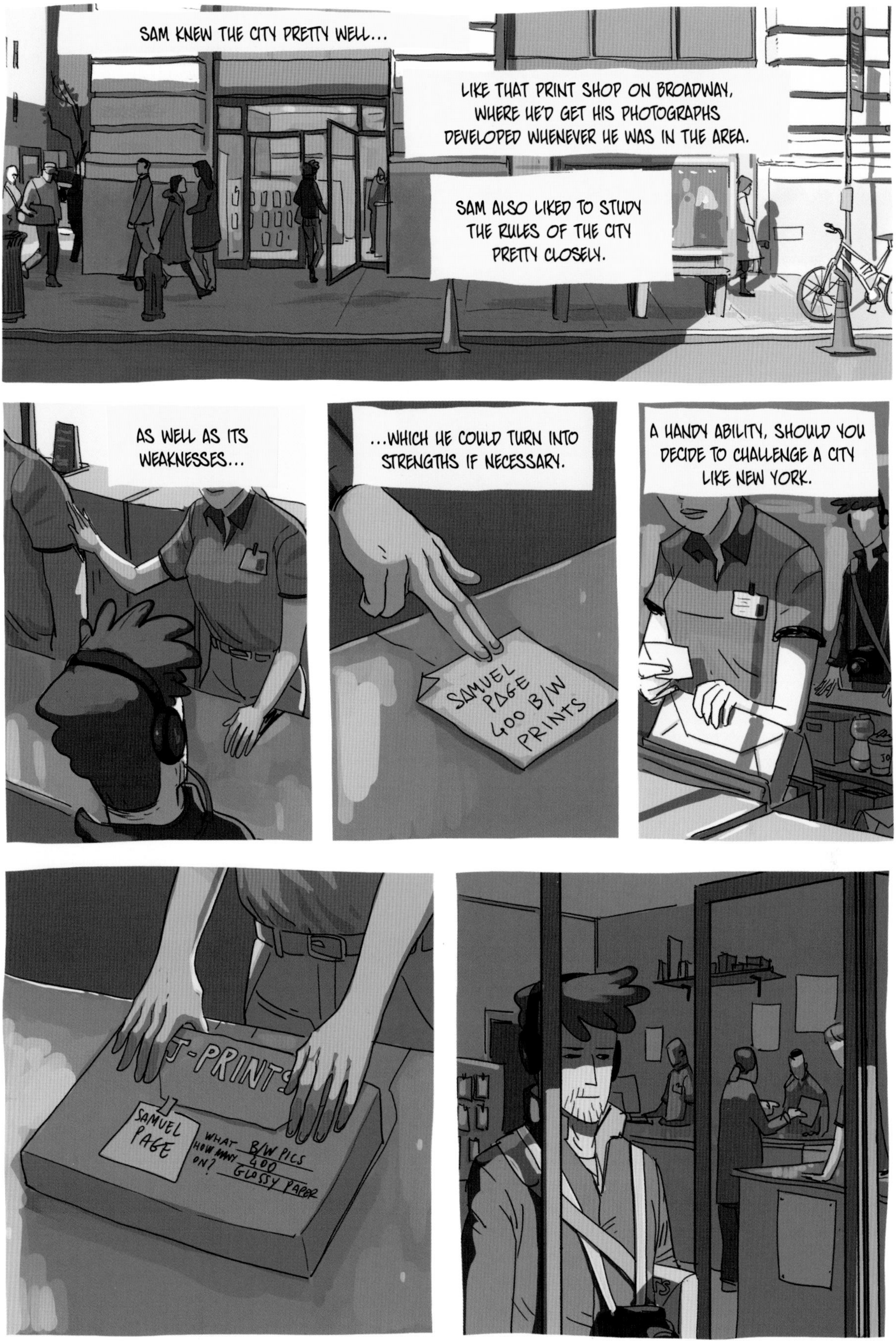
SAM KNEW THE CITY PRETTY WELL...
LIKE THAT PRINT SHOP ON BROADWAY, WHERE HE'D GET HIS PHOTOGRAPHS DEVELOPED WHENEVER HE WAS IN THE AREA.
SAM ALSO LIKED TO STUDY THE RULES OF THE CITY PRETTY CLOSELY.
AS WELL AS ITS WEAKNESSES...
...WHICH HE COULD TURN INTO STRENGTHS IF NECESSARY.
SAMUEL PAGE 400 B/W PRINTS
A HANDY ABILITY, SHOULD YOU DECIDE TO CHALLENGE A CITY LIKE NEW YORK.
J-PRINTS
SAMUEL PAGE
WHAT B/W PICS
HOW MANY 400
ON? GLOSSY PAPER

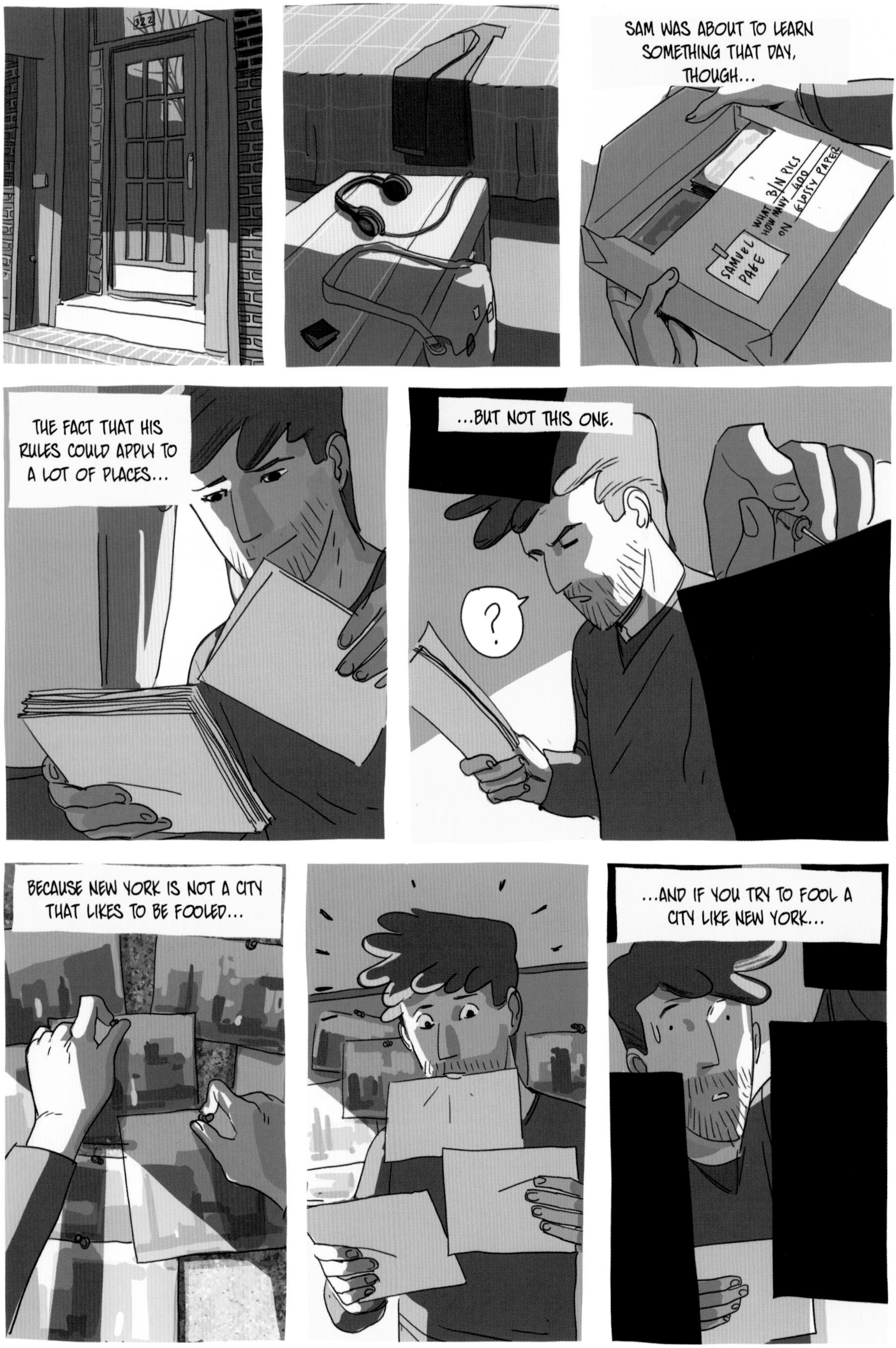
SAM WAS ABOUT TO LEARN SOMETHING THAT DAY, THOUGH...
WHAT B/N PICS
HOW MANY 400
ON GLOSSY PAPER
SAMUEL PAGE
THE FACT THAT HIS RULES COULD APPLY TO A LOT OF PLACES...
...BUT NOT THIS ONE.
?
BECAUSE NEW YORK IS NOT A CITY THAT LIKES TO BE FOOLED...
...AND IF YOU TRY TO FOOL A CITY LIKE NEW YORK...

MOST OF THE TIME...

... NEW YORK...

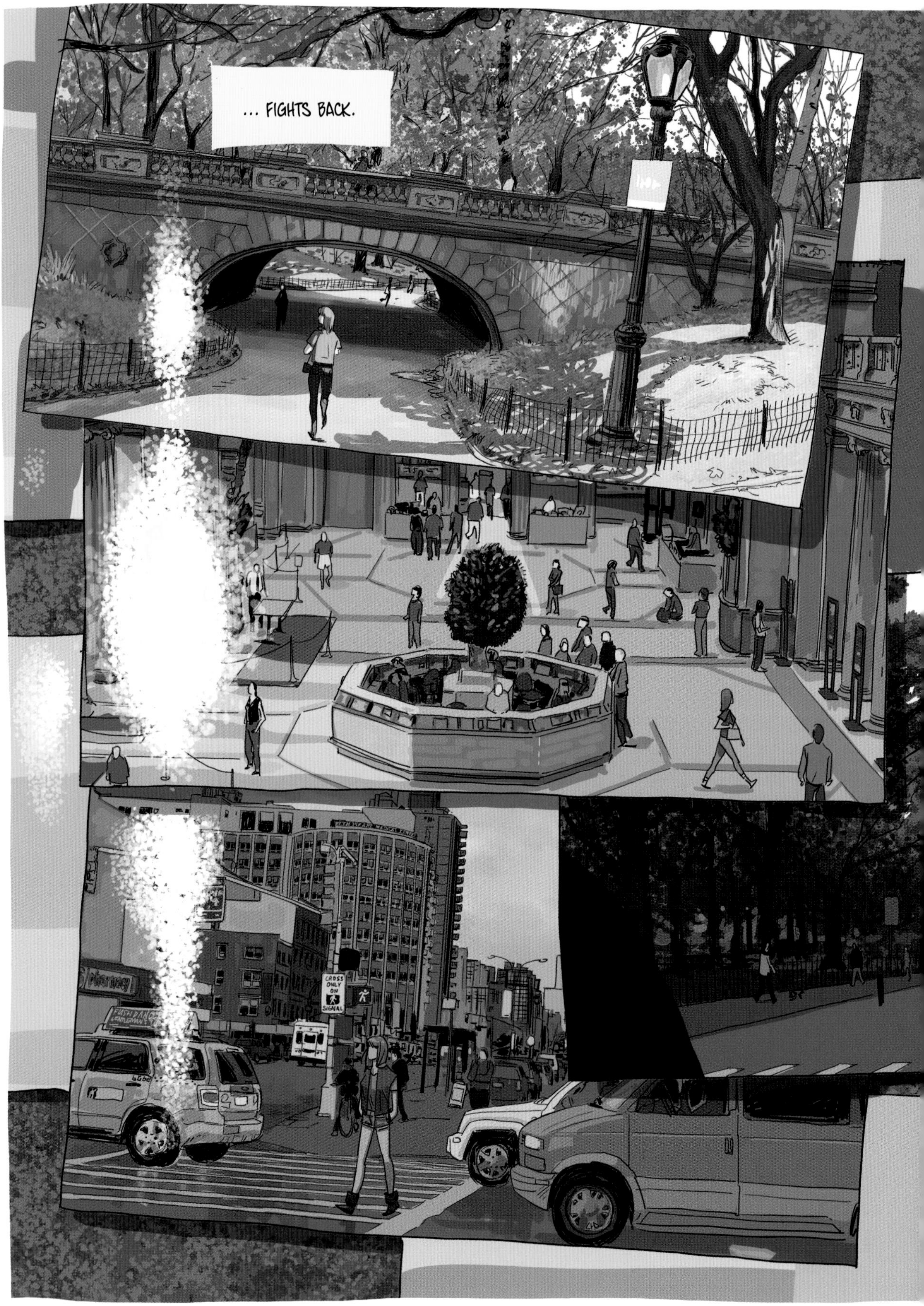
... FIGHTS BACK.
CROSS ONLY ON SIGNAL

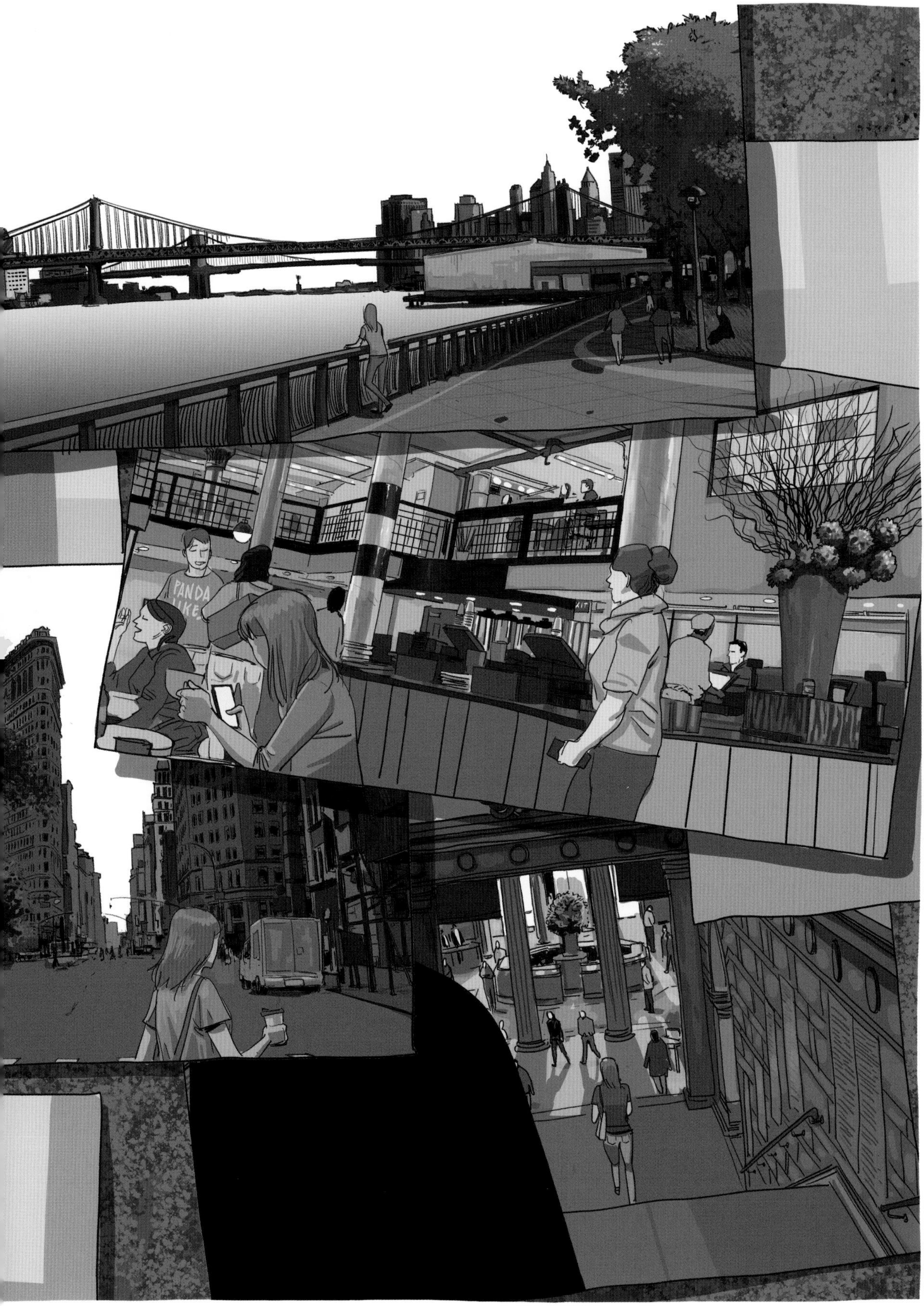
PANDA

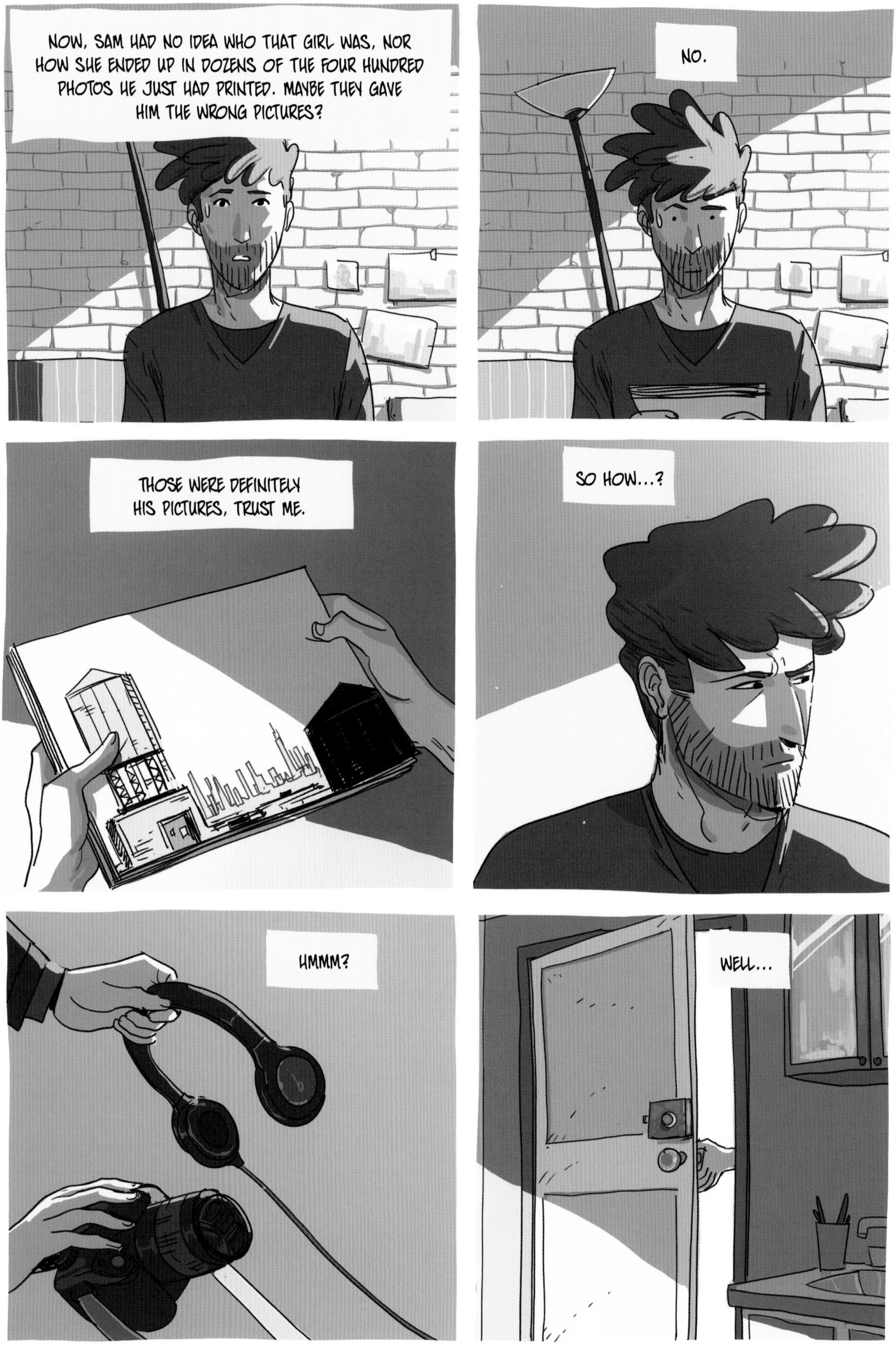
NOW, SAM HAD NO IDEA WHO THAT GIRL WAS, NOR HOW SHE ENDED UP IN DOZENS OF THE FOUR HUNDRED PHOTOS HE JUST HAD PRINTED. MAYBE THEY GAVE HIM THE WRONG PICTURES?
NO.
THOSE WERE DEFINITELY HIS PICTURES, TRUST ME.
SO HOW...?
HMMM?
WELL...

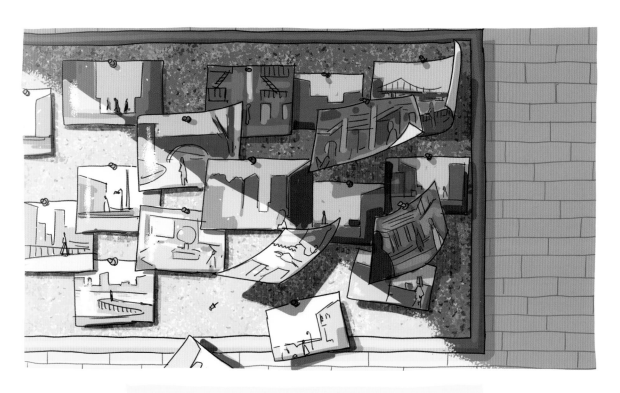

YOU'VE CERTAINLY REALIZED BY NOW THAT SAM IS AN ODD
GUY, WITH HIS OBSESSIONS, HIS RULES, HIS RITUALS.

SURE.

BUT WHAT YOU DON'T KNOW IS HOW HIS ECCENTRICITIES SPREAD
LIKE WILDFIRE THROUGH EVERY ASPECT OF HIS LIFE.

INCLUDING HIS PROFESSIONAL LIFE.

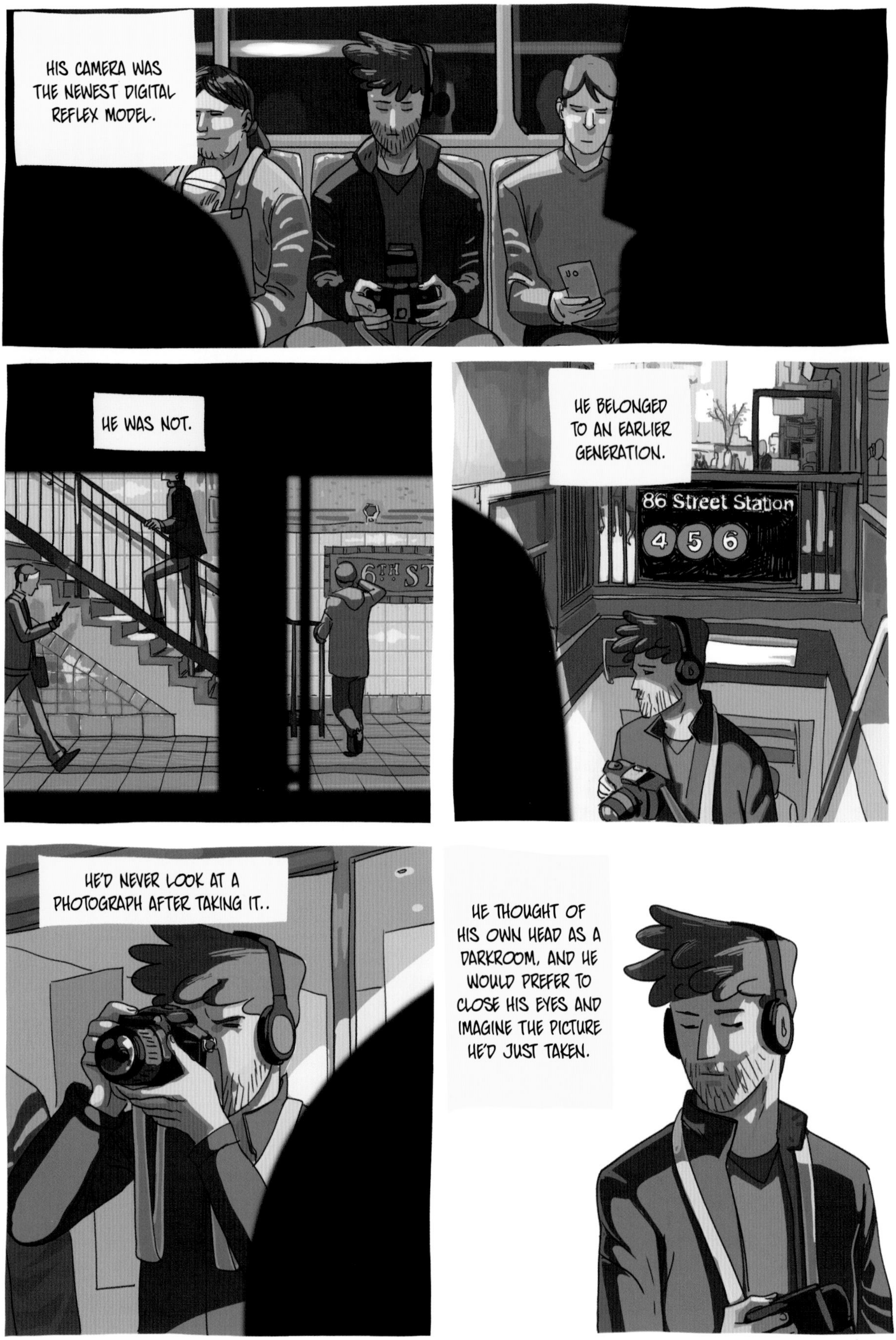
HIS CAMERA WAS THE NEWEST DIGITAL REFLEX MODEL.
HE WAS NOT.
HE BELONGED TO AN EARLIER GENERATION.
86 Street Station
4 5 6
6TH ST
HE'D NEVER LOOK AT A PHOTOGRAPH AFTER TAKING IT..
HE THOUGHT OF HIS OWN HEAD AS A DARKROOM, AND HE WOULD PREFER TO CLOSE HIS EYES AND IMAGINE THE PICTURE HE'D JUST TAKEN.

HE WOULD IMPRINT THE MOMENT
IN HIS BRAIN.

HE KNEW WHAT HE HAD JUST SEEN, AND HE DIDN'T NEED A TINY SCREEN
TO REASSURE HIM A SECOND, A MINUTE, OR EVEN AN HOUR LATER.

HE'D PRINT THAT PHOTO IMMEDIATELY.

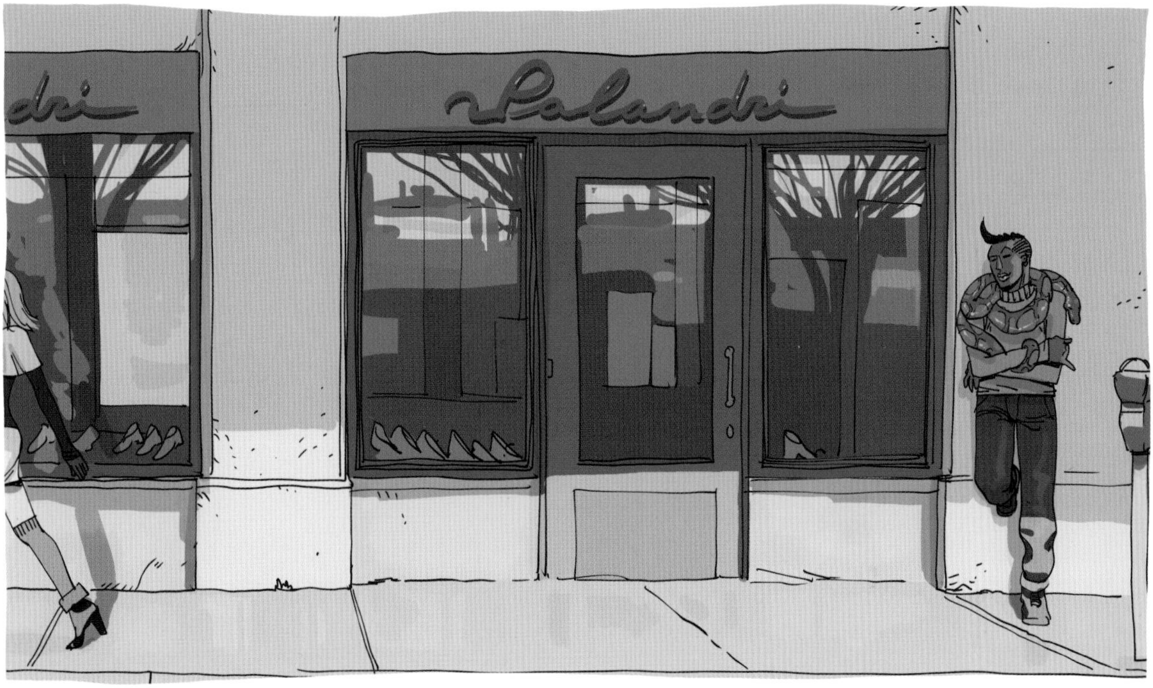
Palandri

IN HIS MEMORY.

AND THAT...

...THAT WAS HOW HE DISTRACTED HIMSELF FROM THE PAIN
AND HIS CONSTANT SEARCH FOR DISTANCE.

THE ONLY TIME HE'D LET
HIMSELF LET GO, BECOMING ONE WITH
THE WORLD AROUND HIM.

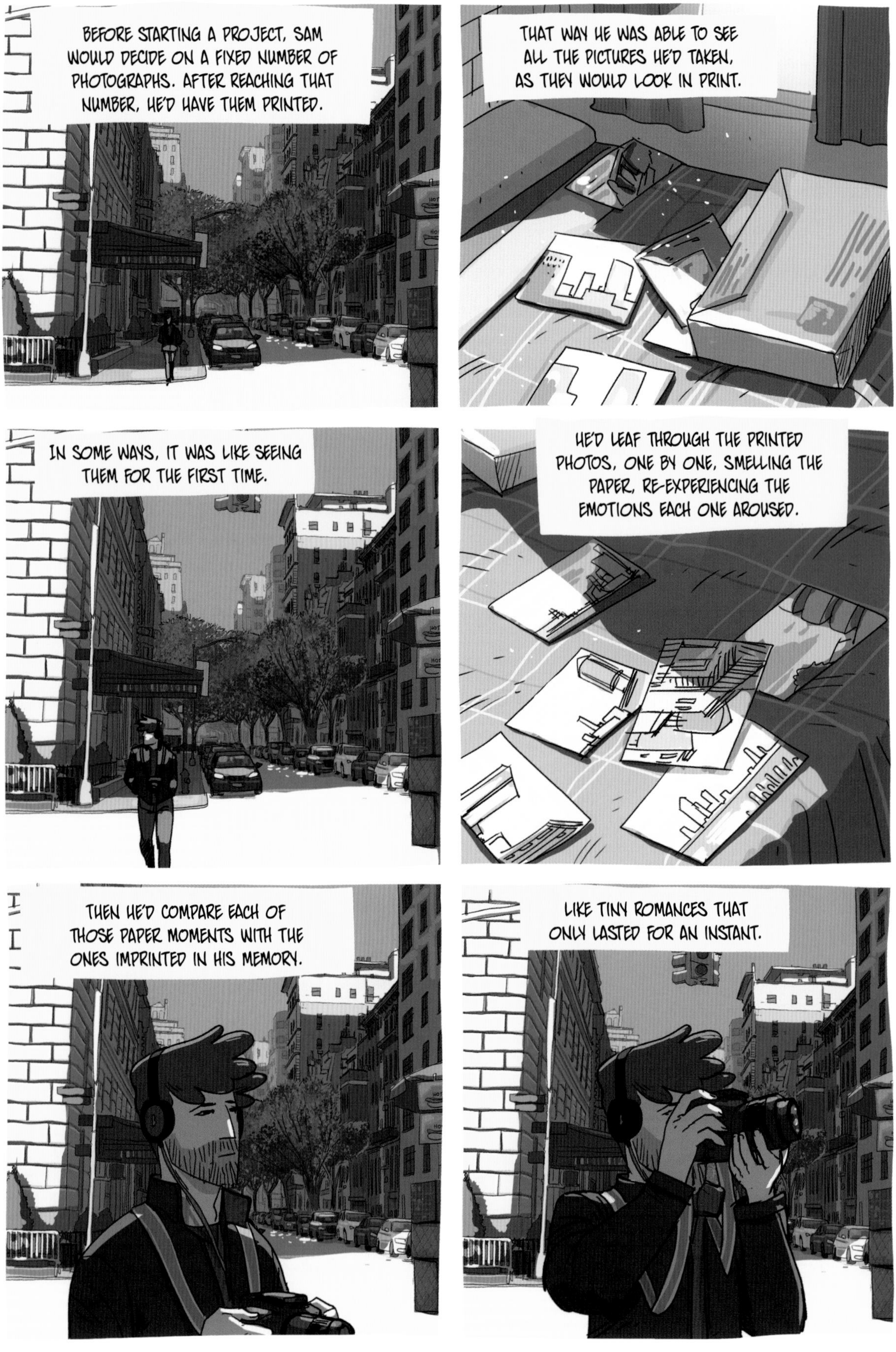
BEFORE STARTING A PROJECT, SAM WOULD DECIDE ON A FIXED NUMBER OF PHOTOGRAPHS. AFTER REACHING THAT NUMBER, HE'D HAVE THEM PRINTED.
THAT WAY HE WAS ABLE TO SEE ALL THE PICTURES HE'D TAKEN, AS THEY WOULD LOOK IN PRINT.
IN SOME WAYS, IT WAS LIKE SEEING THEM FOR THE FIRST TIME.
HE'D LEAF THROUGH THE PRINTED PHOTOS, ONE BY ONE, SMELLING THE PAPER, RE-EXPERIENCING THE EMOTIONS EACH ONE AROUSED.
THEN HE'D COMPARE EACH OF THOSE PAPER MOMENTS WITH THE ONES IMPRINTED IN HIS MEMORY.
LIKE TINY ROMANCES THAT ONLY LASTED FOR AN INSTANT.

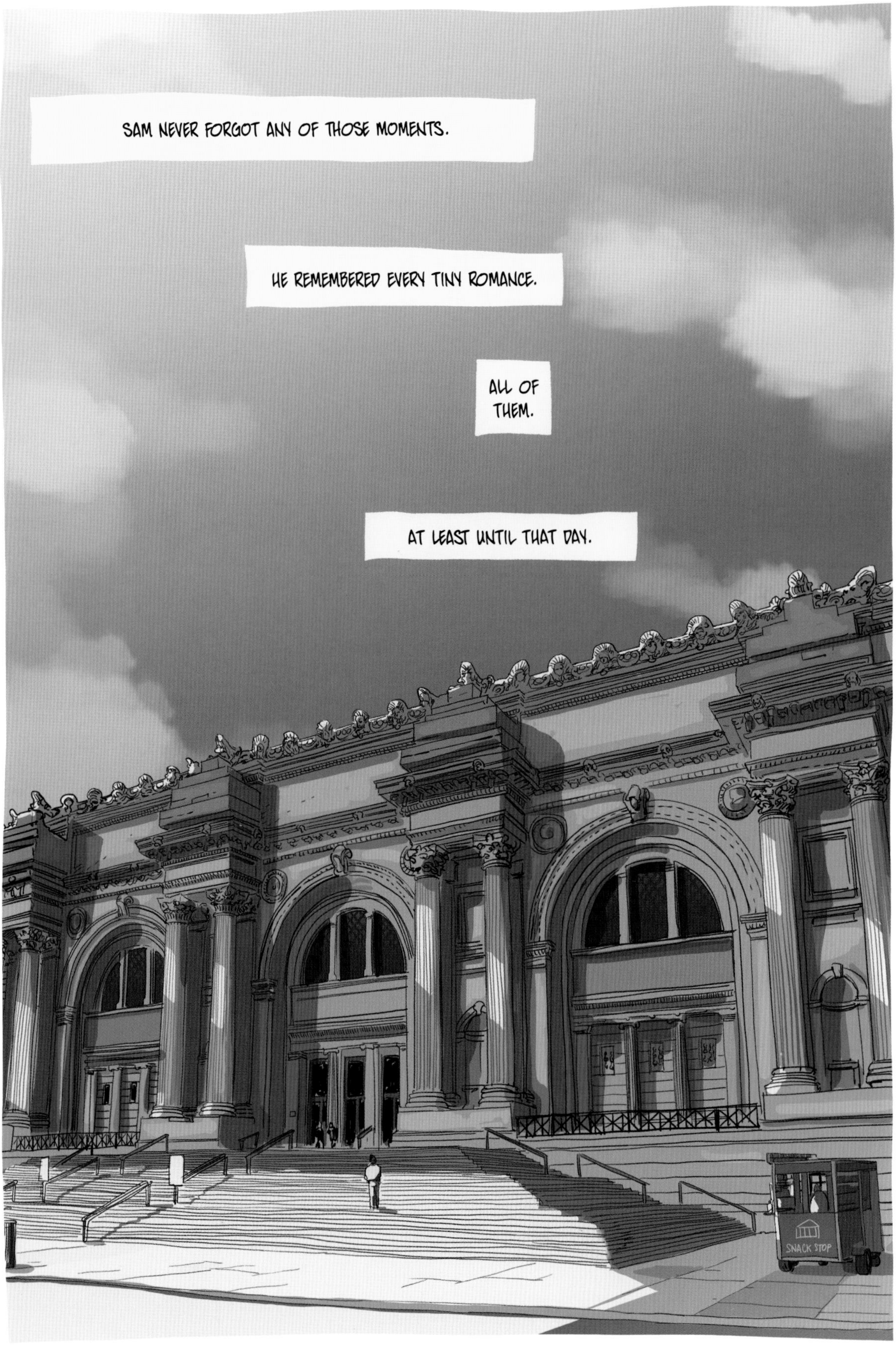
SAM NEVER FORGOT ANY OF THOSE MOMENTS.
HE REMEMBERED EVERY TINY ROMANCE.
ALL OF THEM.
AT LEAST UNTIL THAT DAY.
SNACK STOP

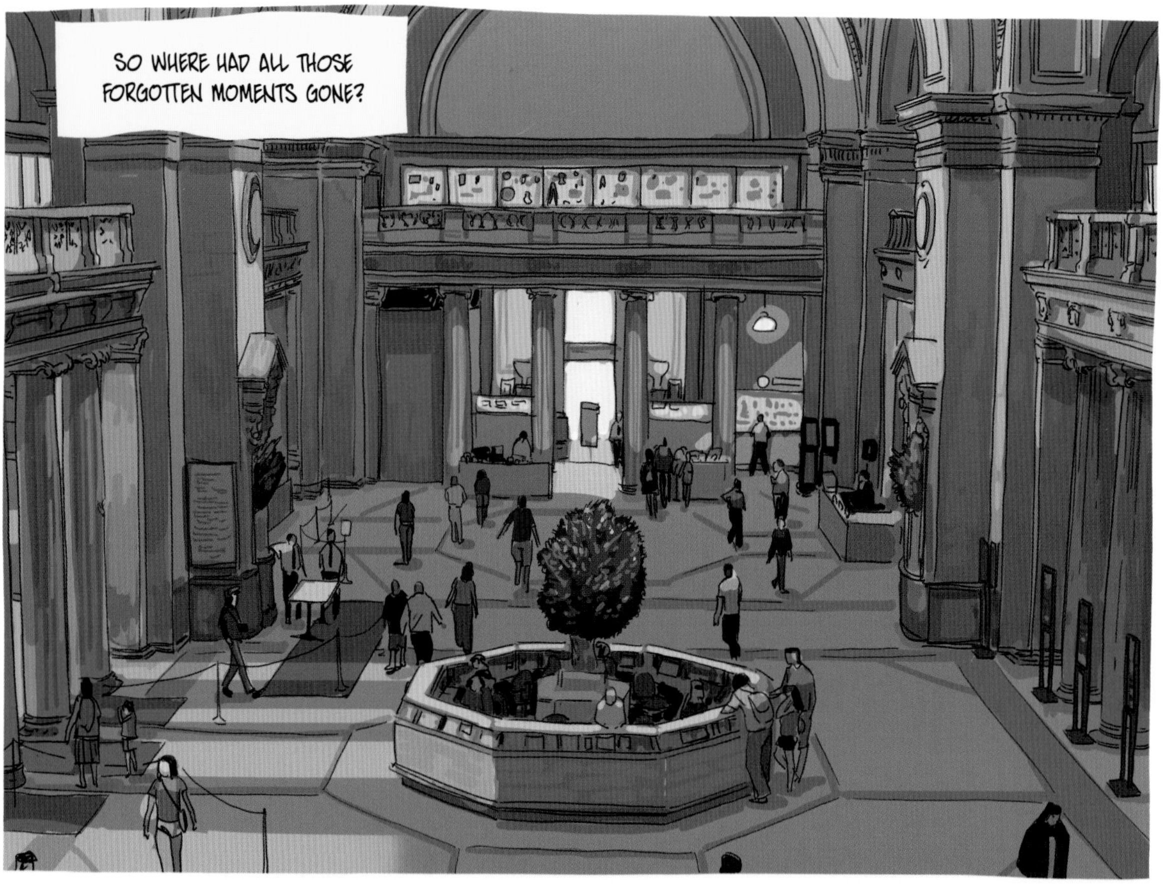
SO WHERE HAD ALL THOSE FORGOTTEN MOMENTS GONE?

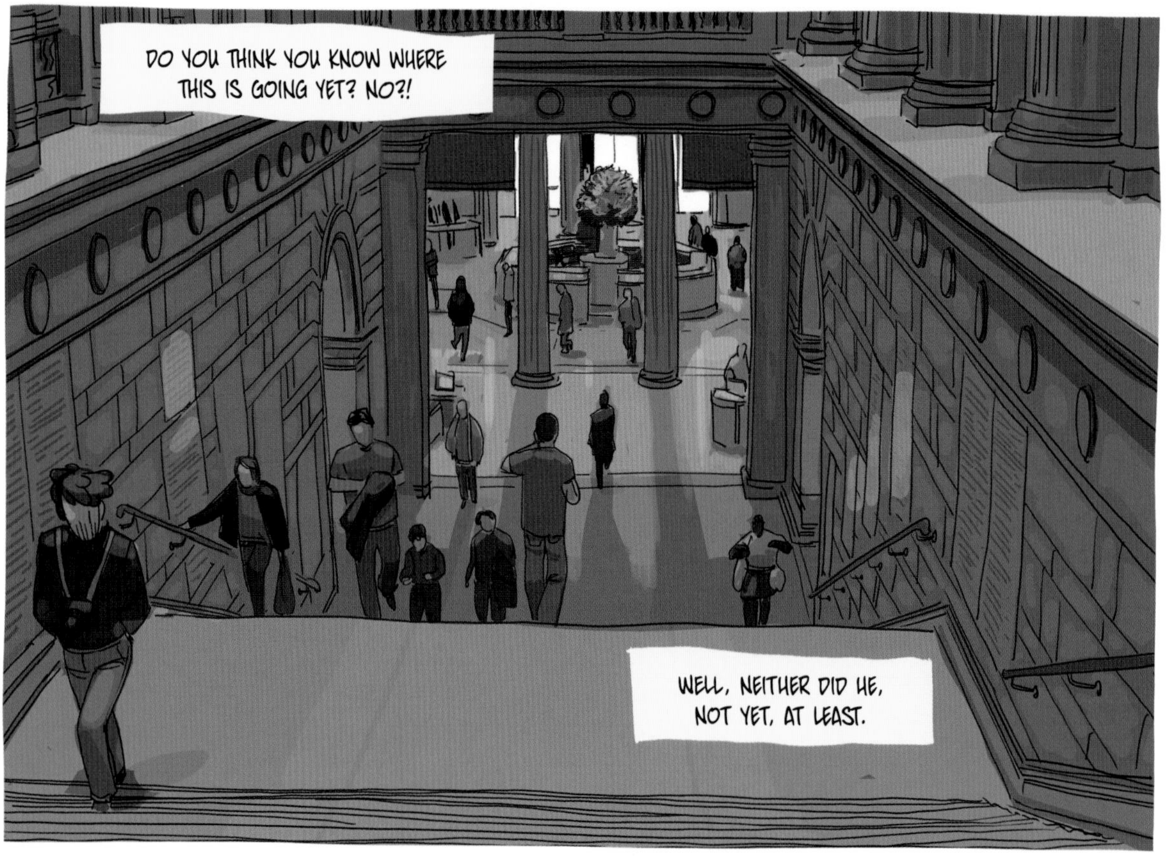
DO YOU THINK YOU KNOW WHERE THIS IS GOING YET? NO?!
WELL, NEITHER DID HE, NOT YET, AT LEAST.

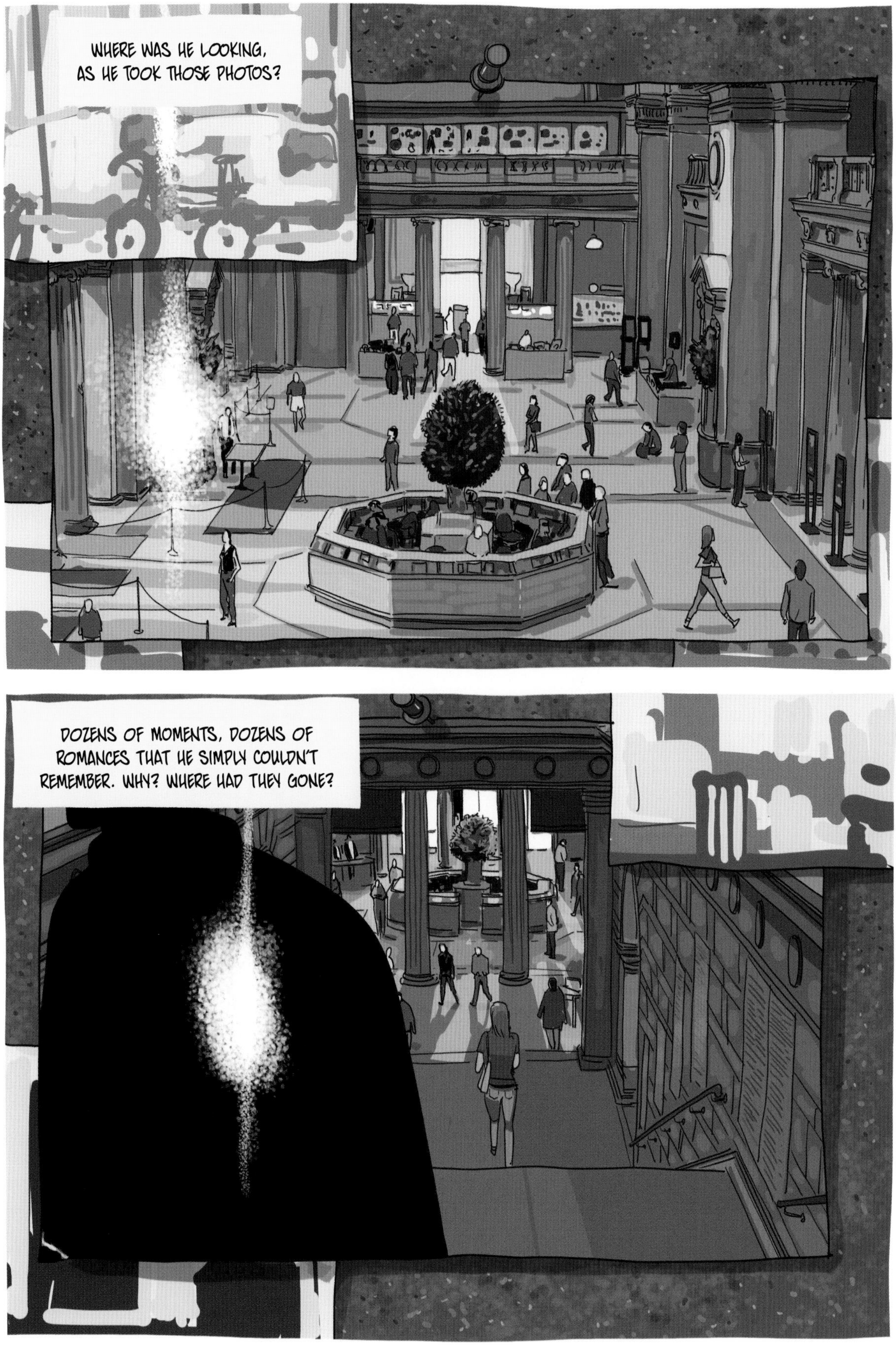
WHERE WAS HE LOOKING, AS HE TOOK THOSE PHOTOS?
DOZENS OF MOMENTS, DOZENS OF ROMANCES THAT HE SIMPLY COULDN'T REMEMBER. WHY? WHERE HAD THEY GONE?

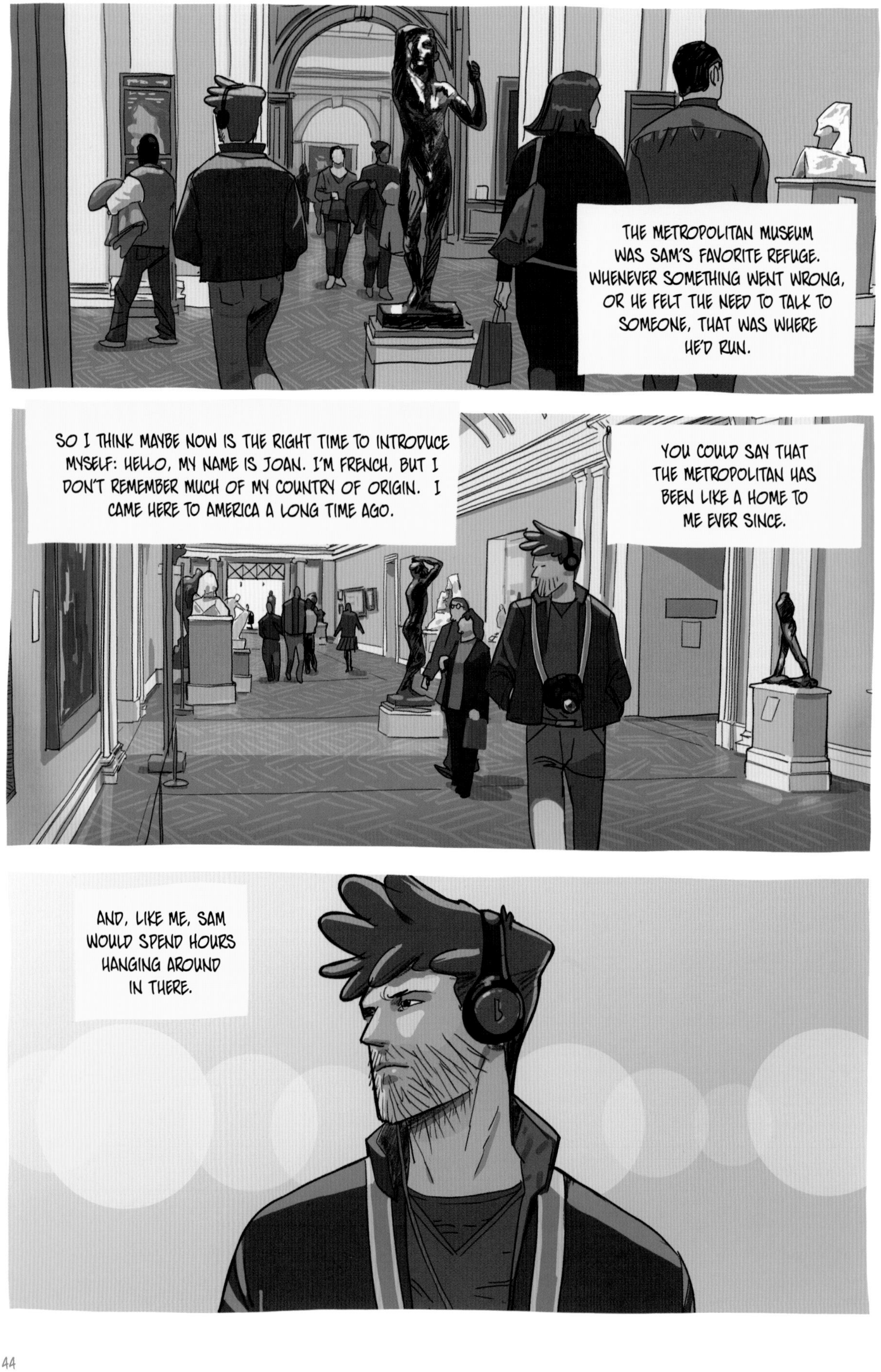
THE METROPOLITAN MUSEUM WAS SAM'S FAVORITE REFUGE. WHENEVER SOMETHING WENT WRONG, OR HE FELT THE NEED TO TALK TO SOMEONE, THAT WAS WHERE HE'D RUN.
SO I THINK MAYBE NOW IS THE RIGHT TIME TO INTRODUCE MYSELF: HELLO, MY NAME IS JOAN. I'M FRENCH, BUT I DON'T REMEMBER MUCH OF MY COUNTRY OF ORIGIN. I CAME HERE TO AMERICA A LONG TIME AGO.
YOU COULD SAY THAT THE METROPOLITAN HAS BEEN LIKE A HOME TO ME EVER SINCE.
AND, LIKE ME, SAM WOULD SPEND HOURS HANGING AROUND IN THERE.

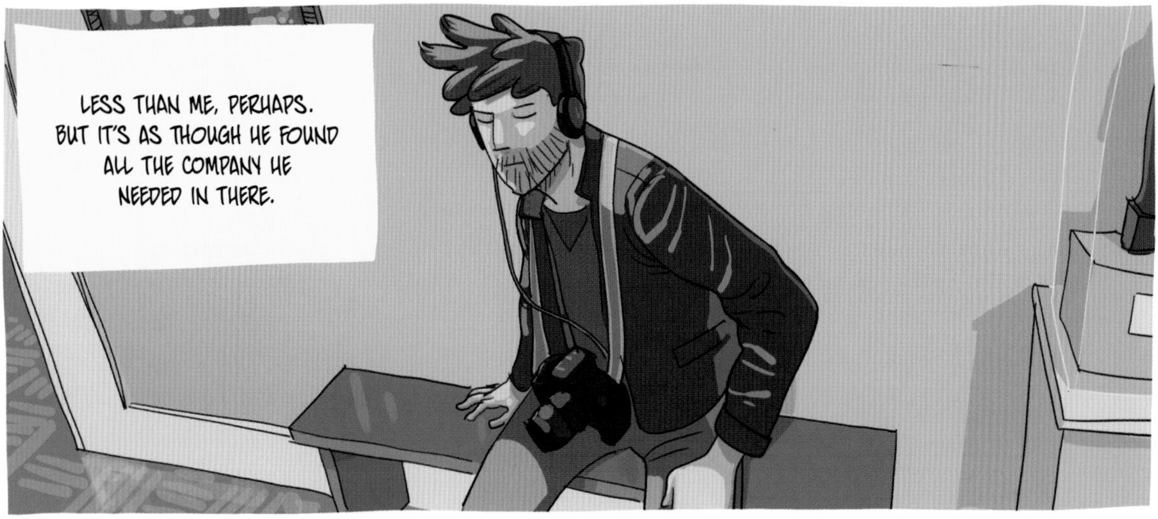
LESS THAN ME, PERHAPS. BUT IT'S AS THOUGH HE FOUND ALL THE COMPANY HE NEEDED IN THERE.

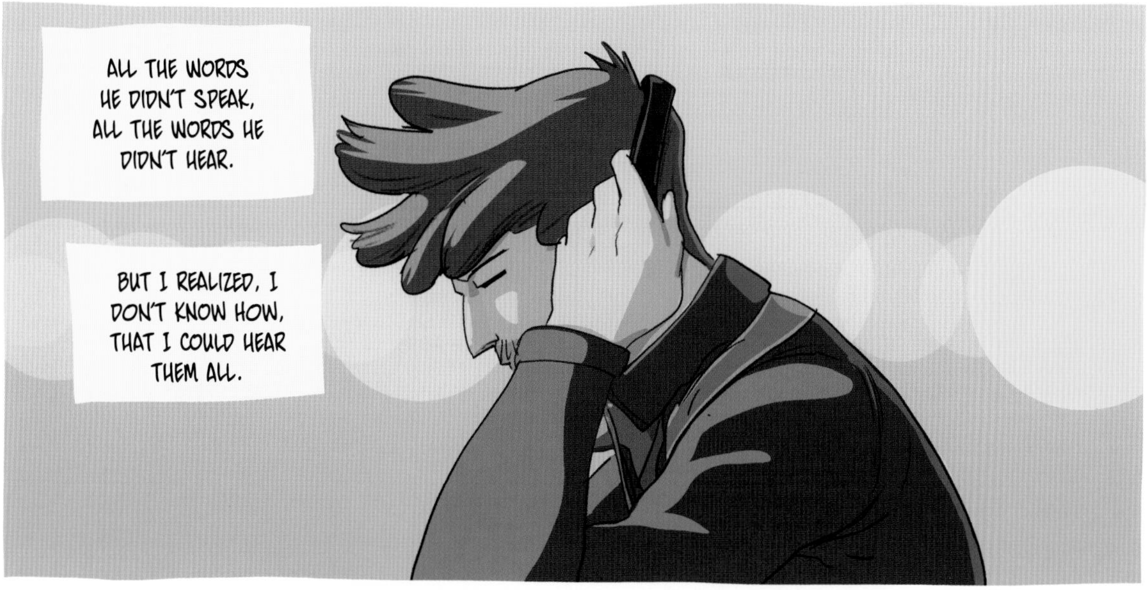
ALL THE WORDS HE DIDN'T SPEAK, ALL THE WORDS HE DIDN'T HEAR.
BUT I REALIZED, I DON'T KNOW HOW, THAT I COULD HEAR THEM ALL.

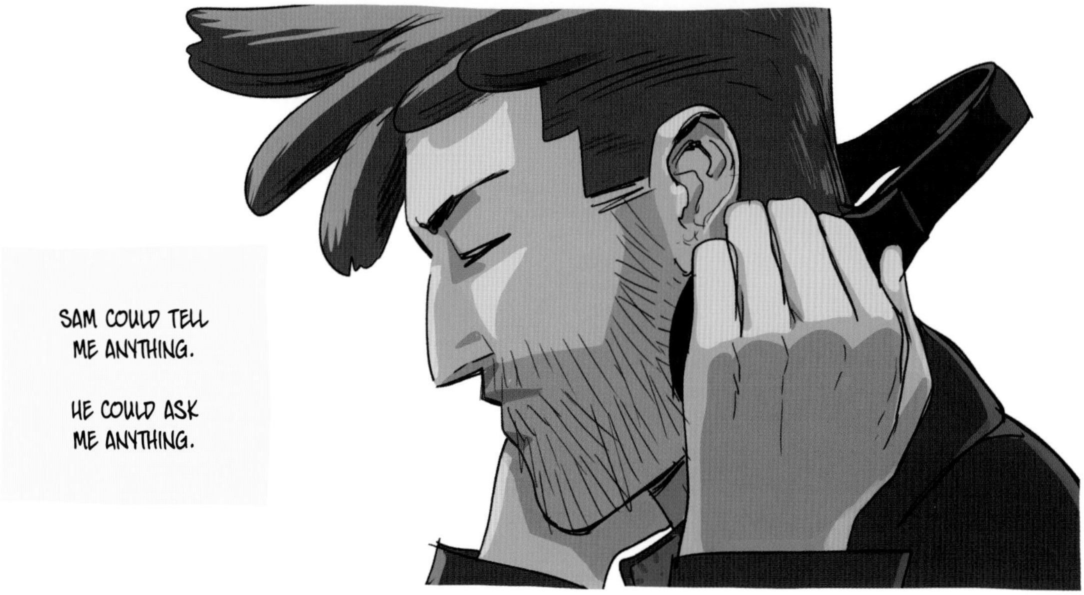
SAM COULD TELL ME ANYTHING.
HE COULD ASK ME ANYTHING.

"WHAT WAS I LOOKING AT WHEN I TOOK THOSE PHOTOS, JOAN?"

"WHY DO I HAVE NO MEMORY OF THOSE MOMENTS?"

"WHAT DOES THIS CITY WANT FROM ME?"

(PLEASE DON'T LAUGH, I CAN'T
DO HIS VOICE VERY WELL.)

BUT THOSE WERE HIS QUESTIONS,
AND I COULD HEAR THEM CLEARLY.

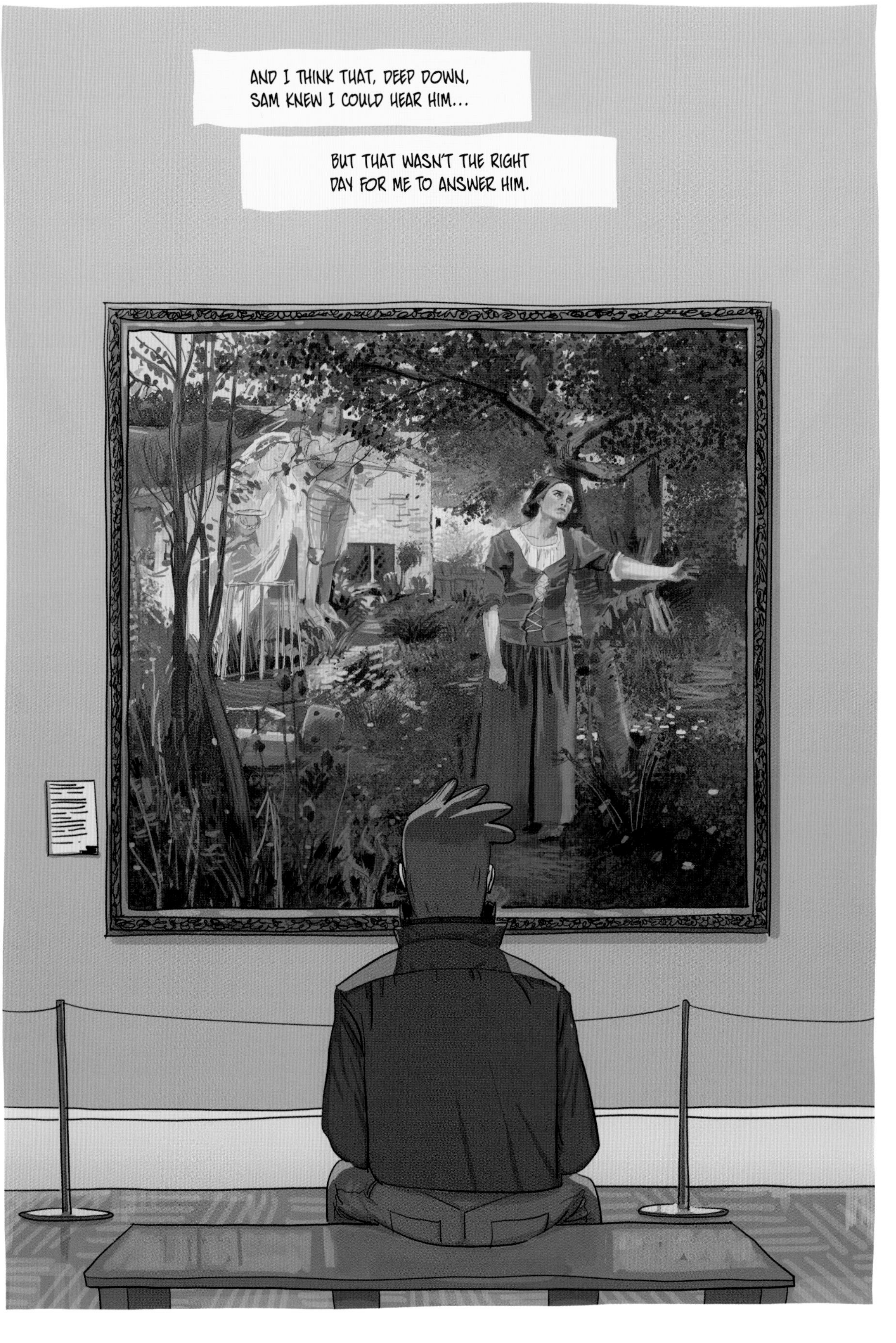
AND I THINK THAT, DEEP DOWN, SAM KNEW I COULD HEAR HIM...
BUT THAT WASN'T THE RIGHT DAY FOR ME TO ANSWER HIM.

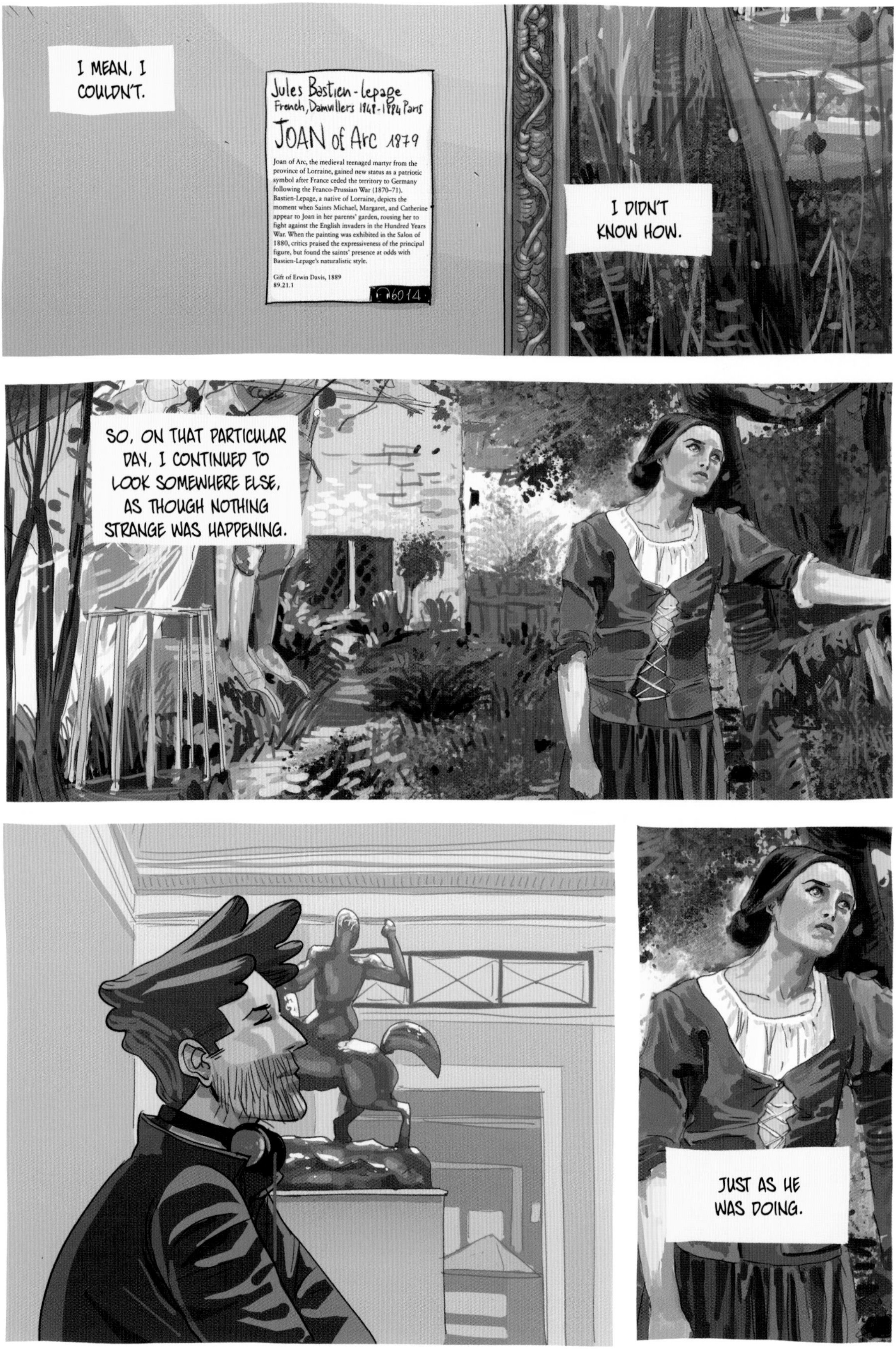
I MEAN, I COULDN'T.
Jules Bastien-lepage
French, Damvillers 1848-1884 Paris
JOAN of Arc 1879
Joan of Arc, the medieval teenaged martyr from the province of Lorraine, gained new status as a patriotic symbol after France ceded the territory to Germany following the Franco-Prussian War (1870–71). Bastien-Lepage, a native of Lorraine, depicts the moment when Saints Michael, Margaret, and Catherine appear to Joan in her parents' garden, rousing her to fight against the English invaders in the Hundred Years War. When the painting was exhibited in the Salon of 1880, critics praised the expressiveness of the principal figure, but found the saints' presence at odds with Bastien-Lepage's naturalistic style.
Gift of Erwin Davis, 1889
89.21.1
6014
I DIDN'T KNOW HOW.
SO, ON THAT PARTICULAR DAY, I CONTINUED TO LOOK SOMEWHERE ELSE, AS THOUGH NOTHING STRANGE WAS HAPPENING.
JUST AS HE WAS DOING.

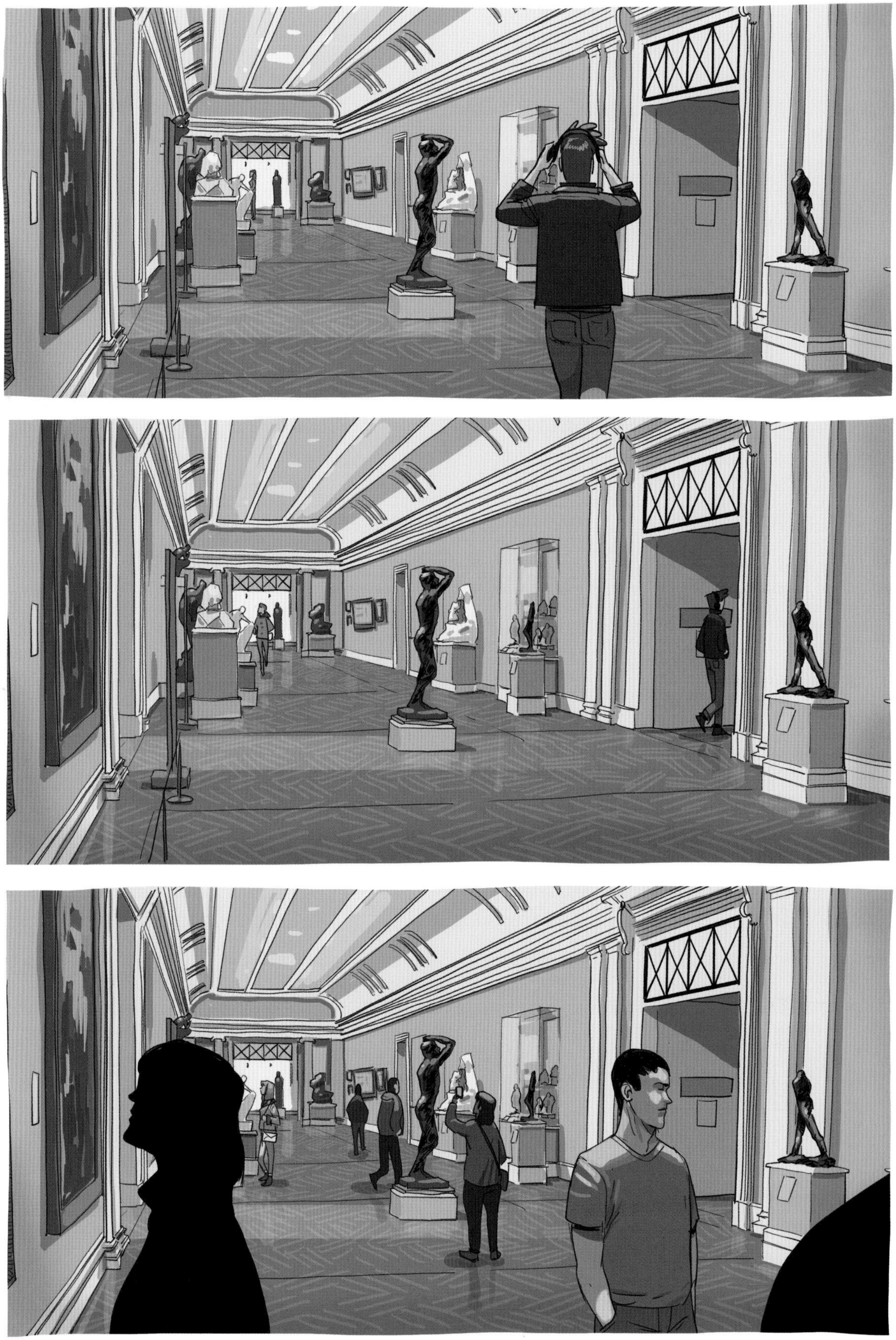

NUMBERS AND RULES

WE WERE TALKING ABOUT
RULES AT THE START OF THIS STORY.
NUMBERS AND RULES.

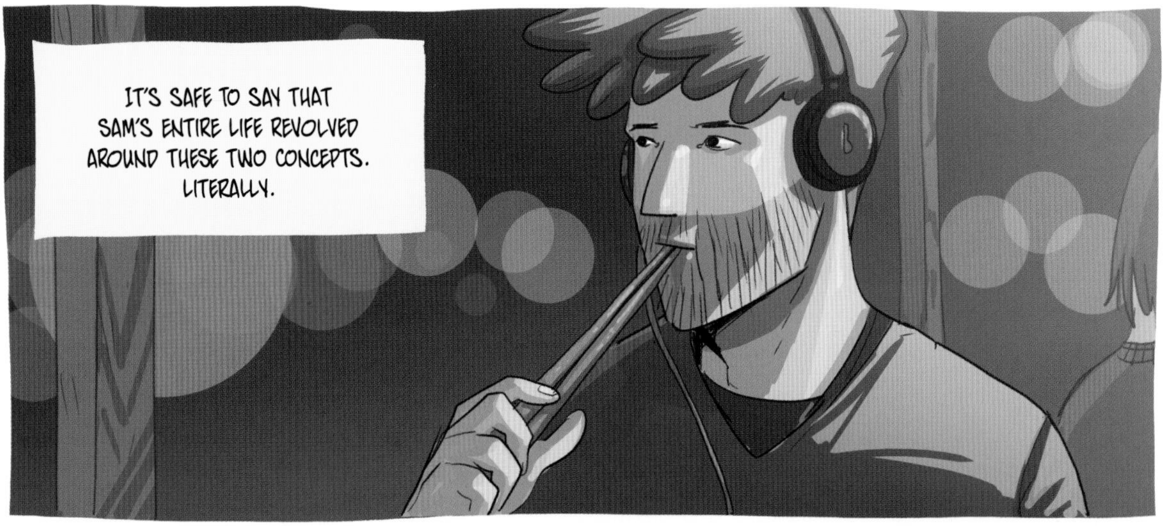
IT'S SAFE TO SAY THAT SAM'S ENTIRE LIFE REVOLVED AROUND THESE TWO CONCEPTS. LITERALLY.

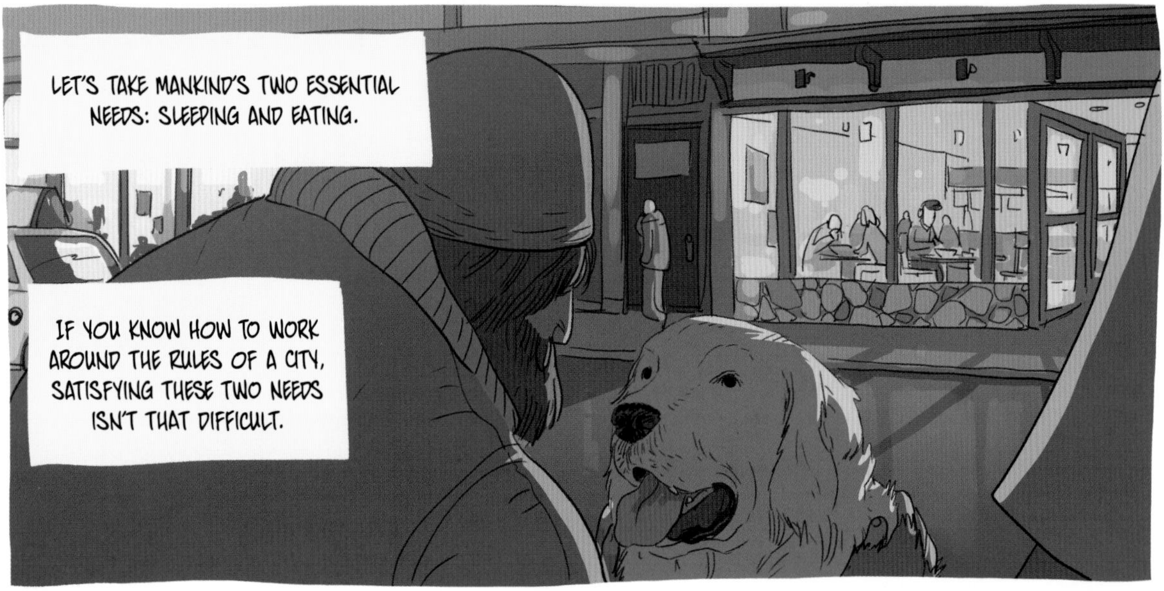
LET'S TAKE MANKIND'S TWO ESSENTIAL NEEDS: SLEEPING AND EATING.
IF YOU KNOW HOW TO WORK AROUND THE RULES OF A CITY, SATISFYING THESE TWO NEEDS ISN'T THAT DIFFICULT.

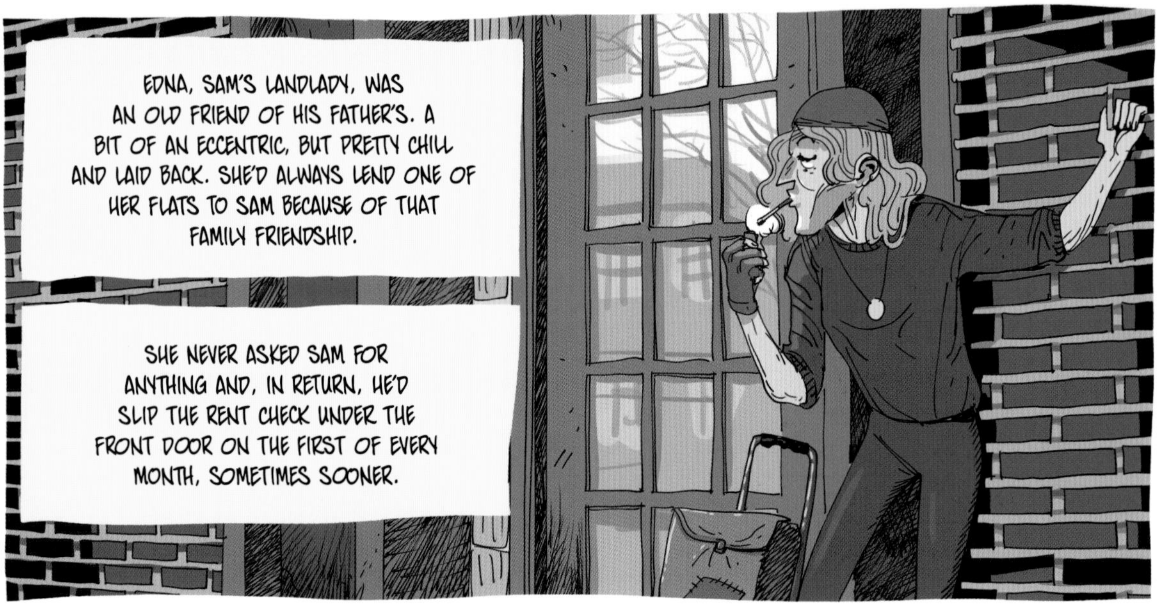
EDNA, SAM'S LANDLADY, WAS AN OLD FRIEND OF HIS FATHER'S. A BIT OF AN ECCENTRIC, BUT PRETTY CHILL AND LAID BACK. SHE'D ALWAYS LEND ONE OF HER FLATS TO SAM BECAUSE OF THAT FAMILY FRIENDSHIP.
SHE NEVER ASKED SAM FOR ANYTHING AND, IN RETURN, HE'D SLIP THE RENT CHECK UNDER THE FRONT DOOR ON THE FIRST OF EVERY MONTH, SOMETIMES SOONER.

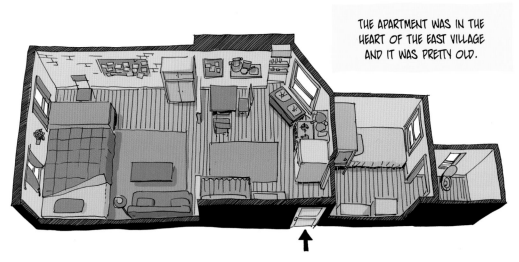

THE APARTMENT WAS IN THE HEART OF THE EAST VILLAGE AND IT WAS PRETTY OLD.

WHEN I SAY PRETTY OLD, I MEAN THE BATHTUB WAS IN THE KITCHEN.

(WHICH ACTUALLY CAME IN PRETTY HANDY WHEN TRYING TO SAVE BOTH WATER AND SOAP -- YOU'VE GOT THE THE CONVENIENT SITUATION OF WASHING THE DISHES WHILE TAKING A SHOWER!)

THE TOILET WAS IN THE GUEST ROOM.

(FOR SAM, IT WAS A SPARE ROOM, FORTUNATELY.)

BUT STILL, IT WAS AN APARTMENT WITH A ROOF, SOLID WALLS, AND REASONABLE RENT. THAT WAS ENOUGH.

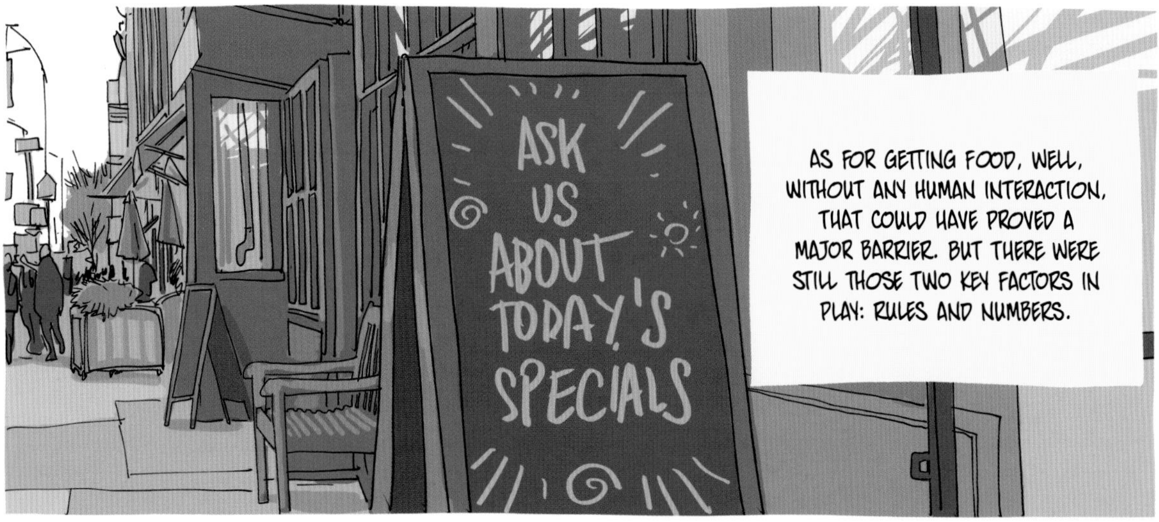
ASK US ABOUT TODAY'S SPECIALS
AS FOR GETTING FOOD, WELL, WITHOUT ANY HUMAN INTERACTION, THAT COULD HAVE PROVED A MAJOR BARRIER. BUT THERE WERE STILL THOSE TWO KEY FACTORS IN PLAY: RULES AND NUMBERS.

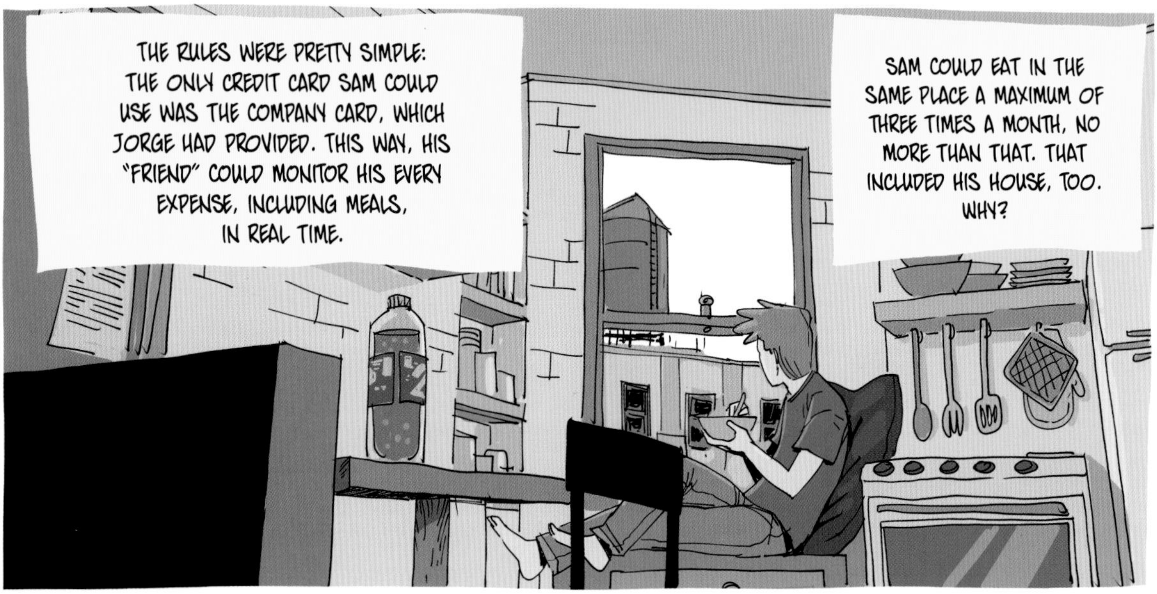
THE RULES WERE PRETTY SIMPLE: THE ONLY CREDIT CARD SAM COULD USE WAS THE COMPANY CARD, WHICH JORGE HAD PROVIDED. THIS WAY, HIS "FRIEND" COULD MONITOR HIS EVERY EXPENSE, INCLUDING MEALS, IN REAL TIME.
SAM COULD EAT IN THE SAME PLACE A MAXIMUM OF THREE TIMES A MONTH, NO MORE THAN THAT. THAT INCLUDED HIS HOUSE, TOO. WHY?

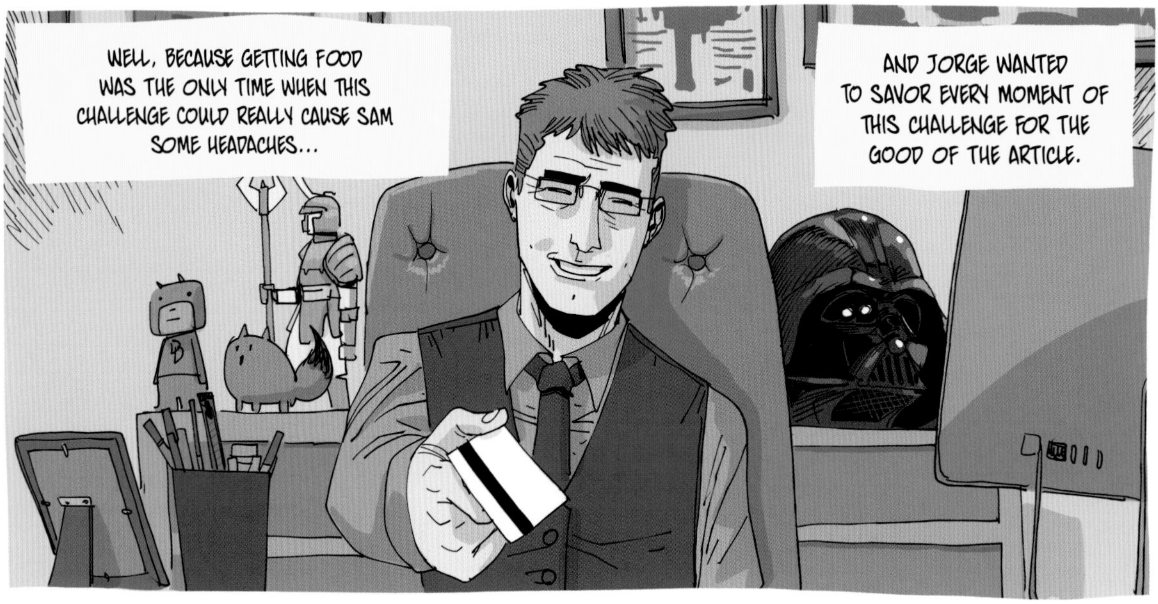
WELL, BECAUSE GETTING FOOD WAS THE ONLY TIME WHEN THIS CHALLENGE COULD REALLY CAUSE SAM SOME HEADACHES...
AND JORGE WANTED TO SAVOR EVERY MOMENT OF THIS CHALLENGE FOR THE GOOD OF THE ARTICLE.

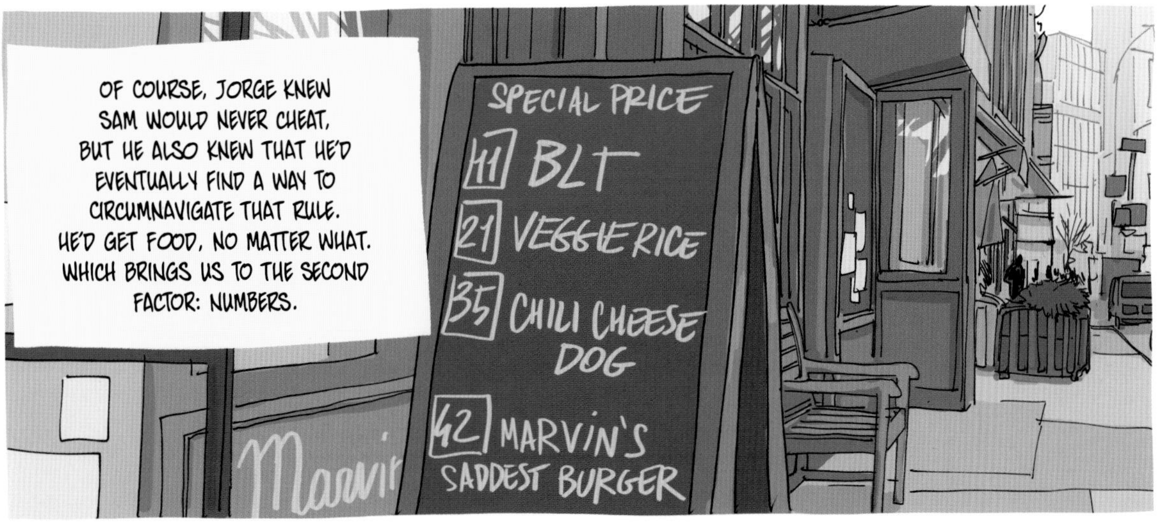
OF COURSE, JORGE KNEW SAM WOULD NEVER CHEAT, BUT HE ALSO KNEW THAT HE'D EVENTUALLY FIND A WAY TO CIRCUMNAVIGATE THAT RULE. HE'D GET FOOD, NO MATTER WHAT. WHICH BRINGS US TO THE SECOND FACTOR: NUMBERS.
SPECIAL PRICE
11 BLT
21 VEGGIE RICE
35 CHILI CHEESE DOG
42 MARVIN'S SADDEST BURGER

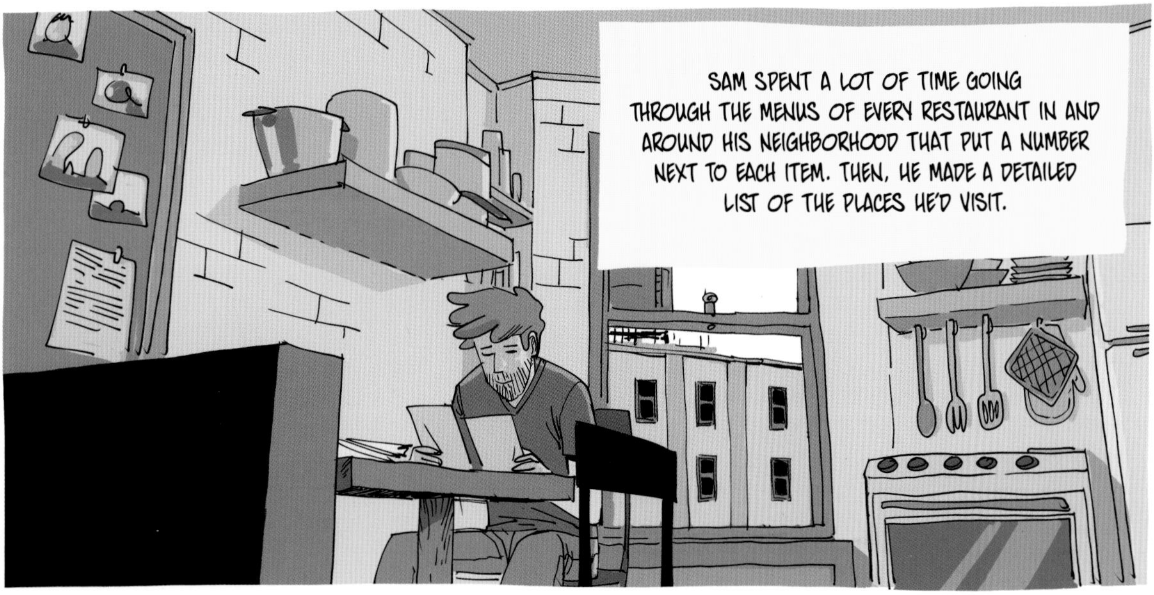
SAM SPENT A LOT OF TIME GOING THROUGH THE MENUS OF EVERY RESTAURANT IN AND AROUND HIS NEIGHBORHOOD THAT PUT A NUMBER NEXT TO EACH ITEM. THEN, HE MADE A DETAILED LIST OF THE PLACES HE'D VISIT.

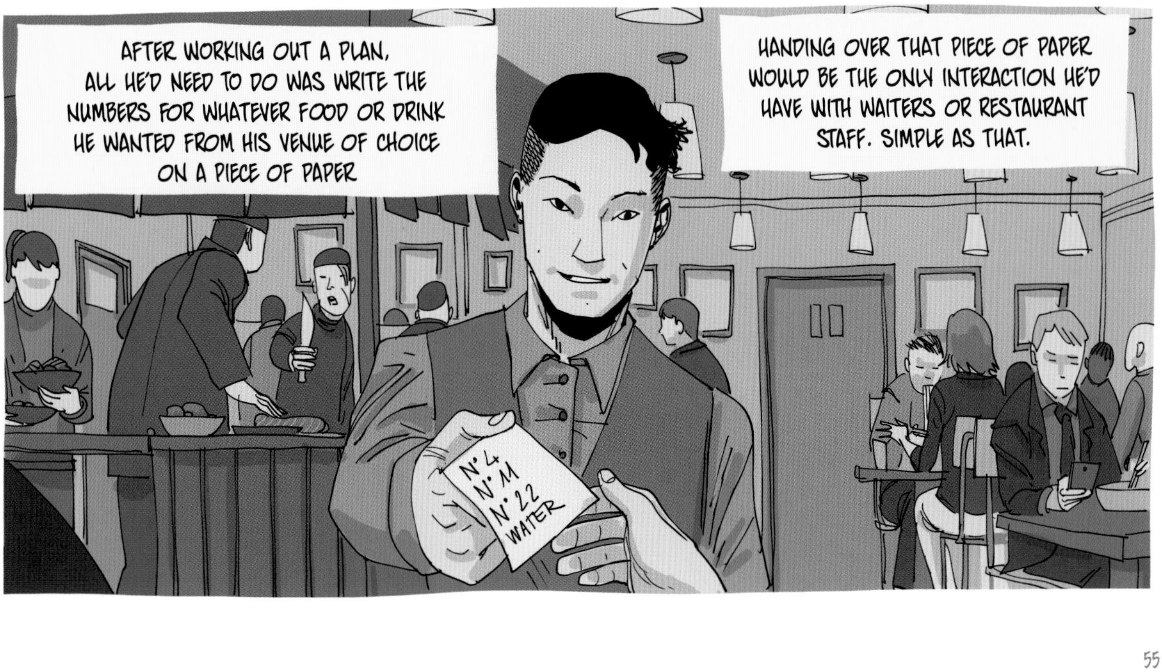
AFTER WORKING OUT A PLAN, ALL HE'D NEED TO DO WAS WRITE THE NUMBERS FOR WHATEVER FOOD OR DRINK HE WANTED FROM HIS VENUE OF CHOICE ON A PIECE OF PAPER
HANDING OVER THAT PIECE OF PAPER WOULD BE THE ONLY INTERACTION HE'D HAVE WITH WAITERS OR RESTAURANT STAFF. SIMPLE AS THAT.
N° 4
N° 11
N° 22
WATER

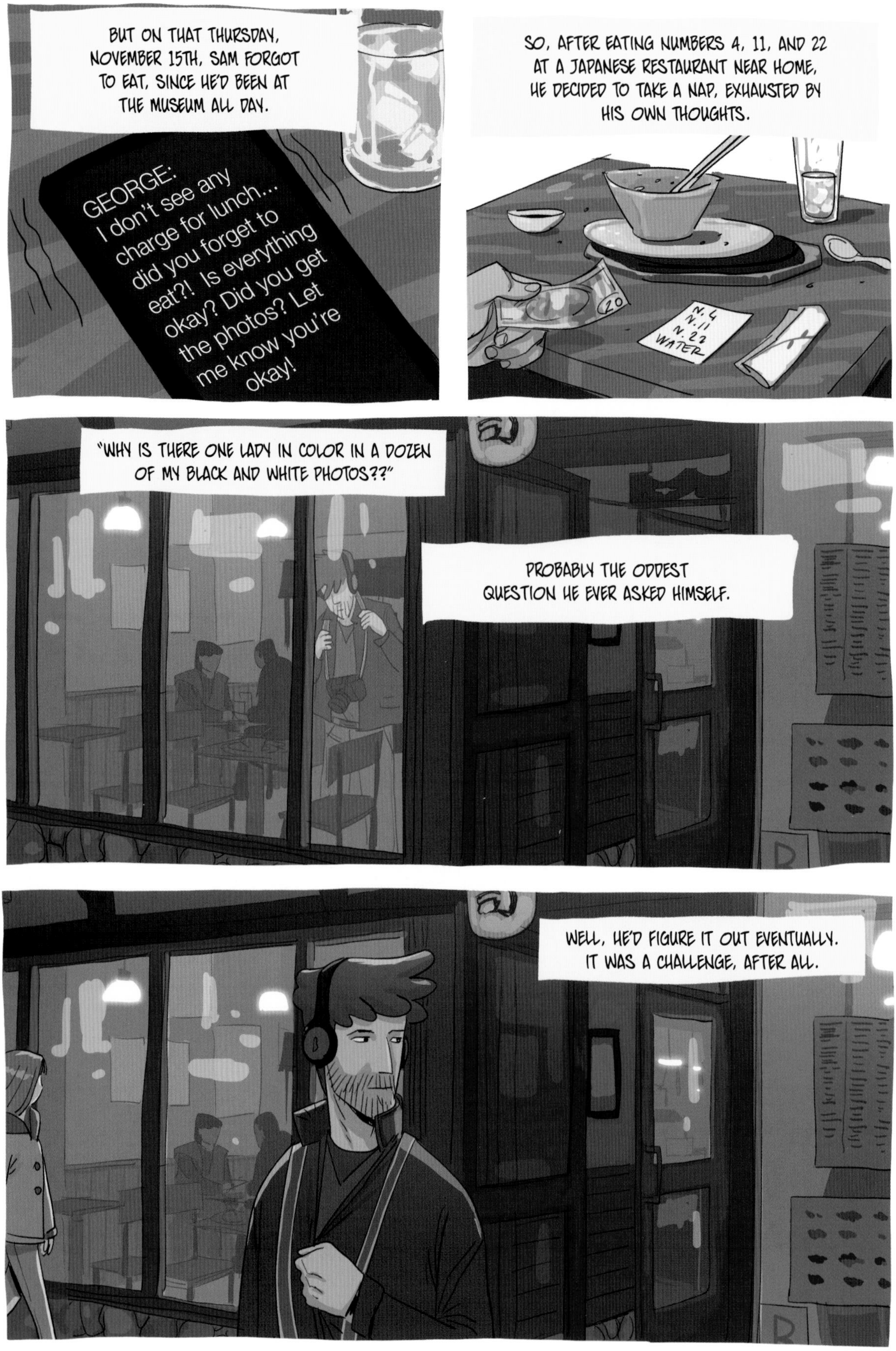
BUT ON THAT THURSDAY, NOVEMBER 15TH, SAM FORGOT TO EAT, SINCE HE'D BEEN AT THE MUSEUM ALL DAY.
GEORGE: I don't see any charge for lunch... did you forget to eat?! Is everything okay? Did you get the photos? Let me know you're okay!
SO, AFTER EATING NUMBERS 4, 11, AND 22 AT A JAPANESE RESTAURANT NEAR HOME, HE DECIDED TO TAKE A NAP, EXHAUSTED BY HIS OWN THOUGHTS.
20
N. 4
N. 11
N. 22
WATER
"WHY IS THERE ONE LADY IN COLOR IN A DOZEN OF MY BLACK AND WHITE PHOTOS??"
PROBABLY THE ODDEST QUESTION HE EVER ASKED HIMSELF.
WELL, HE'D FIGURE IT OUT EVENTUALLY. IT WAS A CHALLENGE, AFTER ALL.

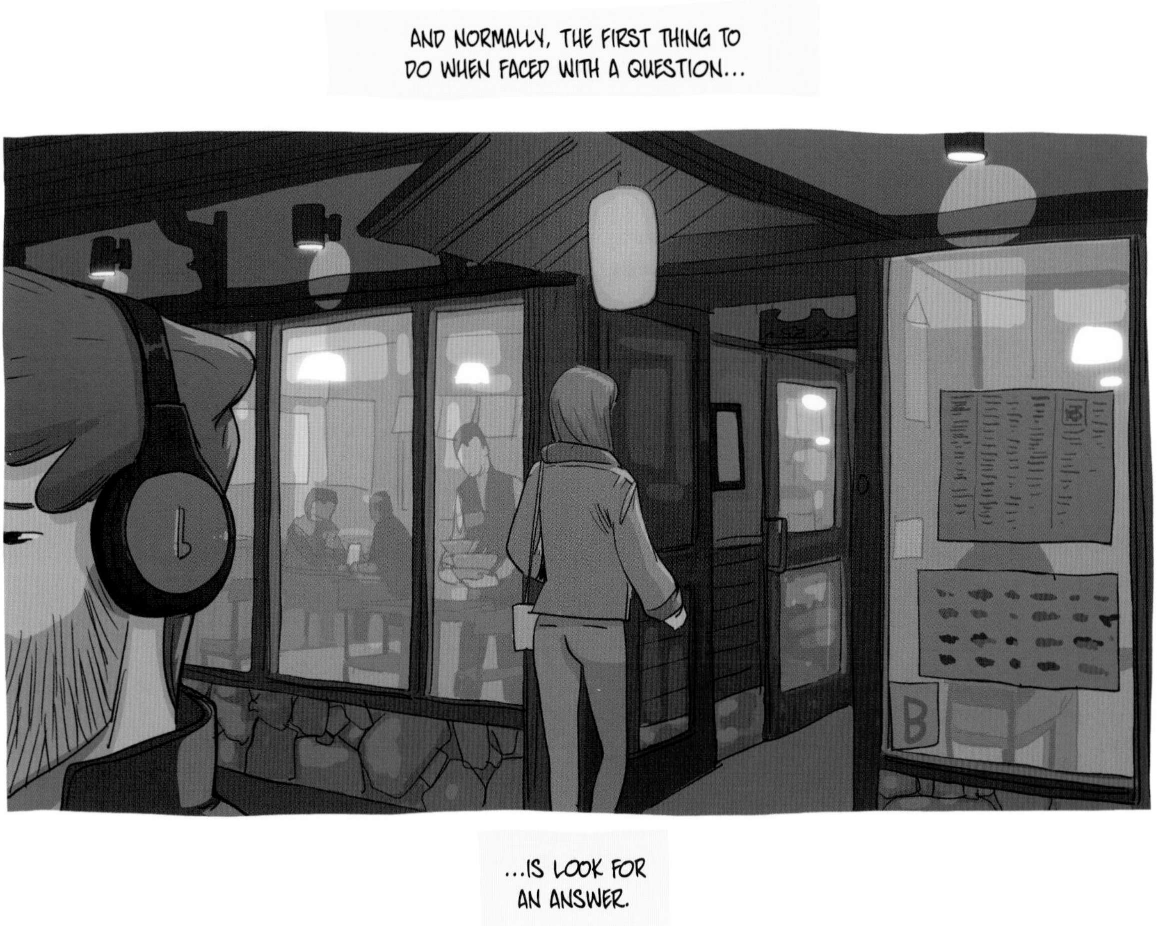
AND NORMALLY, THE FIRST THING TO DO WHEN FACED WITH A QUESTION...
...IS LOOK FOR AN ANSWER.
B

NOVEMBER 16TH

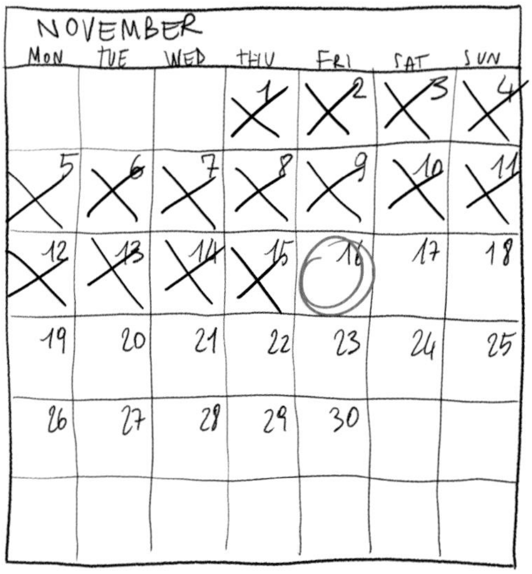
NOVEMBER
MON TUE WED THU FRI SAT SUN
1 2 3 4
5 6 7 8 9 10 11
12 13 14 15 16 17 18
19 20 21 22 23 24 25
26 27 28 29 30

(…) I LOVE JAZZ. IN SUMMER, THEY'LL OFTEN ORGANIZE
JAZZ CONCERTS IN THE CENTER OF MADISON SQUARE PARK.

I NEVER WENT TO ANY OF THEM.

FRANKLY, ALL I LISTEN TO IS CHET BAKER.

AND TO BE HONEST, I ONLY KNOW ONE OF HIS SONGS.

IN FACT, IT'S THE ONLY JAZZ SONG I KNOW.

NOVEMBER 20TH

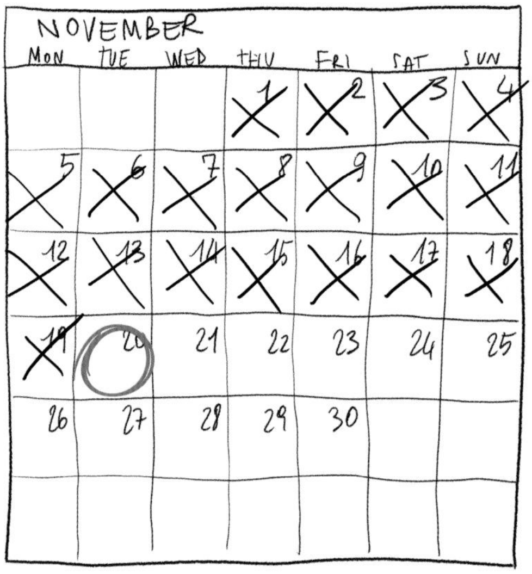
NOVEMBER
MON TUE WED THU FRI SAT SUN
1 2 3 4
5 6 7 8 9 10 11
12 13 14 15 16 17 18
19 20 21 22 23 24 25
26 27 28 29 30

(...) OF ALL THE MANY PLACES THE CITY OFFERED,
I WENT BACK TO CENTRAL PARK THE MOST.

ANYONE WHO SAYS THERE'S ONLY ONE CENTRAL PARK IS WRONG.

THERE ARE THOUSANDS OF CENTRAL PARKS.

ONE FOR EVERY SEASON, CLIMATE, OR WEATHER.

AND ONE FOR EVERY SECOND, MINUTE, AND HOUR OF THE DAY.

ONE FOR EVERY FALLING LEAF.

AND ONE FOR EVERY SINGLE RAY OF SUNSHINE THAT
FILTERS THROUGH THE TREE BRANCHES.

THERE'S A CENTRAL PARK FOR EVERY SNOWFLAKE THAT FALLS.

AND ONE FOR EVERY HORSE APPLE STUCK TO THE WHEELS OF A CARRIAGE.

WHOEVER SAYS THERE'S ONLY ONE CENTRAL PARK IS WRONG.

HONESTLY, I'VE NEVER SEEN THE SAME CENTRAL PARK TWICE IN MY LIFE (...)

NOVEMBER 24TH

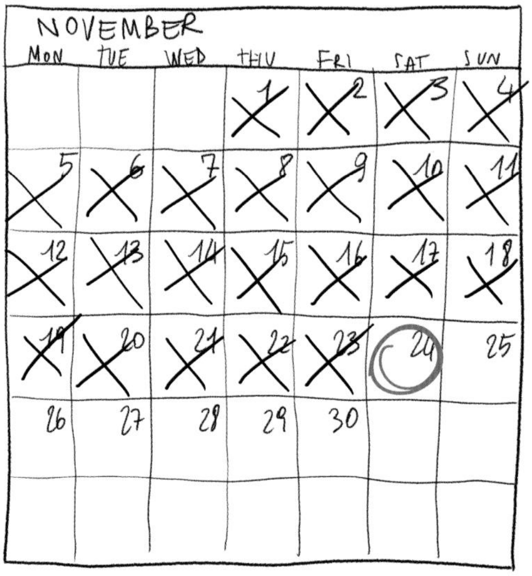
NOVEMBER
MON TUE WED THU FRI SAT SUN
1 2 3 4
5 6 7 8 9 10 11
12 13 14 15 16 17 18
19 20 21 22 23 24 25
26 27 28 29 30

(...) THERE WAS A CAFE ON 15TH THAT I'D GO TO OFTEN.

THE DECAF WASN'T ALL THAT GOOD.

AND THE MUFFINS WERE SORT OF DRY.

I DON'T REALLY RECALL MUCH ABOUT THE STAFF
OR OTHER CUSTOMERS.

SO WHY GO BACK THERE?

I THINK IT WAS BECAUSE THERE WAS AN ALLEY ACROSS THE STREET.
A NARROW ALLEY, BETWEEN TWO BUILDINGS.

AN ALLEY WHERE THE SETTING WINTER SUN
WOULD CUT THROUGH THE PLACE WITH AN INTENSITY
BEFORE LANDING ON MY BACK

I'M PRETTY SURE THAT WAS THE ONLY REASON.

THE WARMTH OF A NARROW
SUN ON MY BACK.

THE BOX

(...) NOTHING. THIS CITY JUST COULDN'T GIVE ME AN ANSWER. OR MAYBE I COULDN'T HEAR IT, BUT IT'S TRUE THAT SHE HAS HER OWN LANGUAGE, AND LIVING HERE, WELL, IT'S DIFFERENT... VERY DIFFERENT...

DIFFERENT FROM WHAT?

WELL, A DIFFERENT WAY OF LIVING THAN IN ANY OTHER CITY IN THE WORLD, AT LEAST FOR ME.

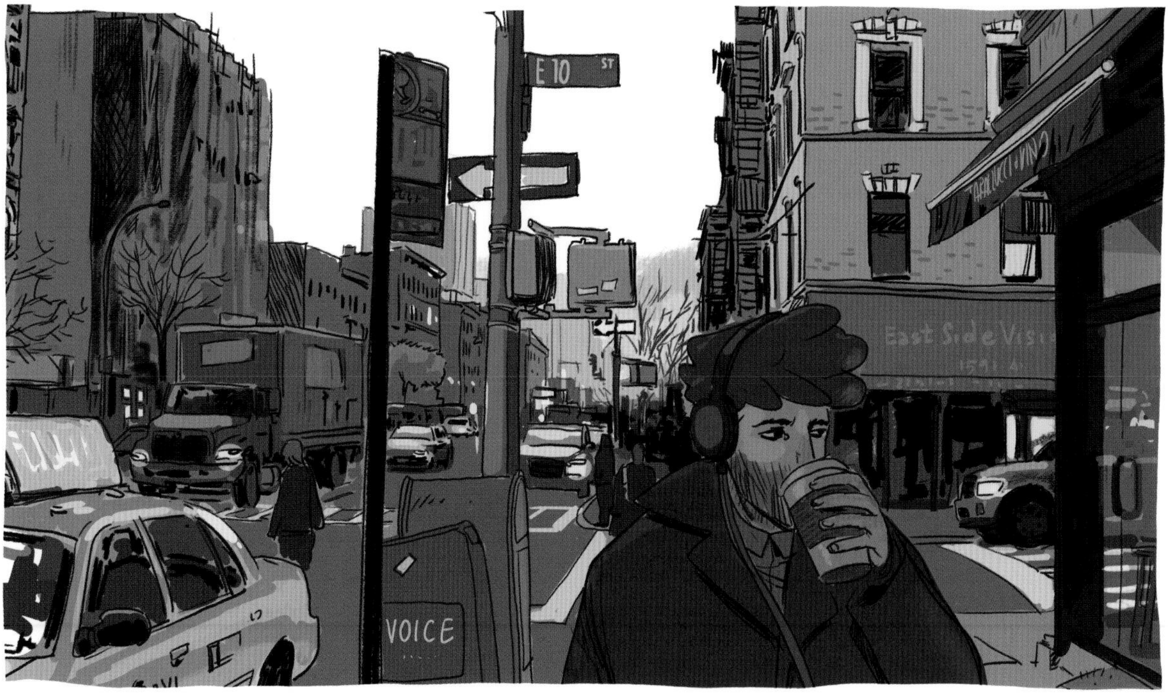
E 10 ST
VOICE

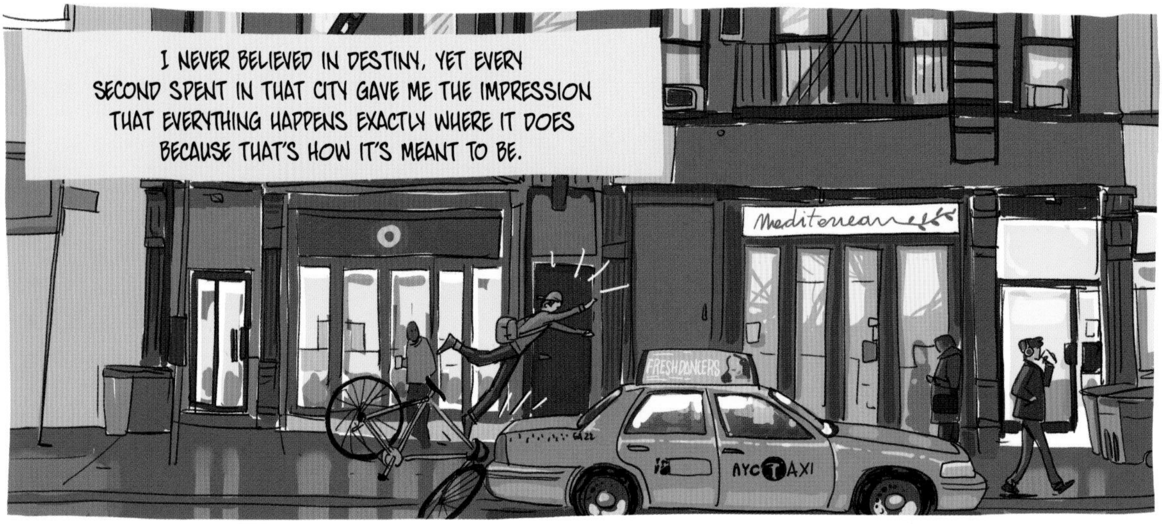
I NEVER BELIEVED IN DESTINY, YET EVERY SECOND SPENT IN THAT CITY GAVE ME THE IMPRESSION THAT EVERYTHING HAPPENS EXACTLY WHERE IT DOES BECAUSE THAT'S HOW IT'S MEANT TO BE.

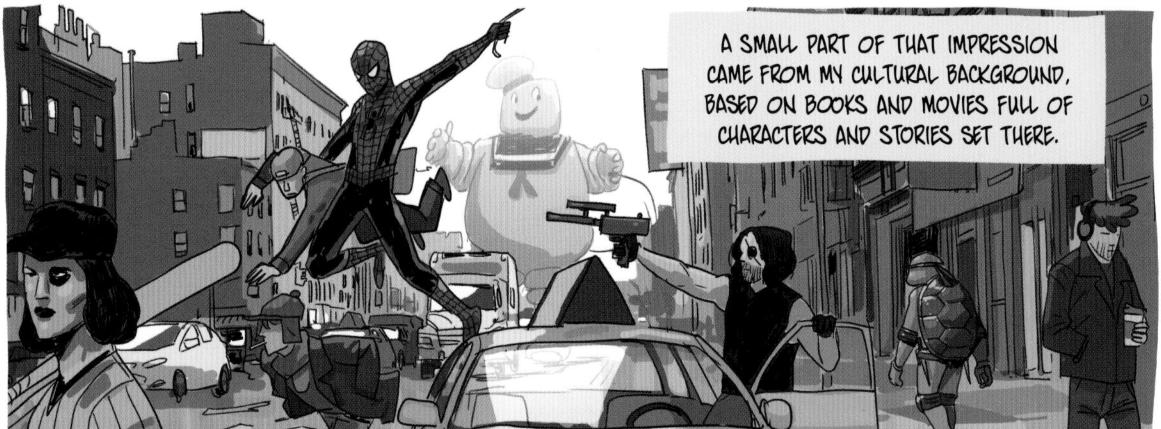
A SMALL PART OF THAT IMPRESSION CAME FROM MY CULTURAL BACKGROUND, BASED ON BOOKS AND MOVIES FULL OF CHARACTERS AND STORIES SET THERE.

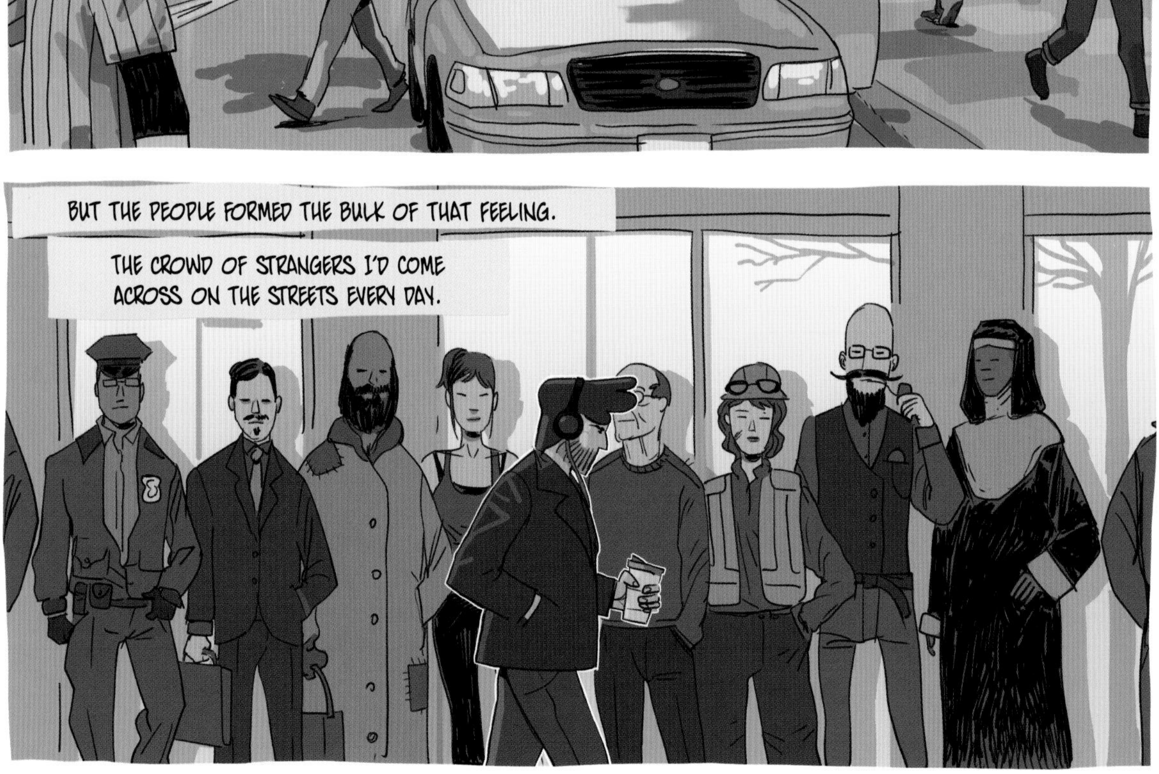
BUT THE PEOPLE FORMED THE BULK OF THAT FEELING.
THE CROWD OF STRANGERS I'D COME ACROSS ON THE STREETS EVERY DAY.

HUNDREDS OF HUMAN RUBBER BANDS, LAUNCHED IN DIFFERENT DIRECTIONS, EACH WITH THEIR OWN THOUGHTS AND DESTINATIONS.

THEIR OWN DREAMS.

TENS OF THOUSANDS OF ELBOWS BUMPING AGAINST EACH OTHER WITHOUT SAYING SORRY, JUST MOVING ON.

MORE THAN ONCE, I FOUND MYSELF WONDERING JUST HOW MUCH A SIMPLE NUDGE COULD AFFECT THE LIFE PATH OF EVERY SINGLE INDIVIDUAL IN NEW YORK CITY.

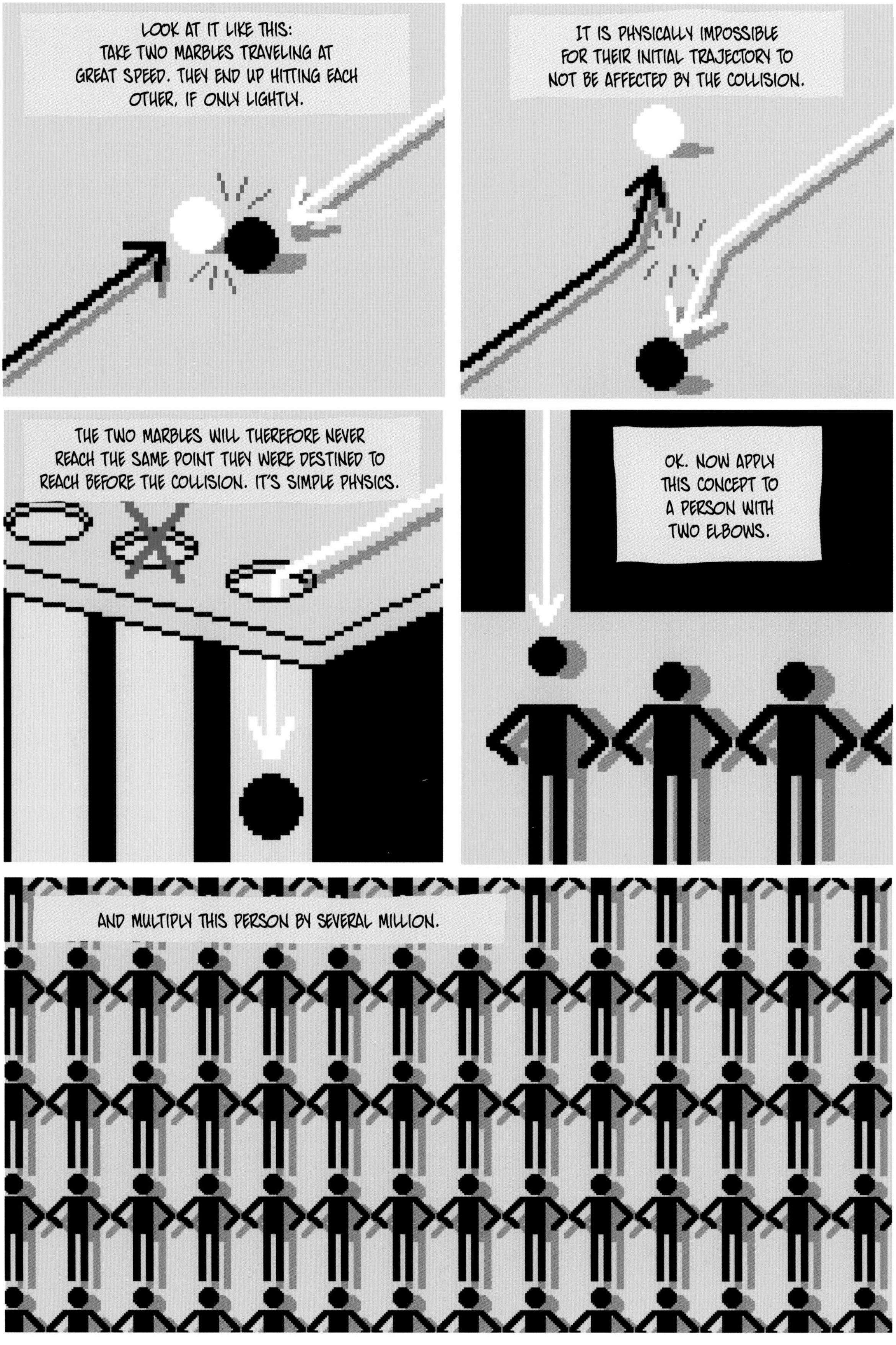
LOOK AT IT LIKE THIS: TAKE TWO MARBLES TRAVELING AT GREAT SPEED. THEY END UP HITTING EACH OTHER, IF ONLY LIGHTLY.
IT IS PHYSICALLY IMPOSSIBLE FOR THEIR INITIAL TRAJECTORY TO NOT BE AFFECTED BY THE COLLISION.
THE TWO MARBLES WILL THEREFORE NEVER REACH THE SAME POINT THEY WERE DESTINED TO REACH BEFORE THE COLLISION. IT'S SIMPLE PHYSICS.
OK. NOW APPLY THIS CONCEPT TO A PERSON WITH TWO ELBOWS.
AND MULTIPLY THIS PERSON BY SEVERAL MILLION.

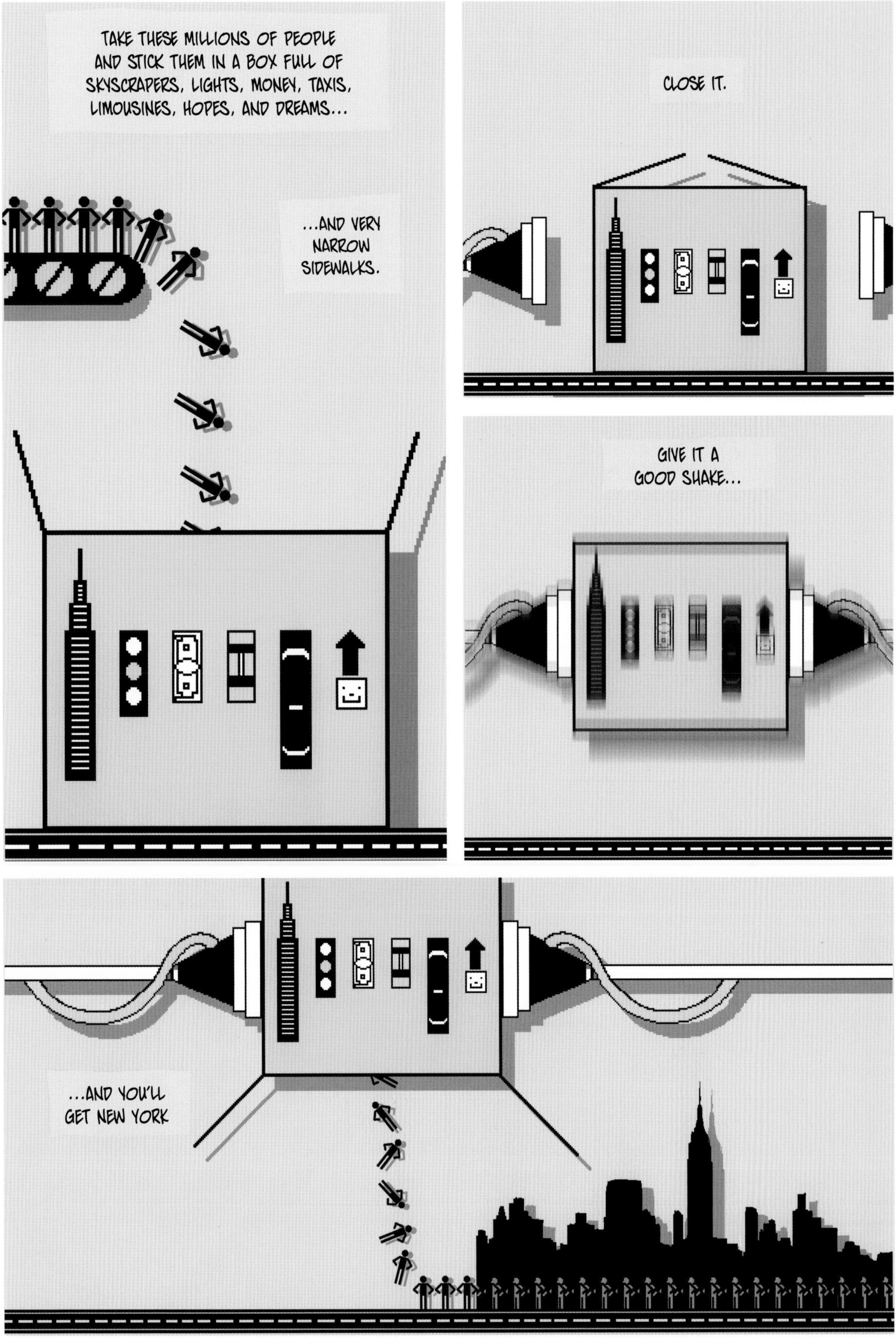
TAKE THESE MILLIONS OF PEOPLE AND STICK THEM IN A BOX FULL OF SKYSCRAPERS, LIGHTS, MONEY, TAXIS, LIMOUSINES, HOPES, AND DREAMS...
...AND VERY NARROW SIDEWALKS.
CLOSE IT.
GIVE IT A GOOD SHAKE...
...AND YOU'LL GET NEW YORK

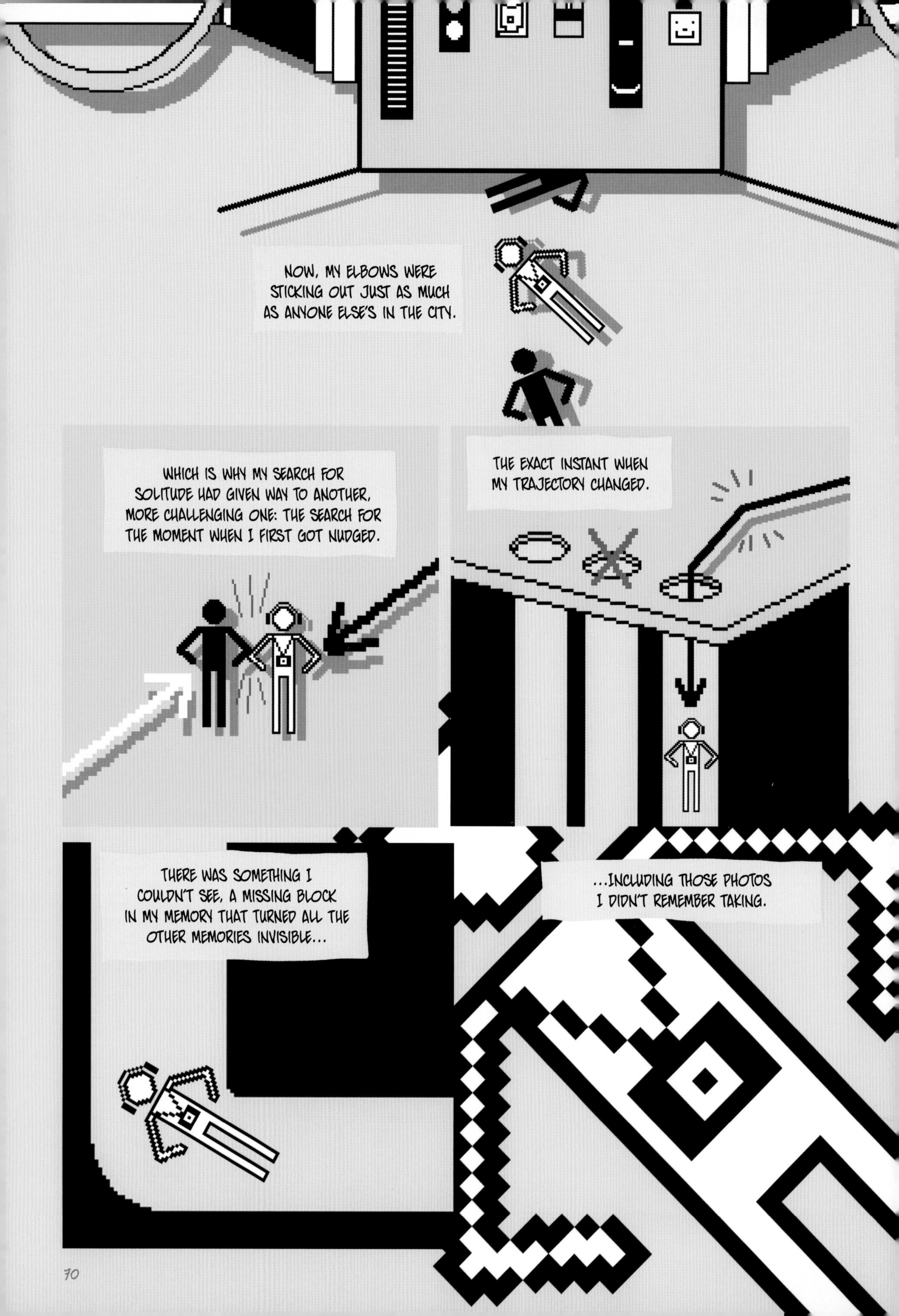
NOW, MY ELBOWS WERE STICKING OUT JUST AS MUCH AS ANYONE ELSE'S IN THE CITY.
WHICH IS WHY MY SEARCH FOR SOLITUDE HAD GIVEN WAY TO ANOTHER, MORE CHALLENGING ONE: THE SEARCH FOR THE MOMENT WHEN I FIRST GOT NUDGED.
THE EXACT INSTANT WHEN MY TRAJECTORY CHANGED.
THERE WAS SOMETHING I COULDN'T SEE, A MISSING BLOCK IN MY MEMORY THAT TURNED ALL THE OTHER MEMORIES INVISIBLE...
...INCLUDING THOSE PHOTOS I DIDN'T REMEMBER TAKING.

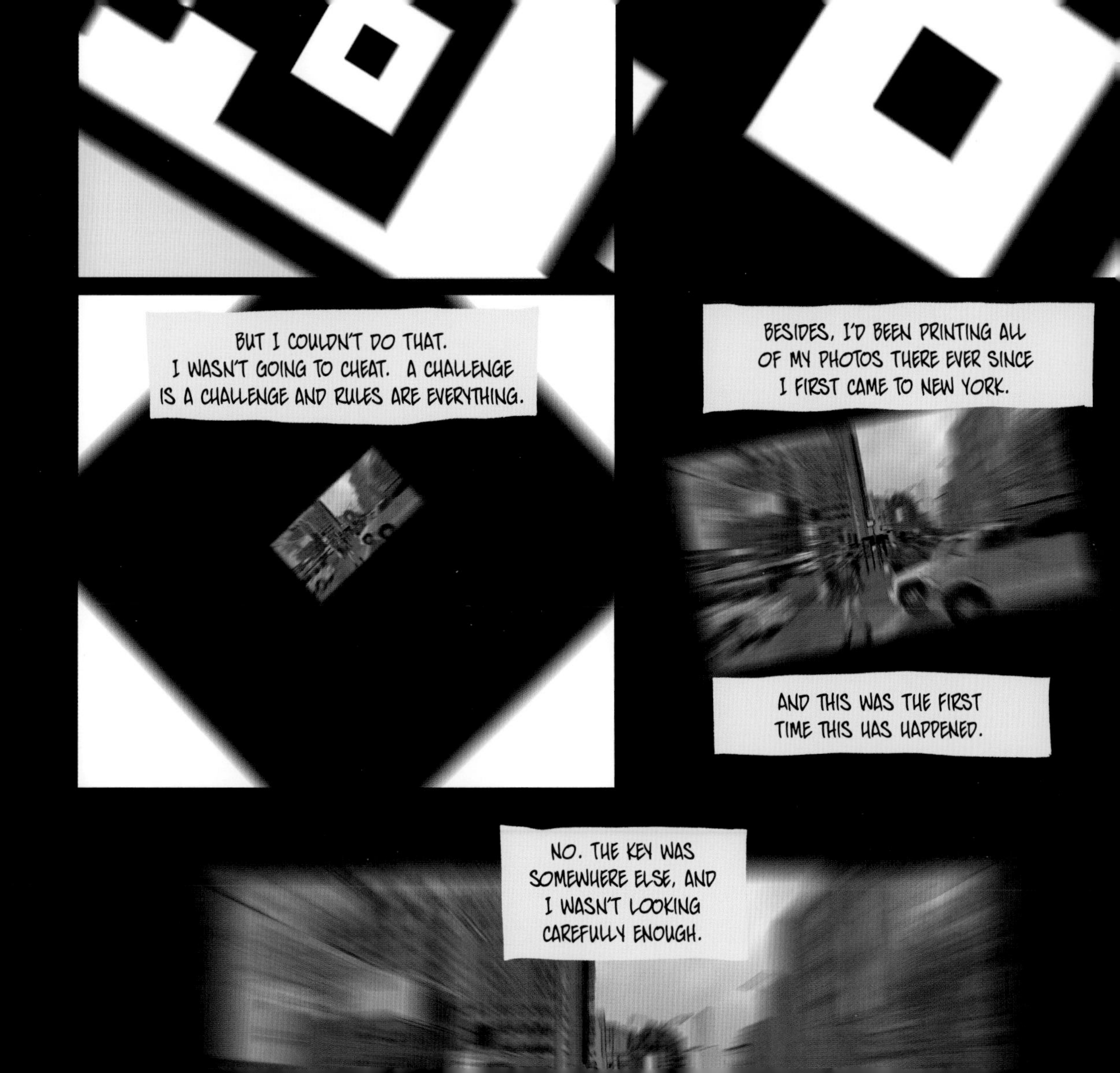
BUT I COULDN'T DO THAT. I WASN'T GOING TO CHEAT. A CHALLENGE IS A CHALLENGE AND RULES ARE EVERYTHING.
BESIDES, I'D BEEN PRINTING ALL OF MY PHOTOS THERE EVER SINCE I FIRST CAME TO NEW YORK.
AND THIS WAS THE FIRST TIME THIS HAS HAPPENED.
NO. THE KEY WAS SOMEWHERE ELSE, AND I WASN'T LOOKING CAREFULLY ENOUGH.

SOMETHING PREVENTED ME FROM REMEMBERING. SOMETHING STOPPED ME FROM FALLING IN LOVE WITH THE MOMENT WHEN I TOOK THE PHOTO. I JUST HAD TO FIGURE OUT WHAT IT WAS.

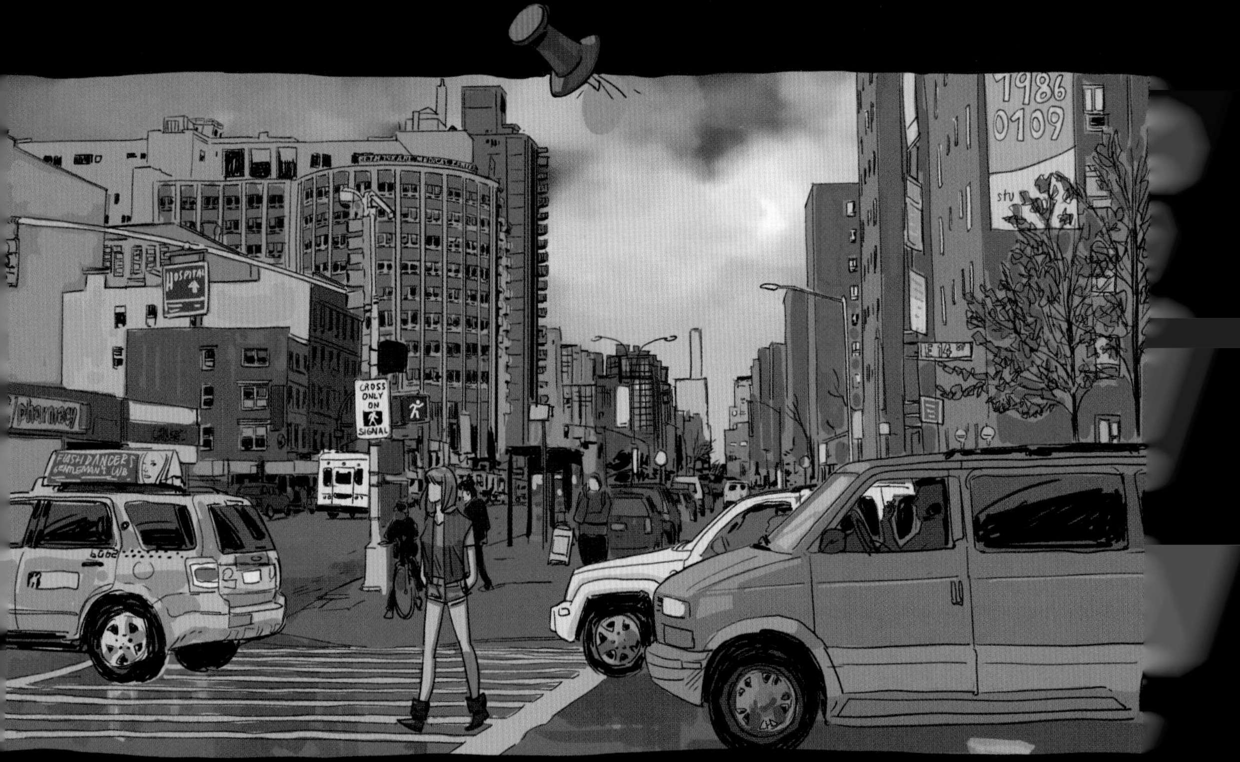

1986
0109
HOSPITAL
CROSS ONLY ON SIGNAL
pharmacy

SO, EVERY DAY, FROM THAT MOMENT FORWARD, I STARTED FOLLOWING THE EXACT SAME SCRIPT (...)

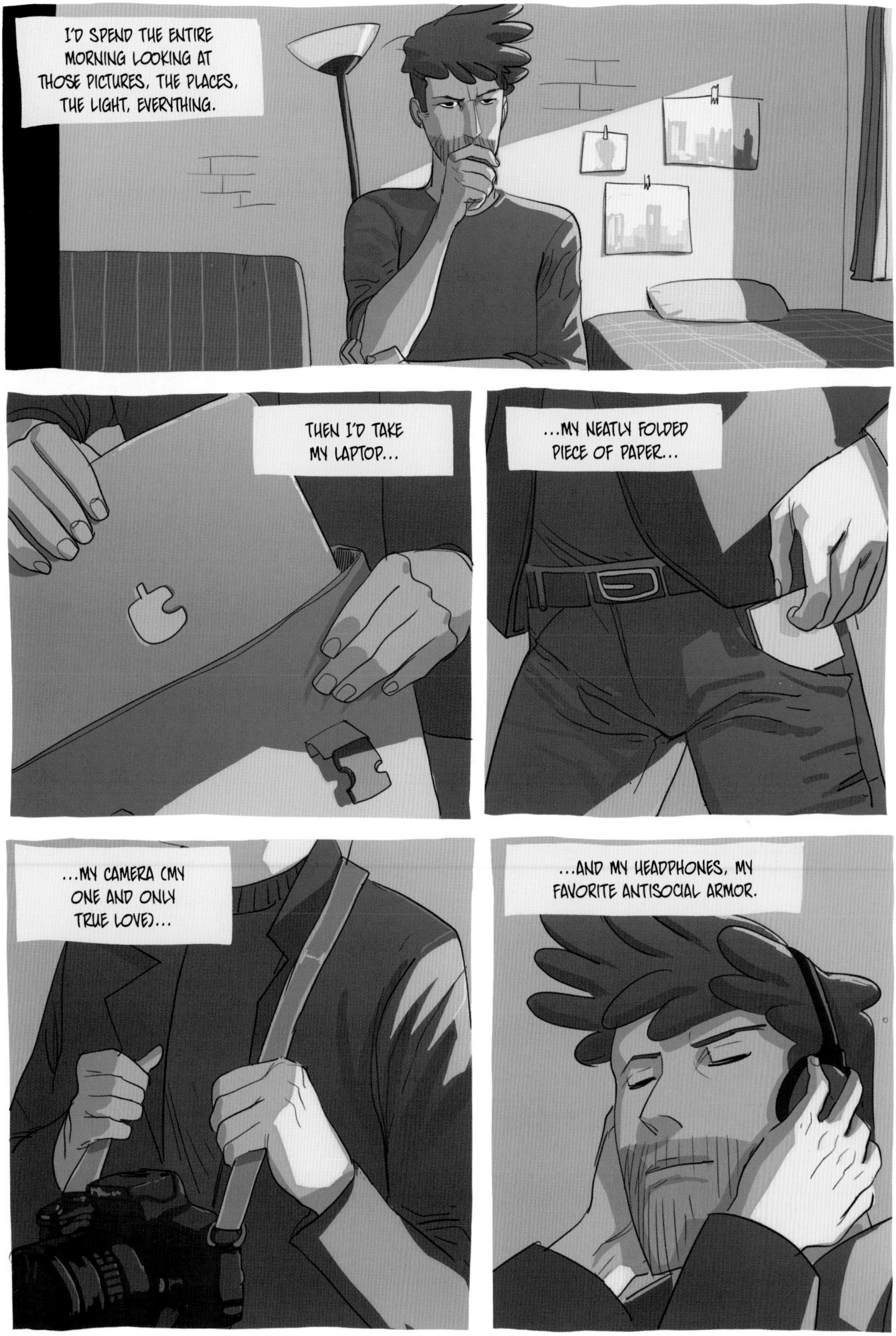
I'D SPEND THE ENTIRE MORNING LOOKING AT THOSE PICTURES, THE PLACES, THE LIGHT, EVERYTHING.
THEN I'D TAKE MY LAPTOP...
...MY NEATLY FOLDED PIECE OF PAPER...
...MY CAMERA (MY ONE AND ONLY TRUE LOVE)...
...AND MY HEADPHONES, MY FAVORITE ANTISOCIAL ARMOR.

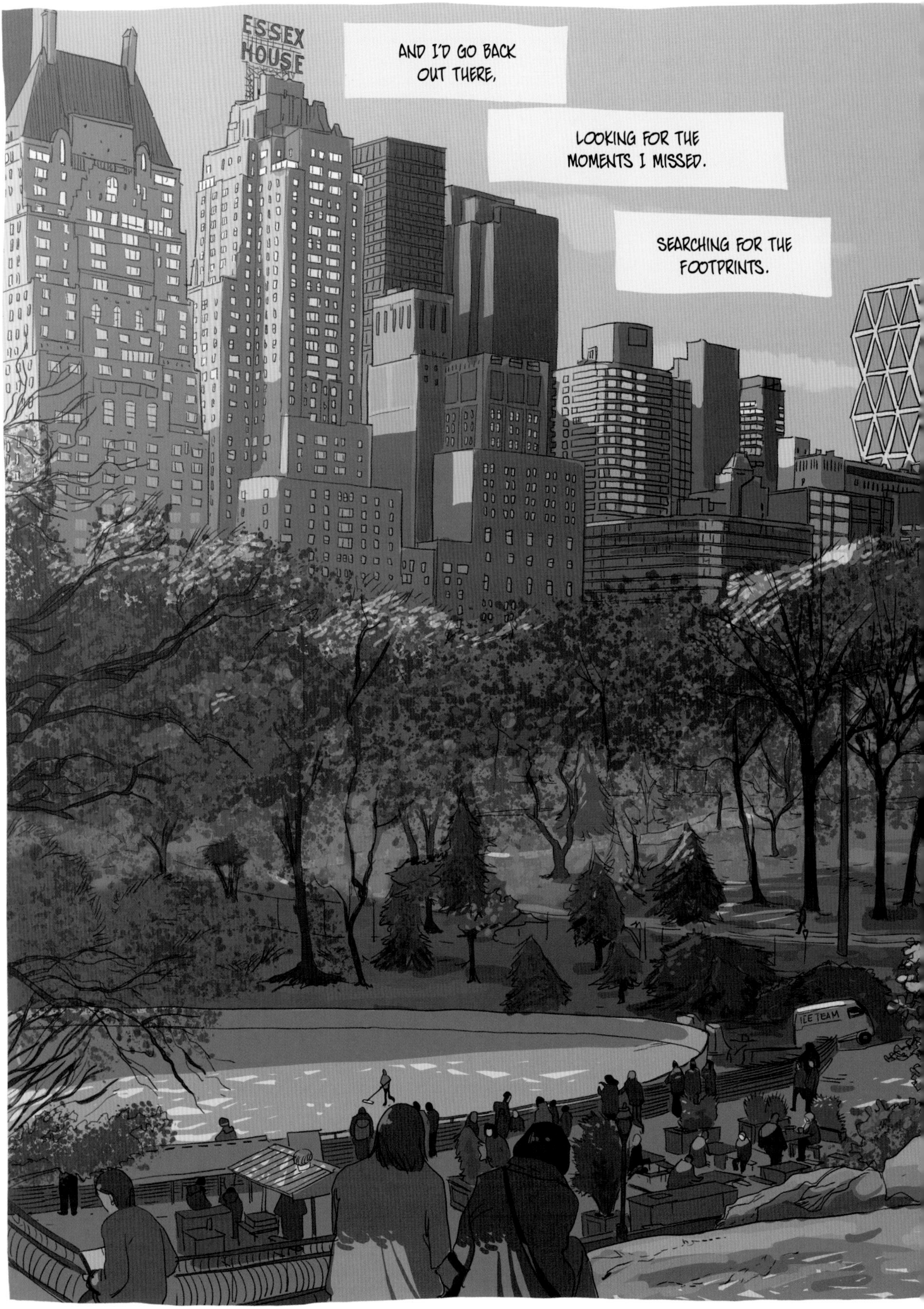
ESSEX HOUSE
AND I'D GO BACK OUT THERE,
LOOKING FOR THE MOMENTS I MISSED.
SEARCHING FOR THE FOOTPRINTS.
ICE TEAM

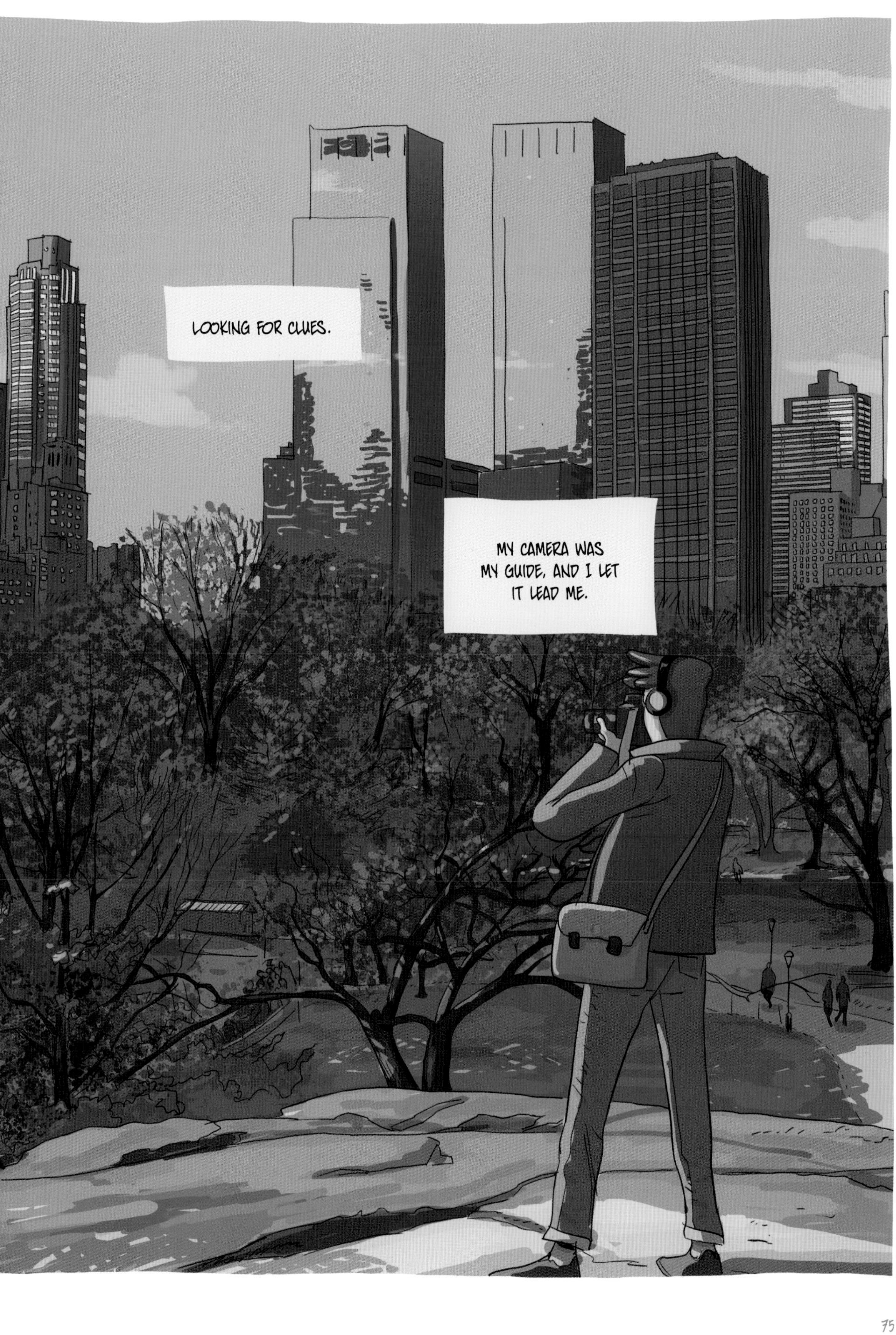
LOOKING FOR CLUES.
MY CAMERA WAS MY GUIDE, AND I LET IT LEAD ME.

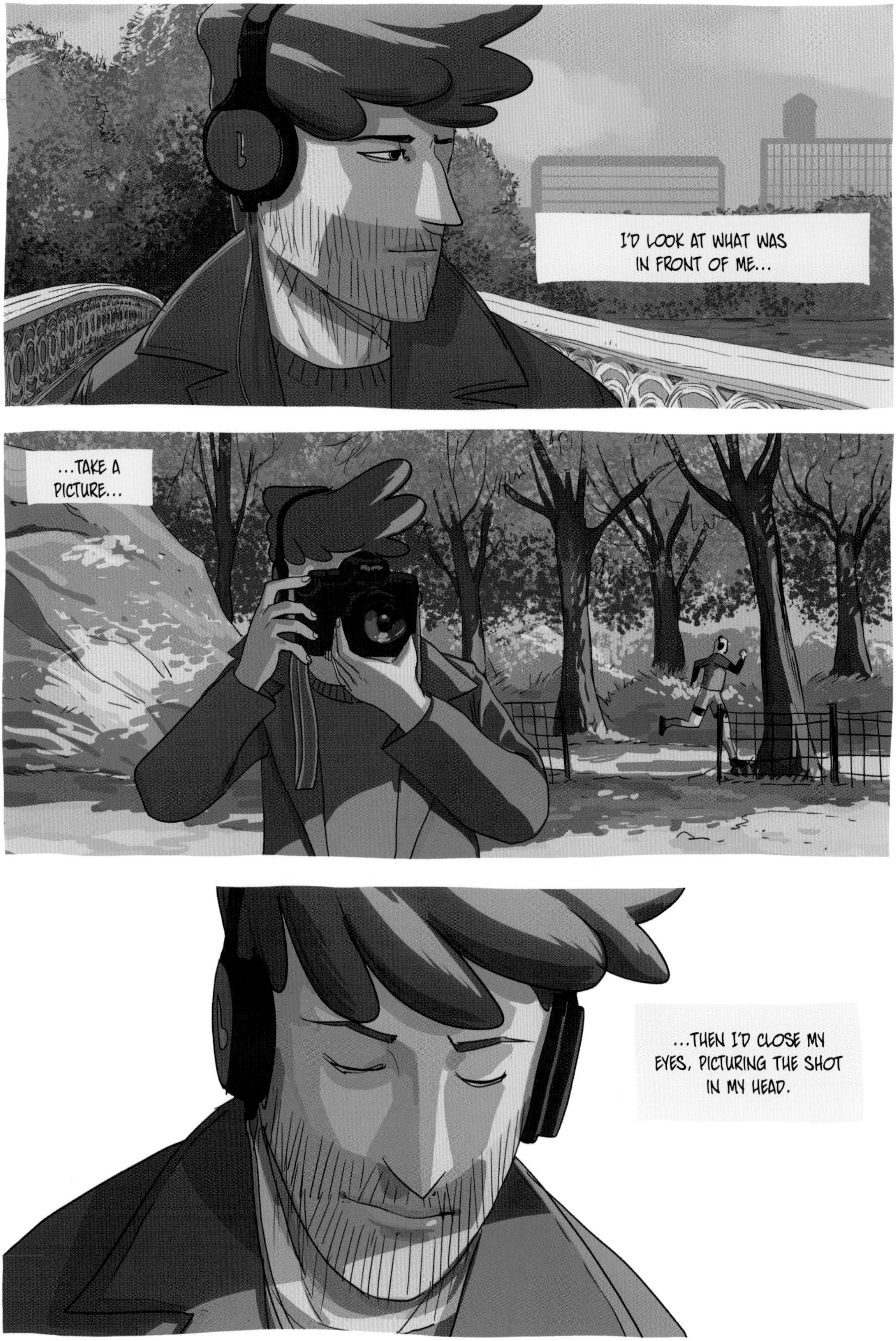
I'D LOOK AT WHAT WAS IN FRONT OF ME...
...TAKE A PICTURE...
...THEN I'D CLOSE MY EYES, PICTURING THE SHOT IN MY HEAD.

AND THERE IT WAS,
JUST AS I IMAGINED IT.

EVERYTHING WENT WELL, FOR A WHILE AT LEAST,
UNTIL ONE AFTERNOON...

THE AFTERNOON OF FRIDAY, NOVEMBER 30TH.

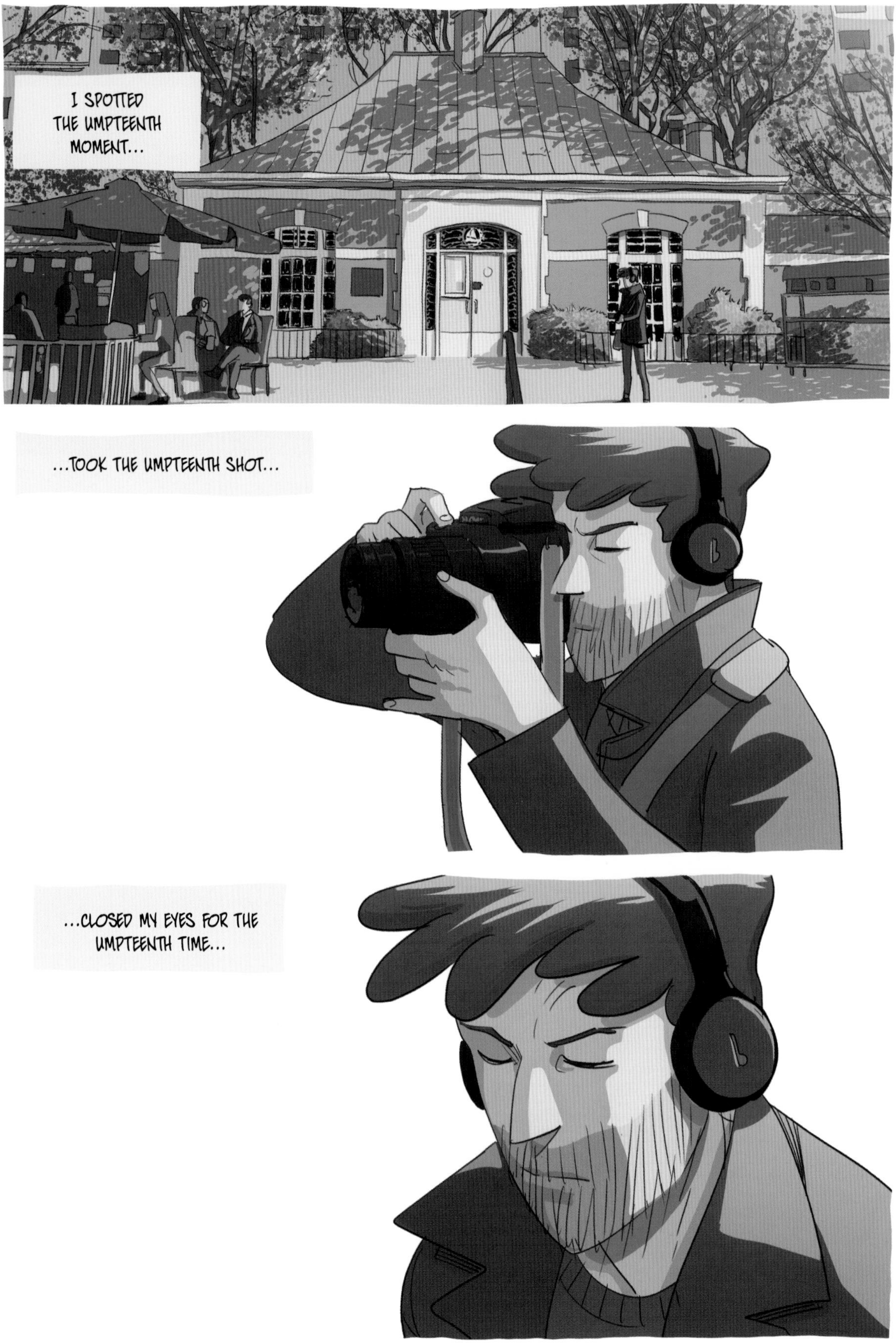
I SPOTTED THE UMPTEENTH MOMENT...
...TOOK THE UMPTEENTH SHOT...
...CLOSED MY EYES FOR THE UMPTEENTH TIME...

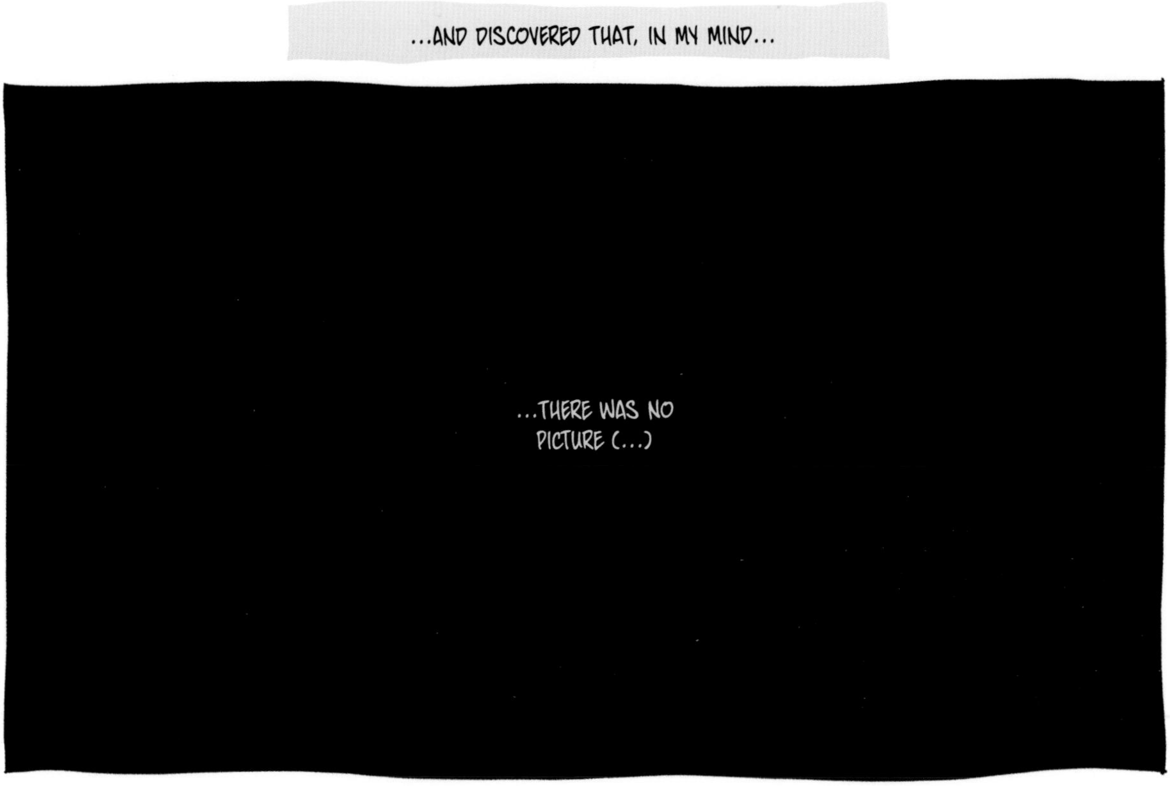
...AND DISCOVERED THAT, IN MY MIND...
...THERE WAS NO PICTURE (...)

NOVEMBER 30TH

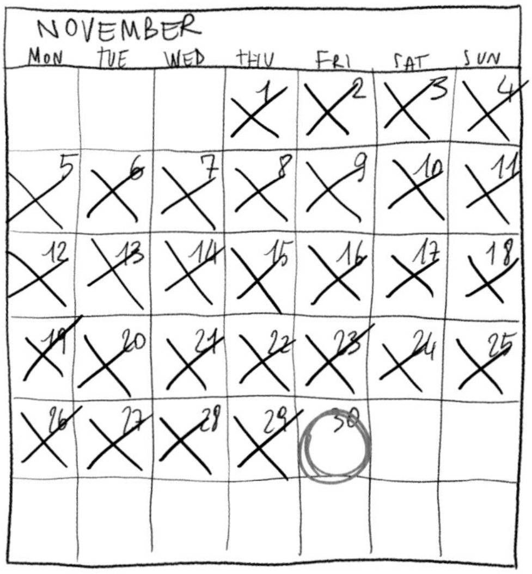
NOVEMBER
MON TUE WED THU FRI SAT SUN
1 2 3 4
5 6 7 8 9 10 11
12 13 14 15 16 17 18
19 20 21 22 23 24 25
26 27 28 29 30

HIS FIRST REACTION WAS TO PANIC, OF COURSE.

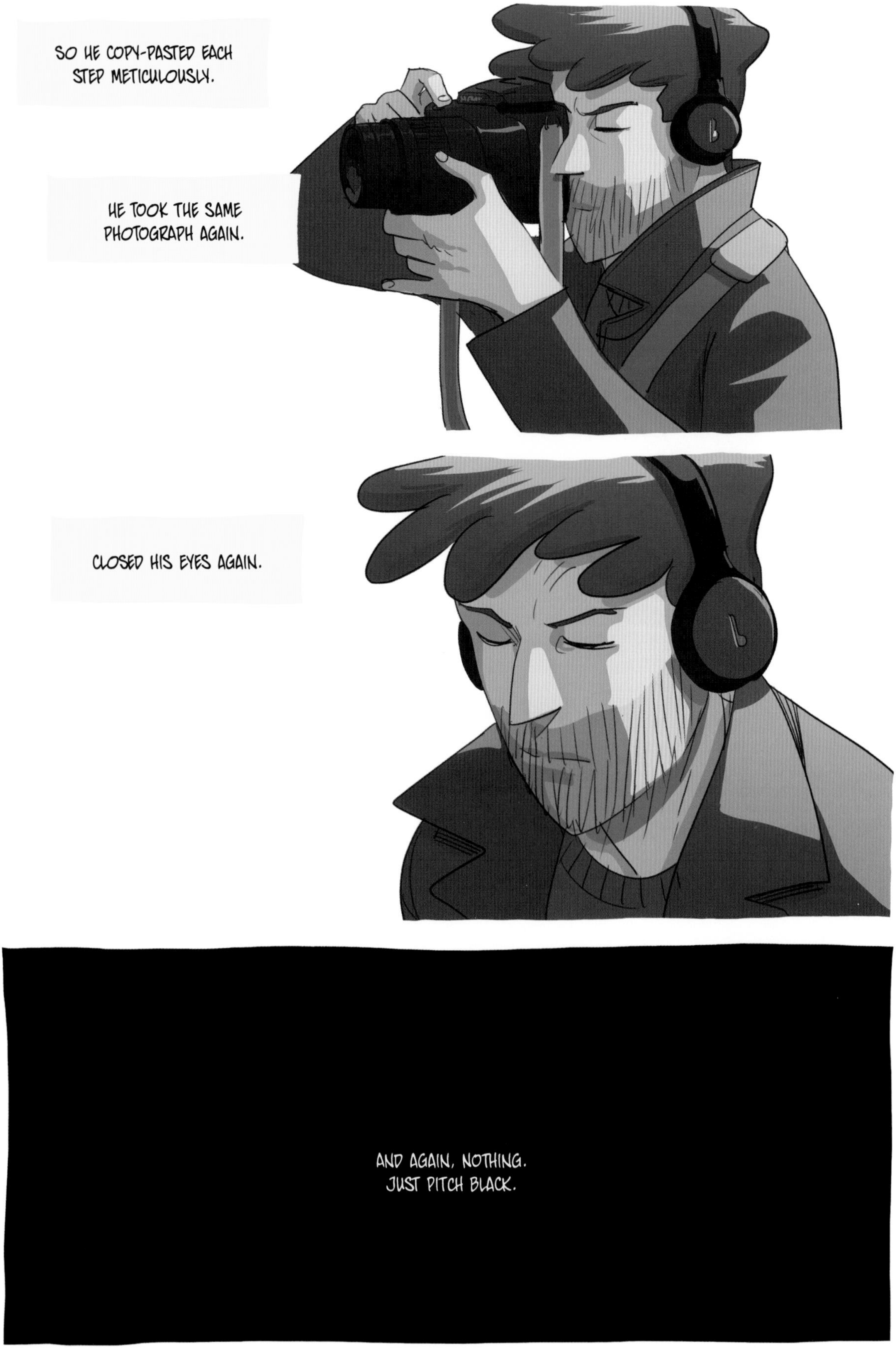
SO HE COPY-PASTED EACH STEP METICULOUSLY.
HE TOOK THE SAME PHOTOGRAPH AGAIN.
CLOSED HIS EYES AGAIN.
AND AGAIN, NOTHING. JUST PITCH BLACK.

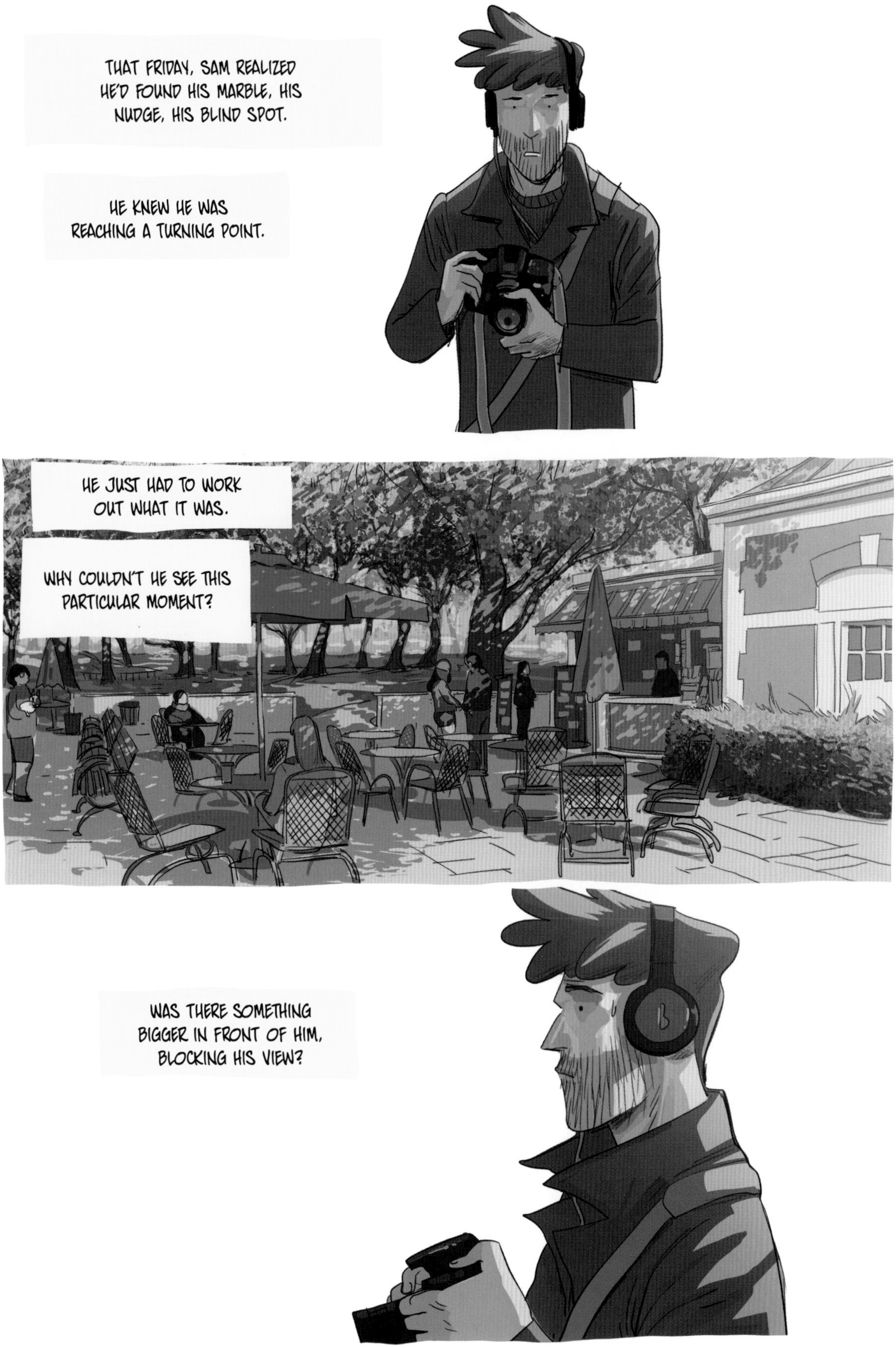
THAT FRIDAY, SAM REALIZED HE'D FOUND HIS MARBLE, HIS NUDGE, HIS BLIND SPOT.
HE KNEW HE WAS REACHING A TURNING POINT.
HE JUST HAD TO WORK OUT WHAT IT WAS.
WHY COULDN'T HE SEE THIS PARTICULAR MOMENT?
WAS THERE SOMETHING BIGGER IN FRONT OF HIM, BLOCKING HIS VIEW?

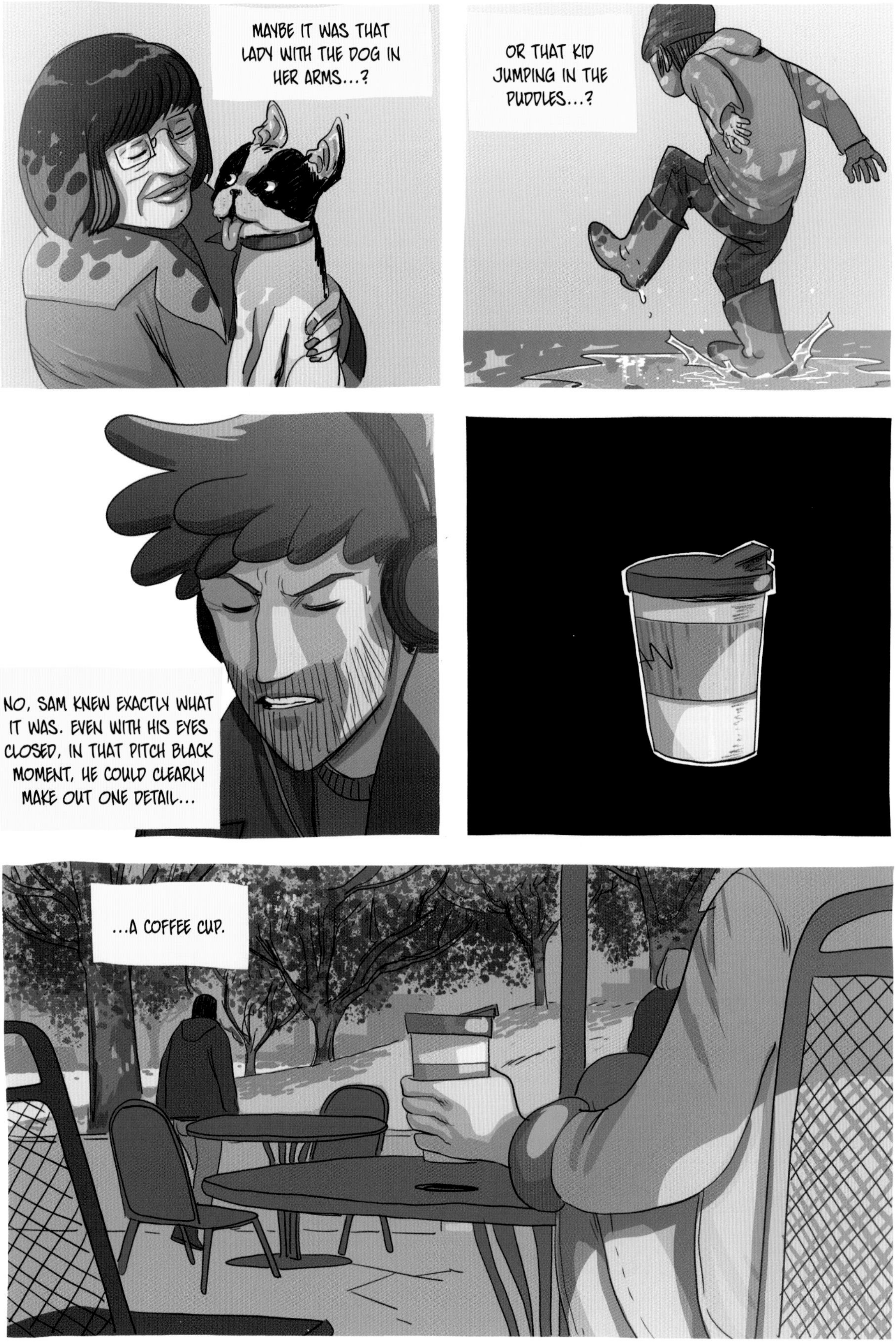
MAYBE IT WAS THAT LADY WITH THE DOG IN HER ARMS...?
OR THAT KID JUMPING IN THE PUDDLES...?
NO, SAM KNEW EXACTLY WHAT IT WAS. EVEN WITH HIS EYES CLOSED, IN THAT PITCH BLACK MOMENT, HE COULD CLEARLY MAKE OUT ONE DETAIL...
...A COFFEE CUP.

NO, NOT THE CUP.

THE PERSON HOLDING IT.

HER...

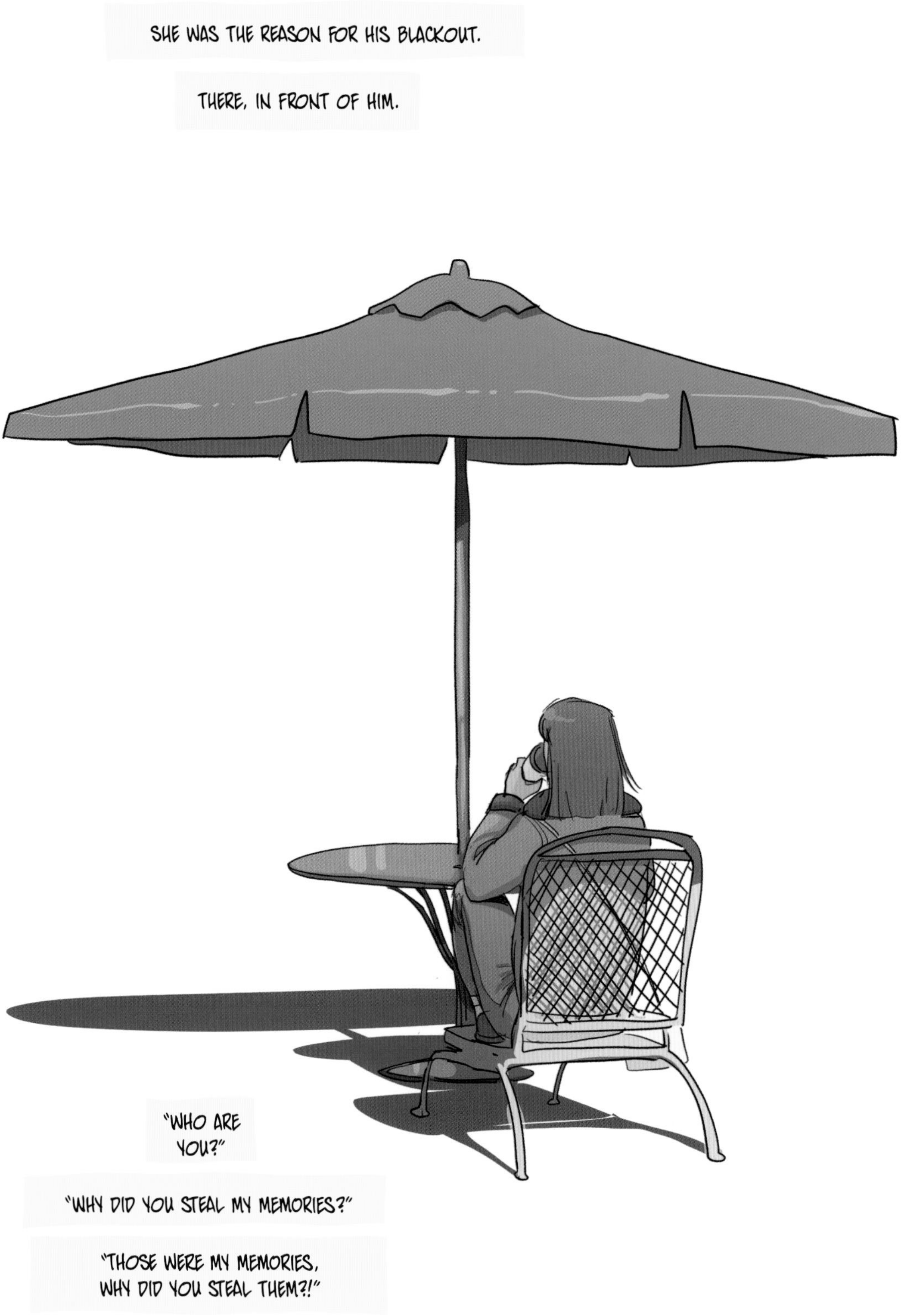
SHE WAS THE REASON FOR HIS BLACKOUT.
THERE, IN FRONT OF HIM.
"WHO ARE YOU?"
"WHY DID YOU STEAL MY MEMORIES?"
"THOSE WERE MY MEMORIES, WHY DID YOU STEAL THEM?!"

THERE WERE A HUNDRED QUESTIONS IN
SAM'S HEAD, BUT HE COULDN'T ASK ANY OF THEM.

HE WASN'T ALLOWED TO TALK TO HER, EVEN THOUGH IT WAS
THE ONE THING HE WANTED TO DO MOST RIGHT NOW.

HE COULDN'T DO IT, HE COULDN'T BREAK THE MOST IMPORTANT
RULE OF THE CHALLENGE. HE'D NEVER FORGIVE HIMSELF.

SO, THAT DAY, HE DECIDED TO BREAK A SMALLER ONE.

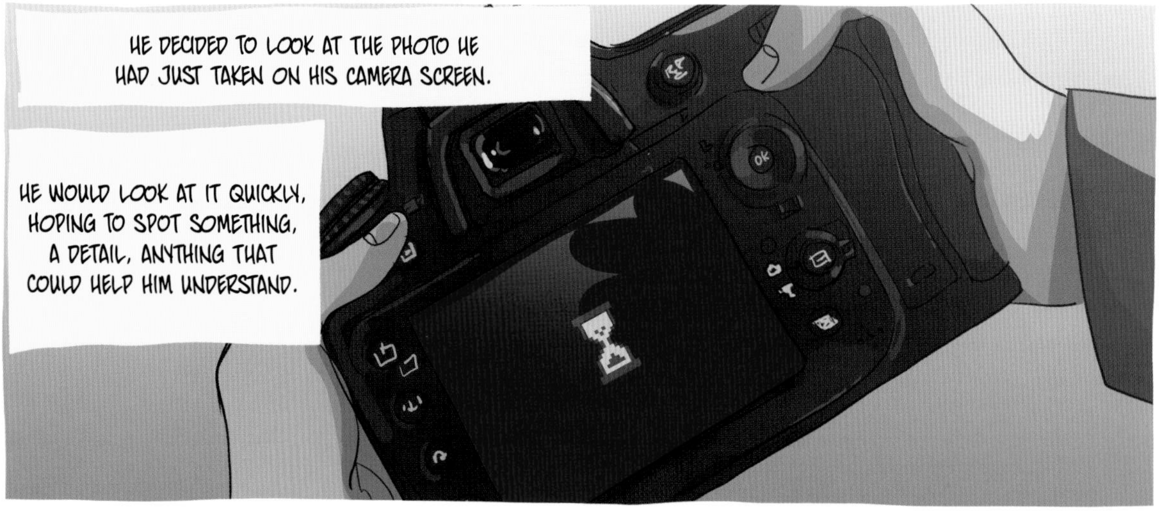
HE DECIDED TO LOOK AT THE PHOTO HE HAD JUST TAKEN ON HIS CAMERA SCREEN.
HE WOULD LOOK AT IT QUICKLY, HOPING TO SPOT SOMETHING, A DETAIL, ANYTHING THAT COULD HELP HIM UNDERSTAND.

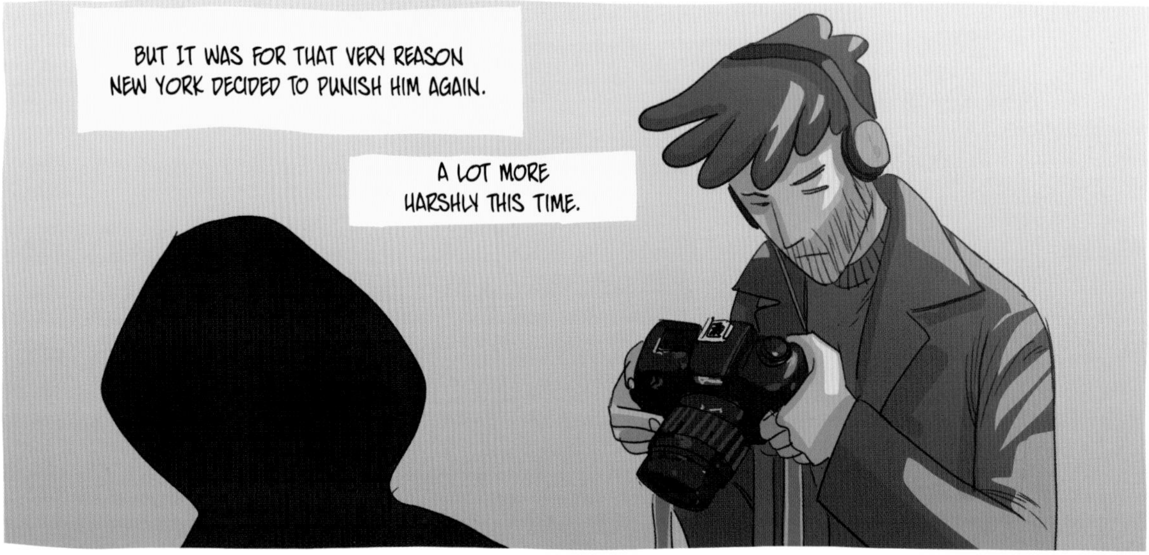
BUT IT WAS FOR THAT VERY REASON NEW YORK DECIDED TO PUNISH HIM AGAIN.
A LOT MORE HARSHLY THIS TIME.

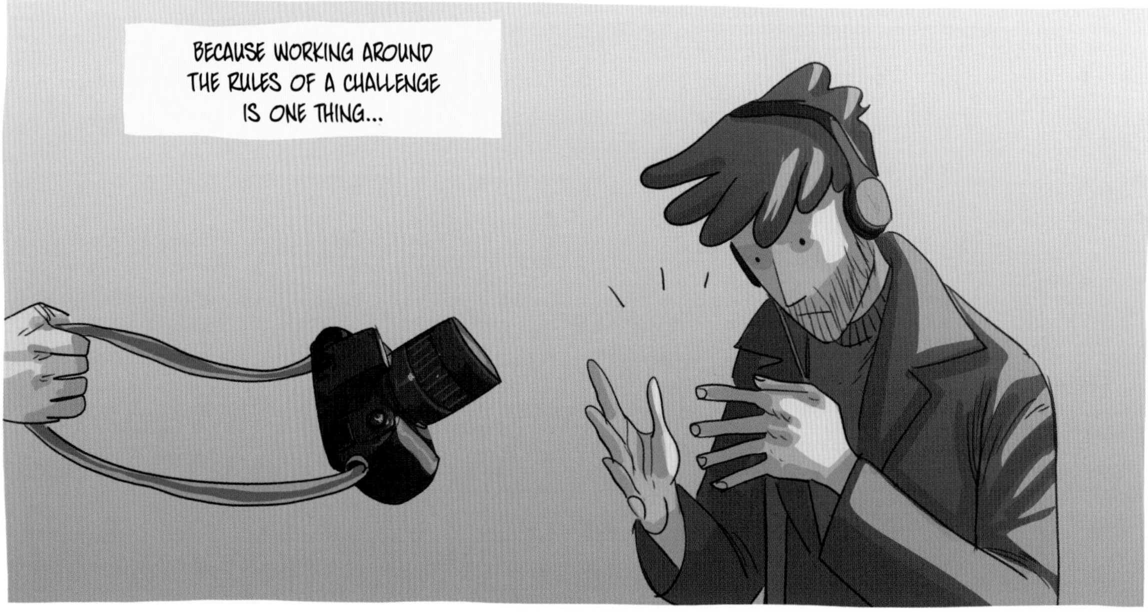
BECAUSE WORKING AROUND THE RULES OF A CHALLENGE IS ONE THING...

...BUT BREAKING THEM IS
ANOTHER MATTER ENTIRELY.

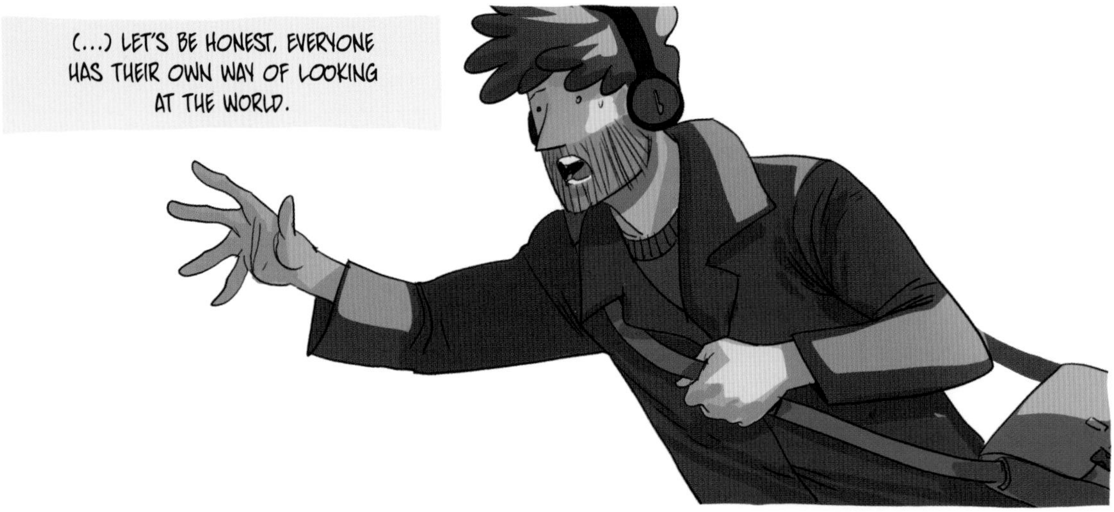
(...) LET'S BE HONEST, EVERYONE HAS THEIR OWN WAY OF LOOKING AT THE WORLD.

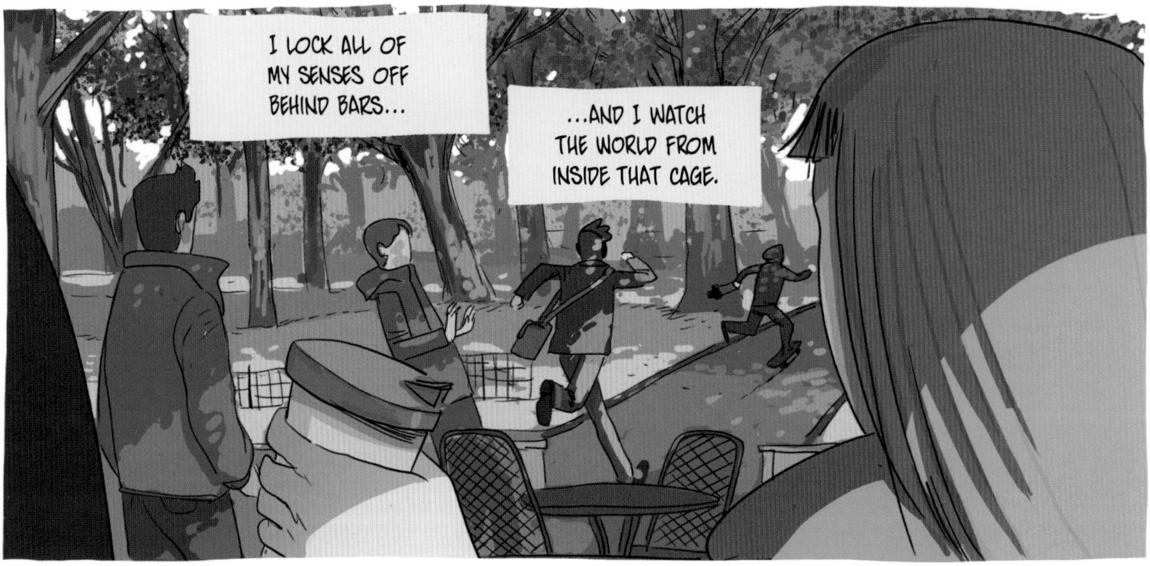
I LOCK ALL OF MY SENSES OFF BEHIND BARS...
...AND I WATCH THE WORLD FROM INSIDE THAT CAGE.

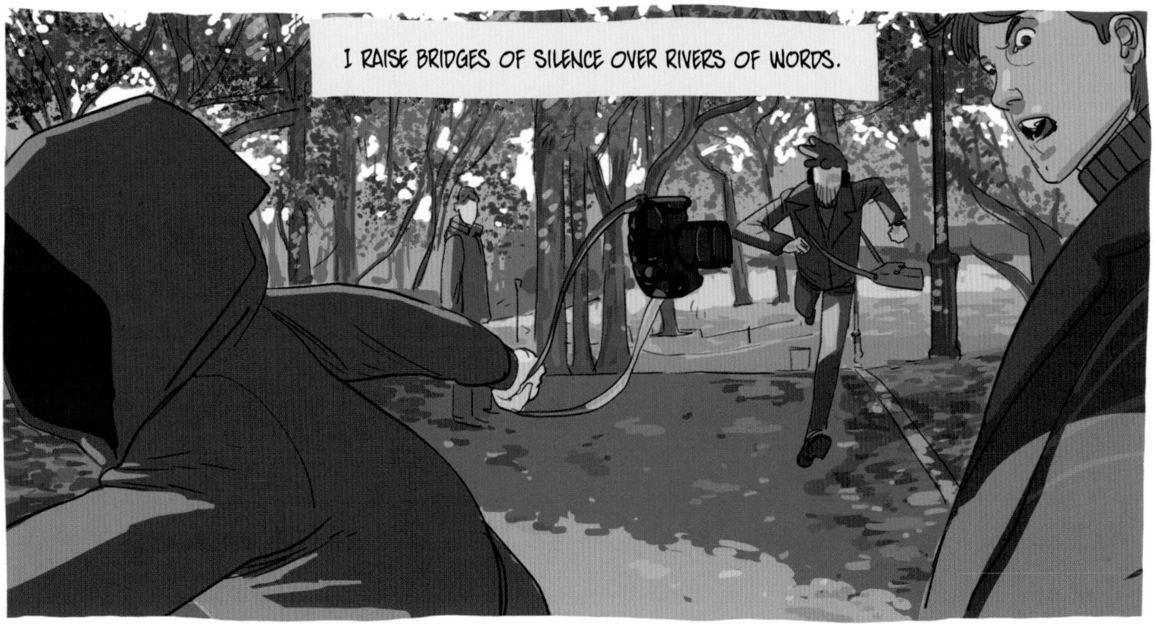
I RAISE BRIDGES OF SILENCE OVER RIVERS OF WORDS.

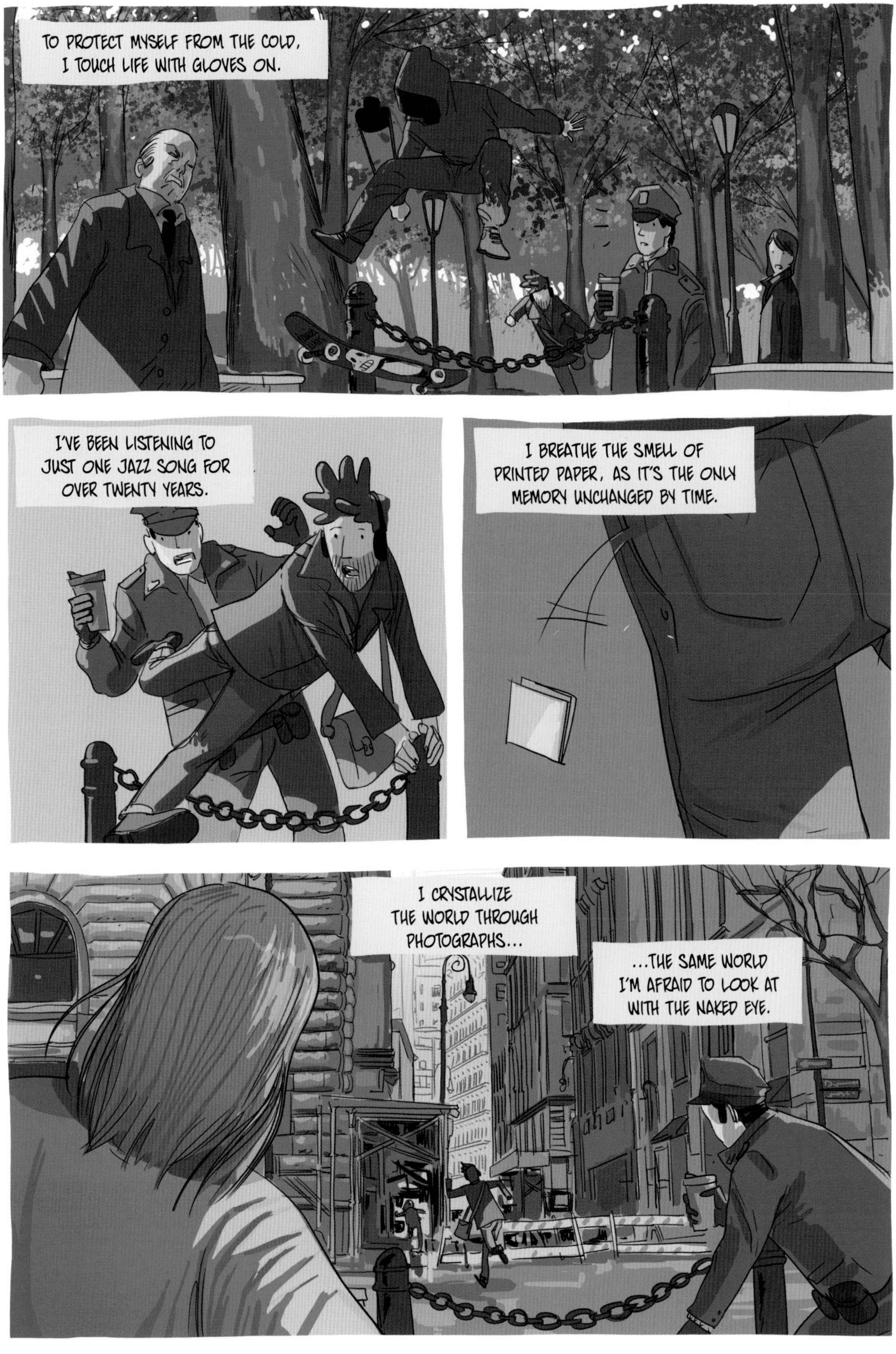
TO PROTECT MYSELF FROM THE COLD, I TOUCH LIFE WITH GLOVES ON.
I'VE BEEN LISTENING TO JUST ONE JAZZ SONG FOR OVER TWENTY YEARS.
I BREATHE THE SMELL OF PRINTED PAPER, AS IT'S THE ONLY MEMORY UNCHANGED BY TIME.
I CRYSTALLIZE THE WORLD THROUGH PHOTOGRAPHS...
...THE SAME WORLD I'M AFRAID TO LOOK AT WITH THE NAKED EYE.

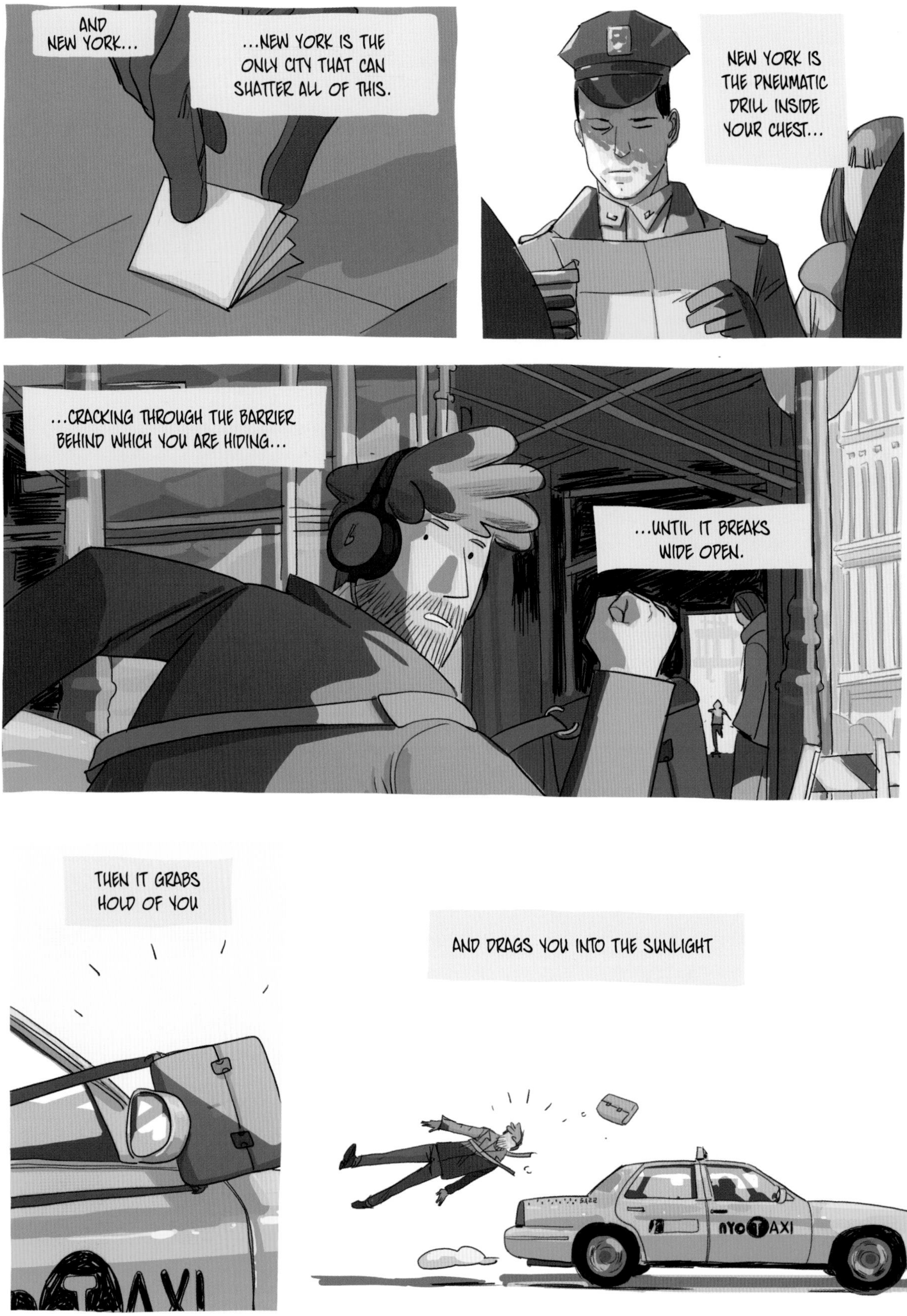
AND NEW YORK...
...NEW YORK IS THE ONLY CITY THAT CAN SHATTER ALL OF THIS.
NEW YORK IS THE PNEUMATIC DRILL INSIDE YOUR CHEST...
...CRACKING THROUGH THE BARRIER BEHIND WHICH YOU ARE HIDING...
...UNTIL IT BREAKS WIDE OPEN.
THEN IT GRABS HOLD OF YOU
AND DRAGS YOU INTO THE SUNLIGHT
NYC TAXI

IN FRONT OF EVERYONE

SO THAT EVERYBODY CAN SEE YOU...

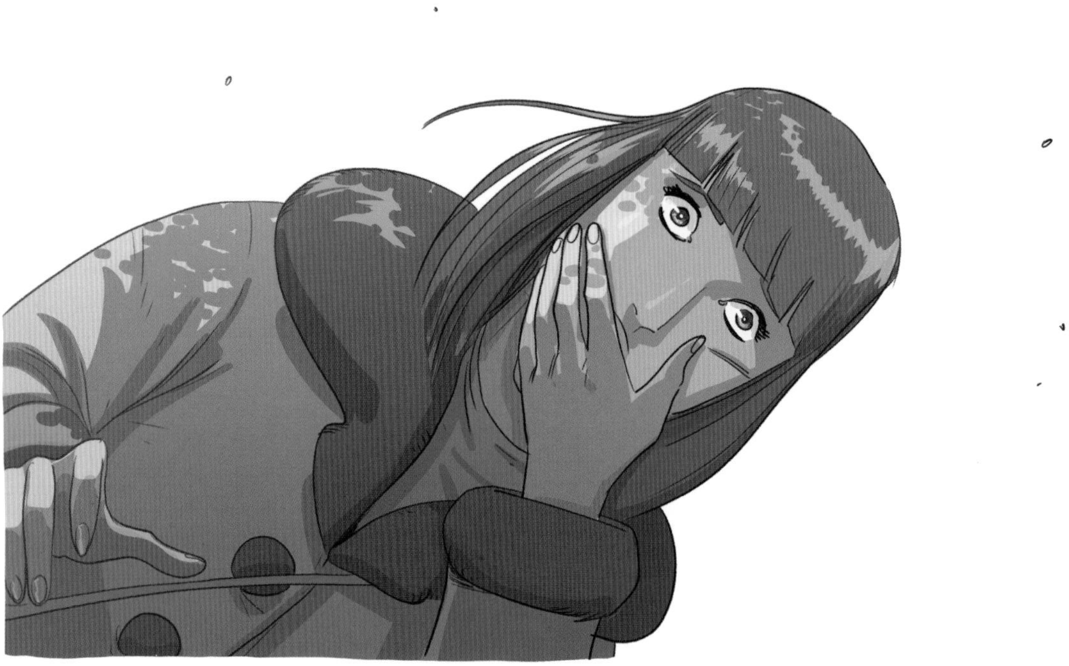

...AND YOU CAN SEE EVERYBODY (...)

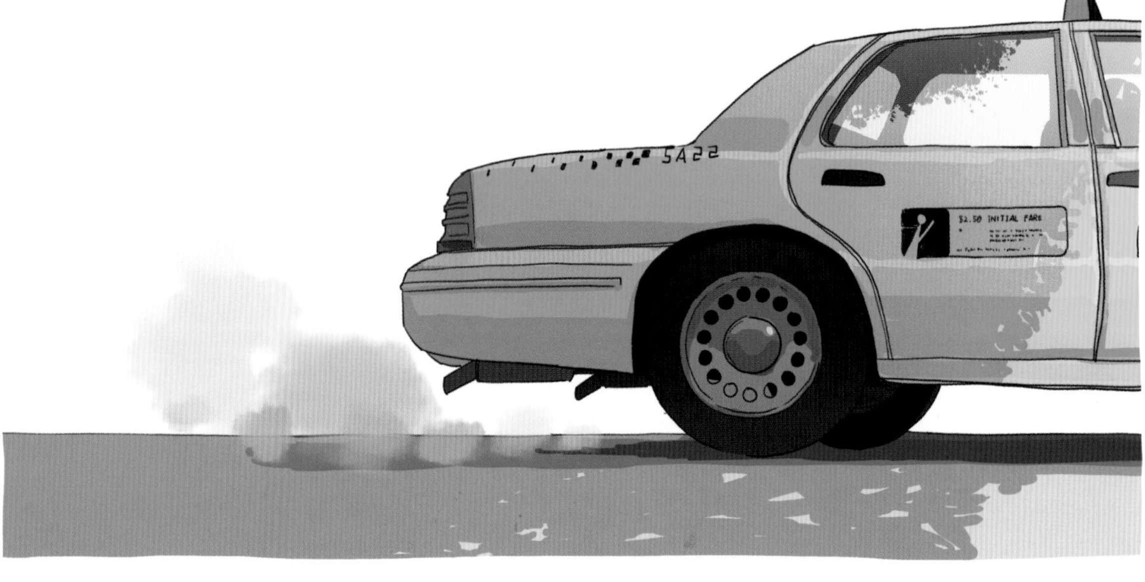
5A22
$2.50 INITIAL FARE

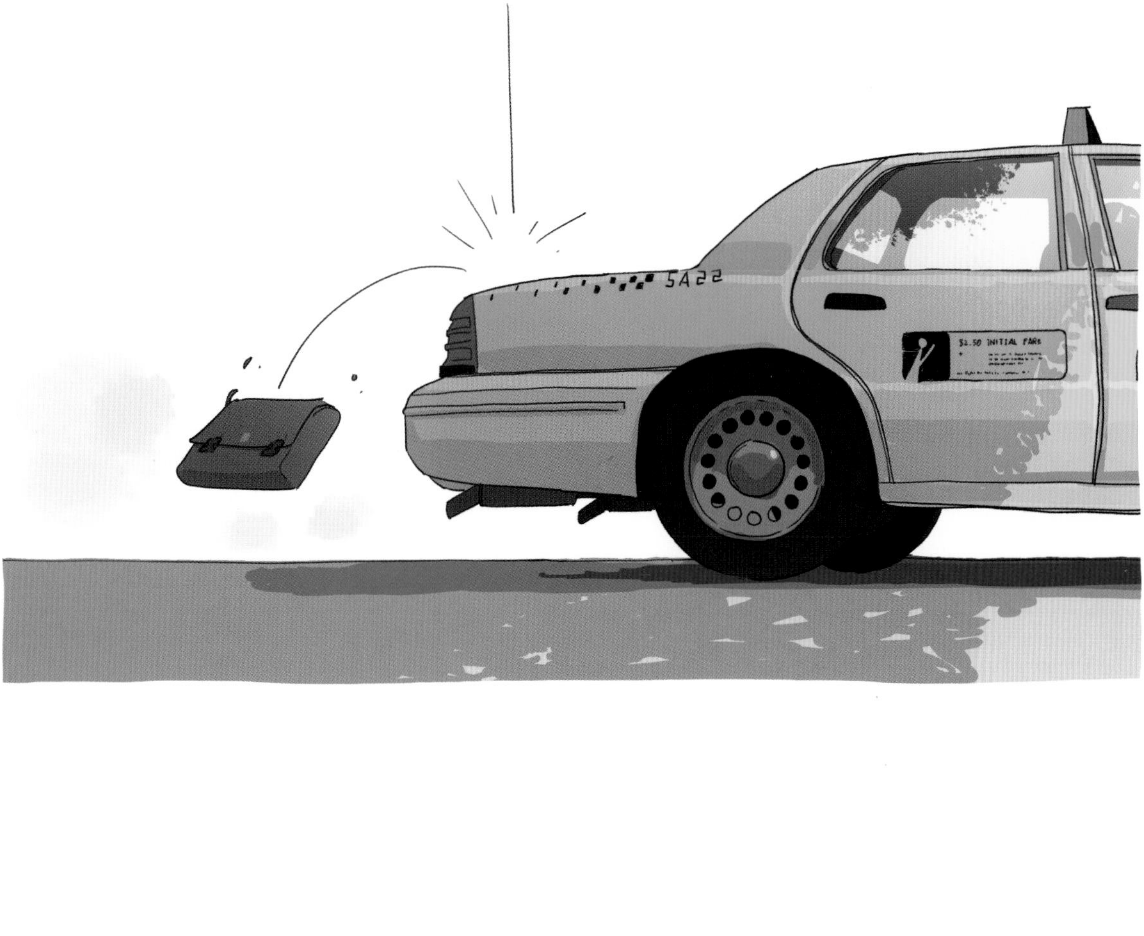
5A22
$2.50 INITIAL FARE

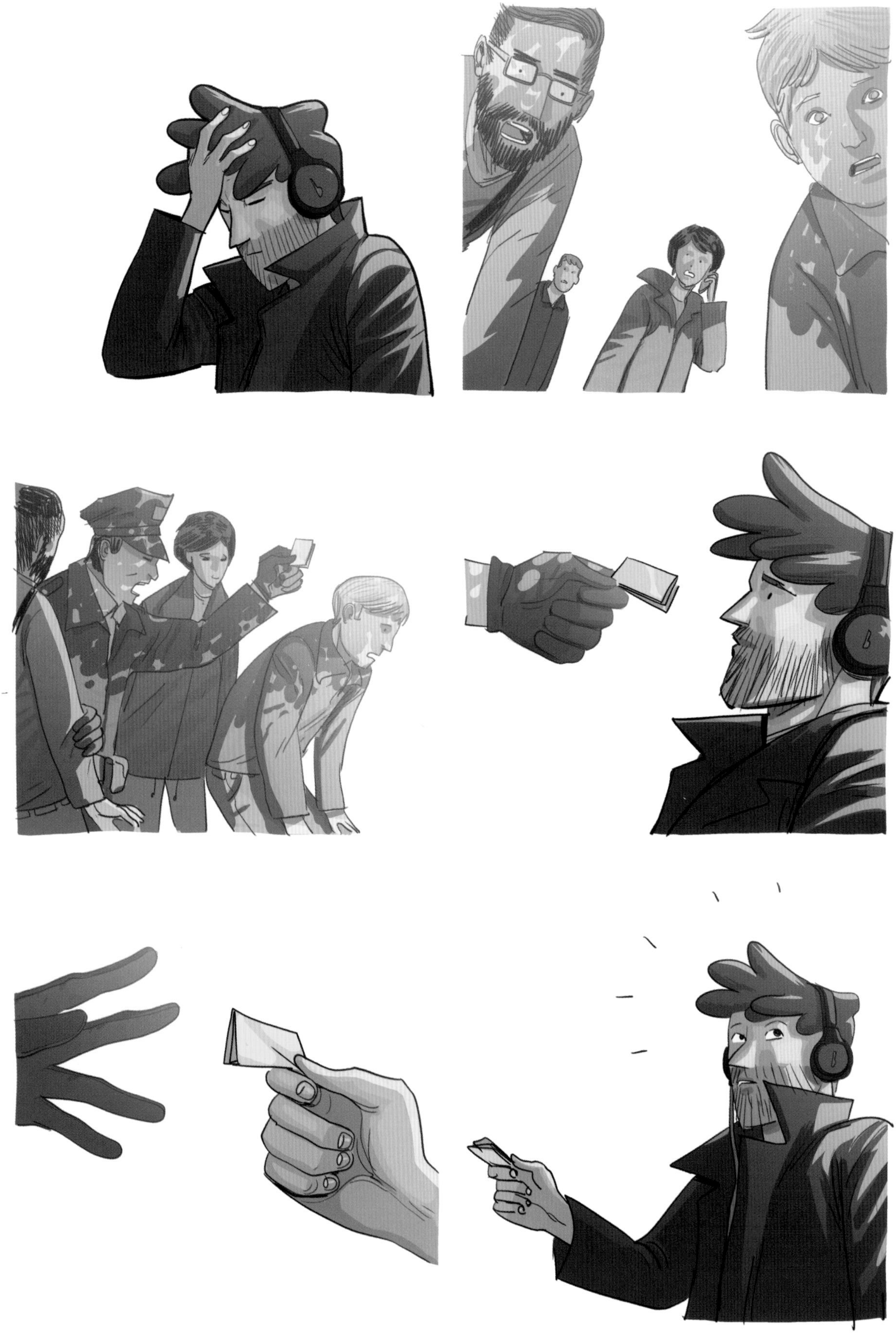

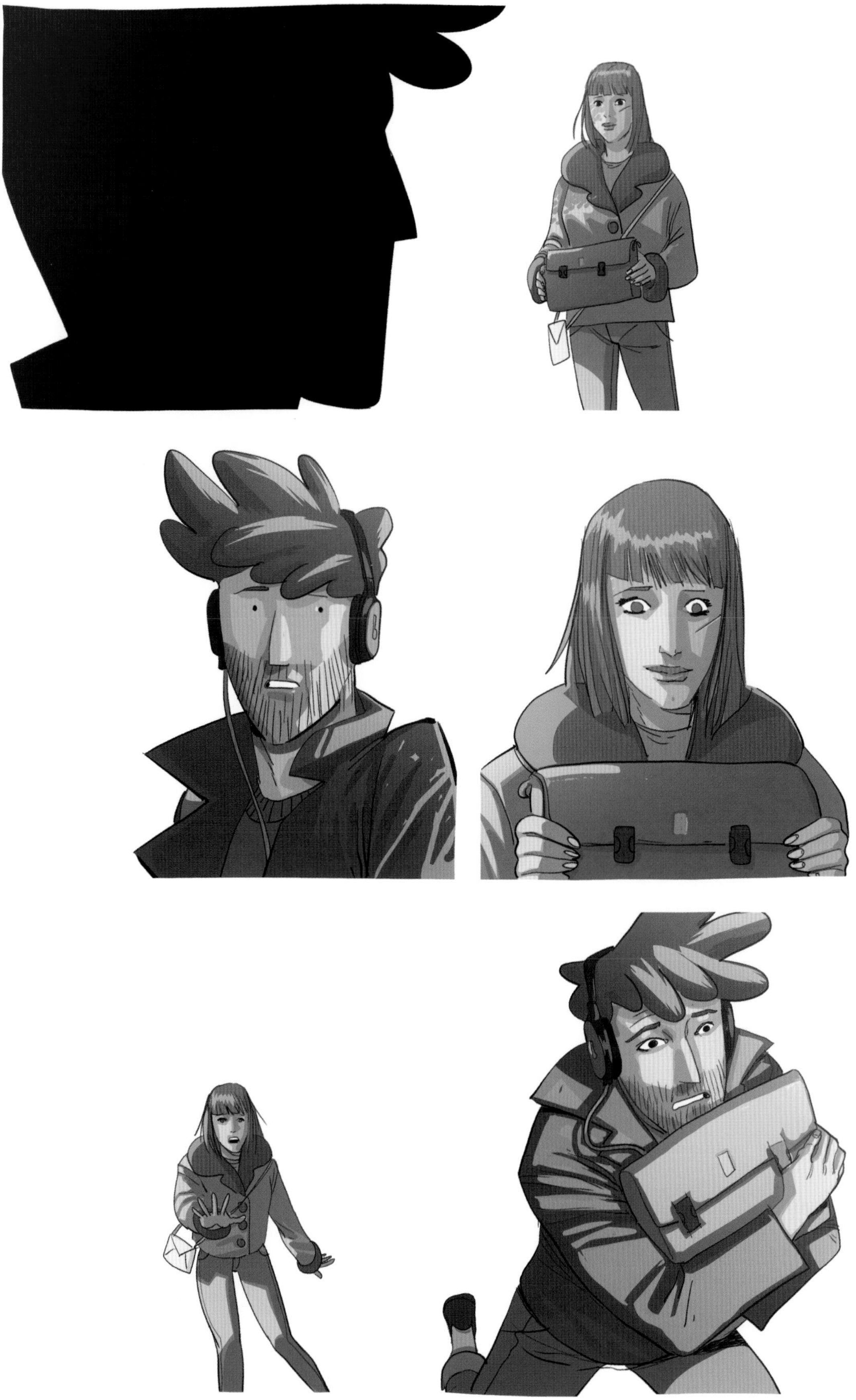

DECEMBER 1ST

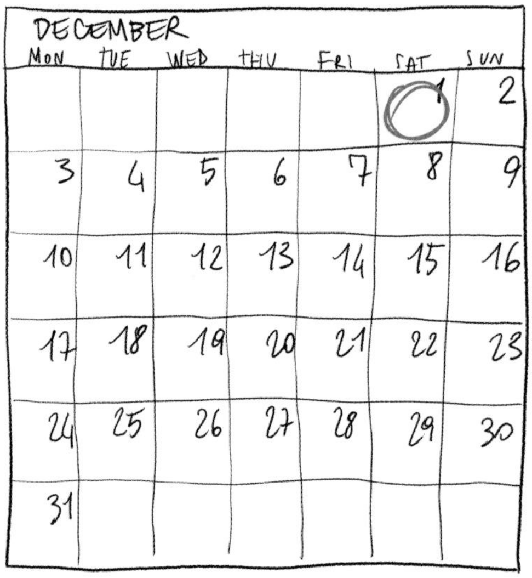

DECEMBER						
MON	TUE	WED	THU	FRI	SAT	SUN
					1	2
3	4	5	6	7	8	9
10	11	12	13	14	15	16
17	18	19	20	21	22	23
24	25	26	27	28	29	30
31						

(...) THESE SELF-IMPOSED RULES COME
FROM A CORE NEED OF MINE:

SUFFER AS LITTLE AS POSSIBLE.

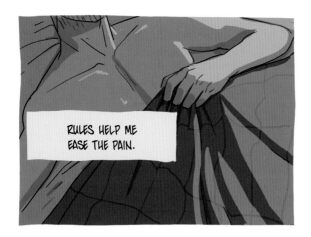

RULES HELP ME
EASE THE PAIN.

OR ENDURE IT.

OR EVEN
OVERCOME IT
UNSCATHED.

RULES ARE
THE REASON WE'RE
STILL ALIVE.

THEY'RE WHAT'S LEFT WHEN
LIFE (OR ANY COMMON ASSHOLE)
HURTS OR ROBS US OF THE TOOLS
WE USE TO FILTER THE WORLD.

FRUSH
FRUSH

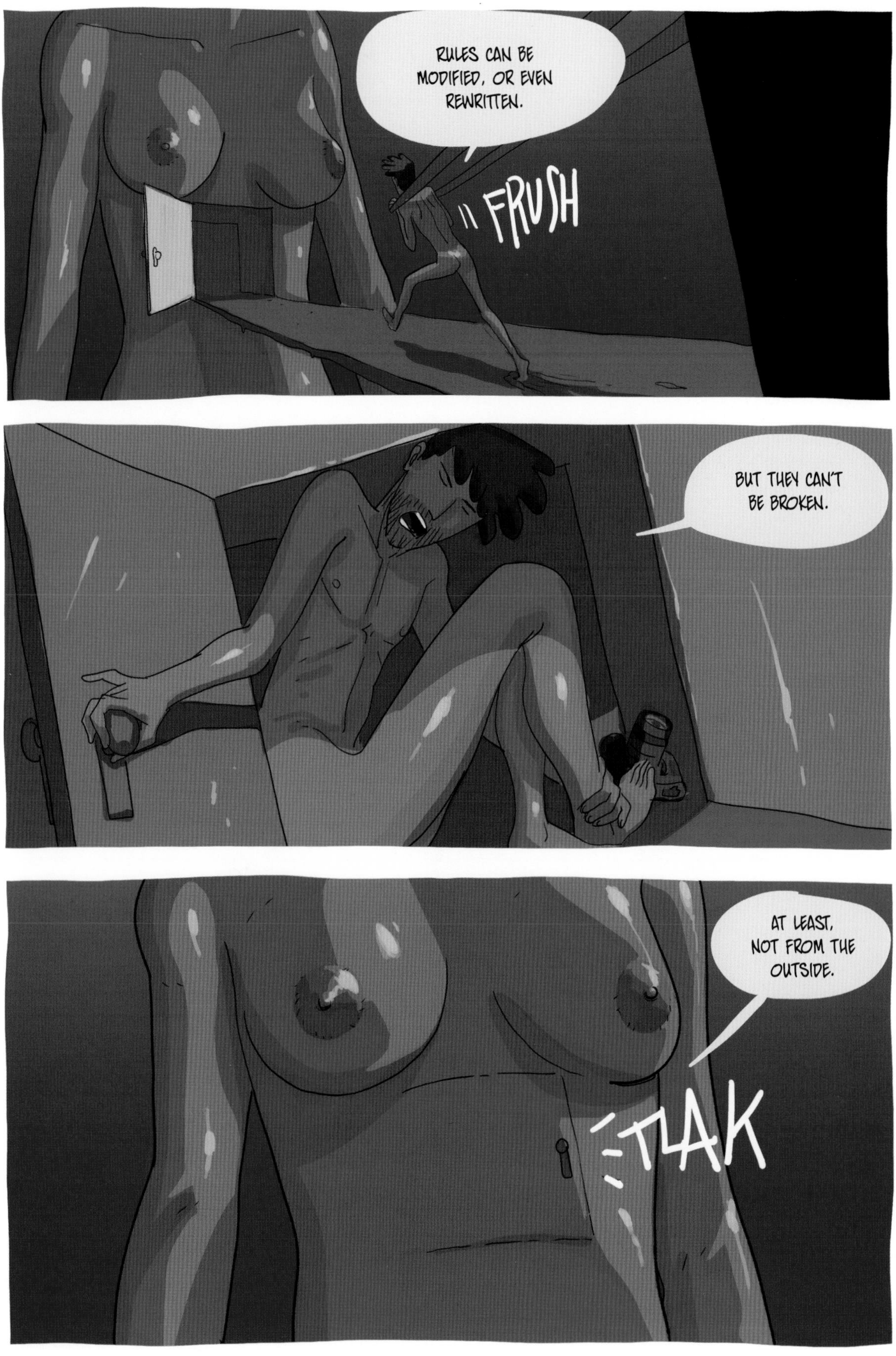
RULES CAN BE MODIFIED, OR EVEN REWRITTEN.
FRUSH
BUT THEY CAN'T BE BROKEN.
AT LEAST, NOT FROM THE OUTSIDE.
TLAK

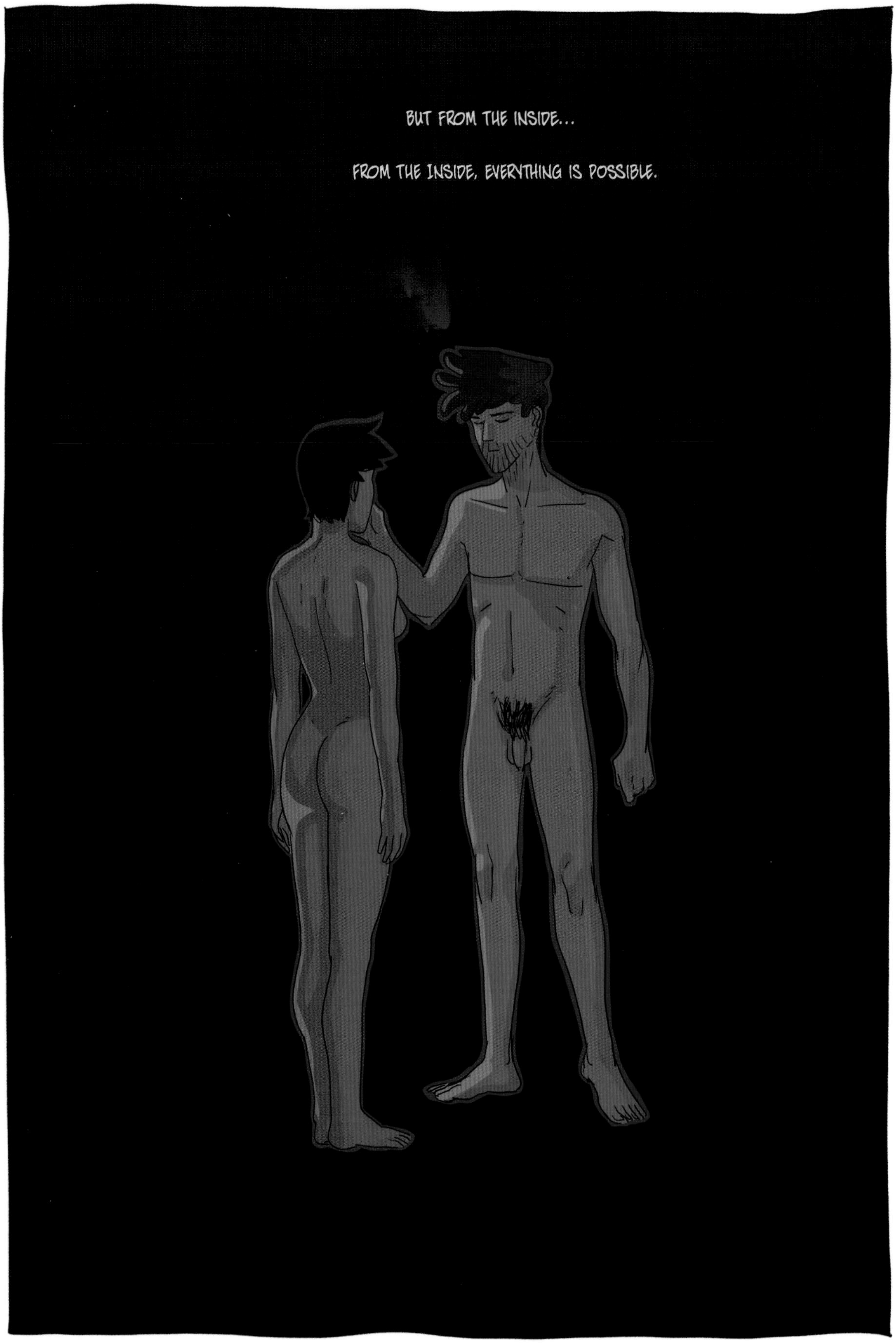

BUT FROM THE INSIDE...

FROM THE INSIDE, EVERYTHING IS POSSIBLE.

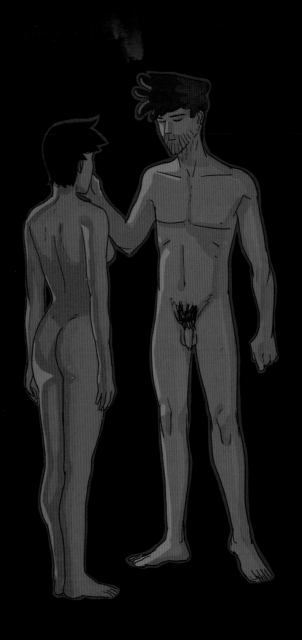

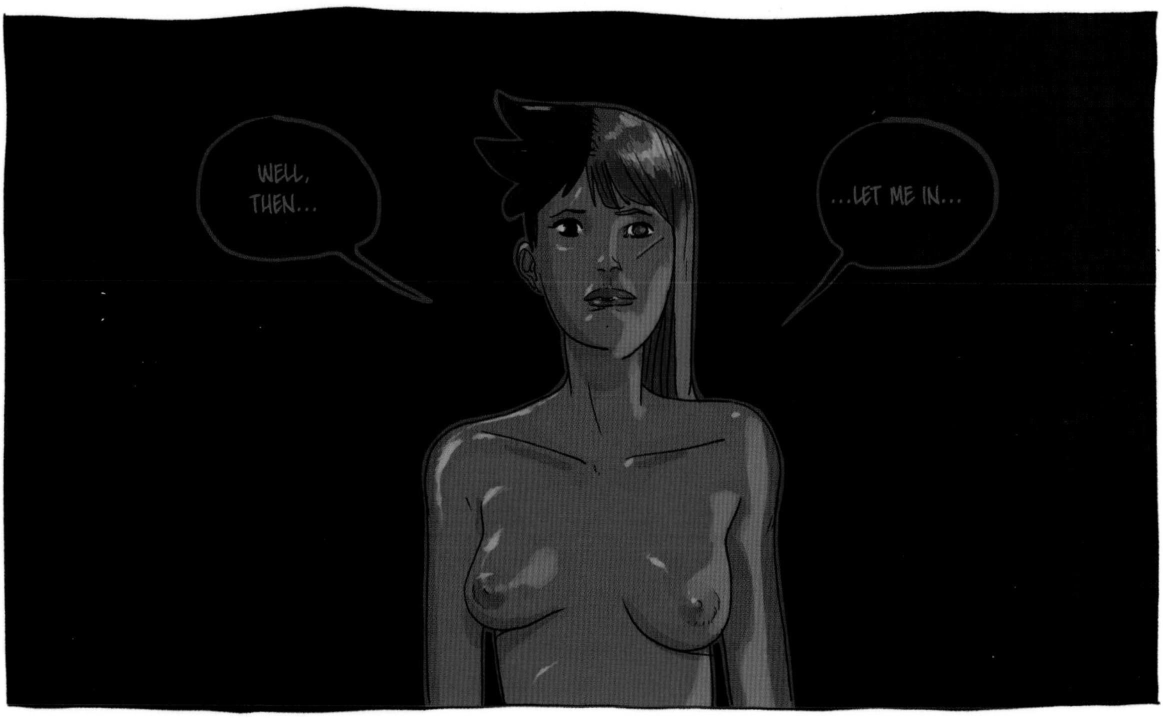
WELL, THEN...
...LET ME IN...

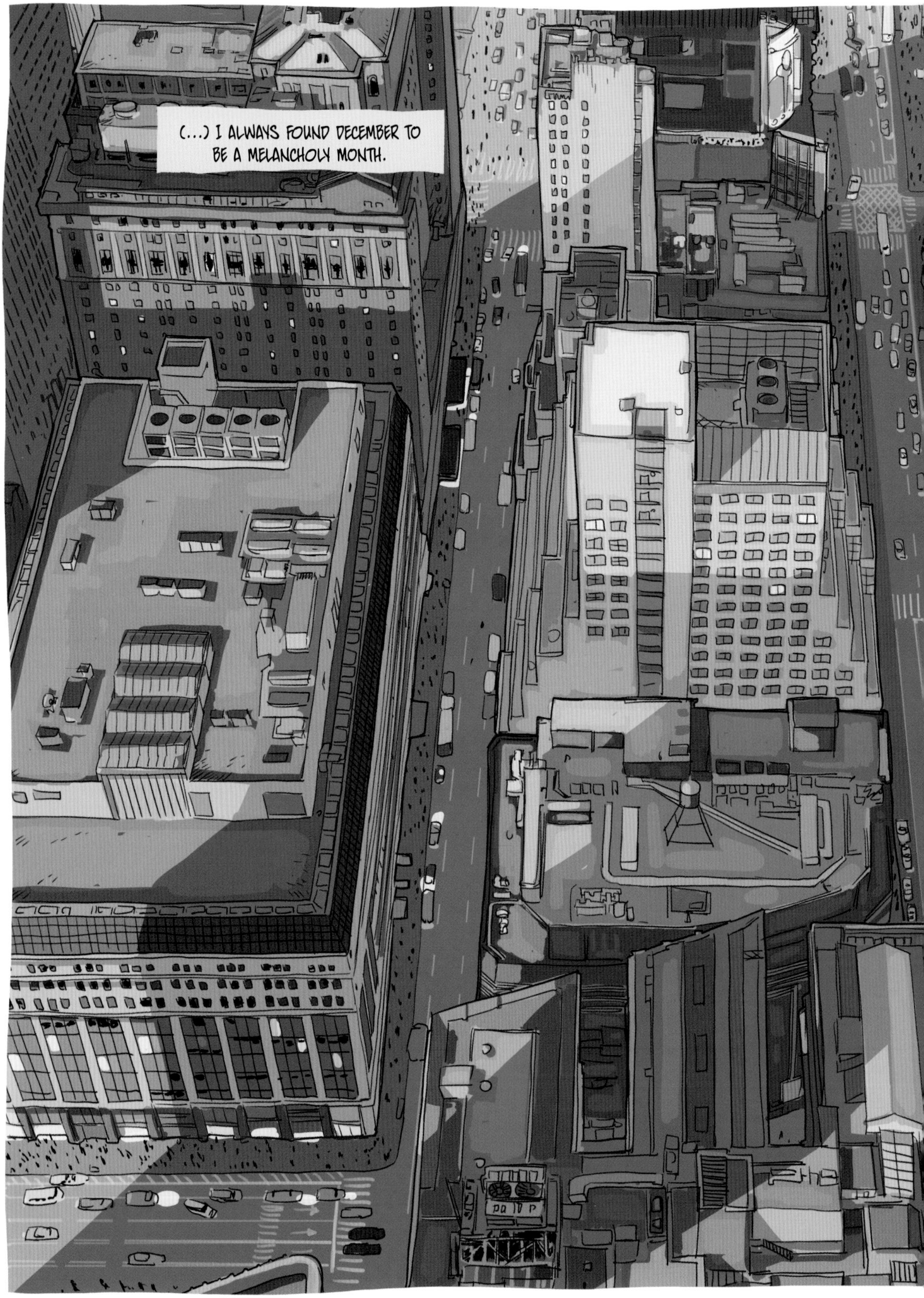
(...) I ALWAYS FOUND DECEMBER TO BE A MELANCHOLY MONTH.

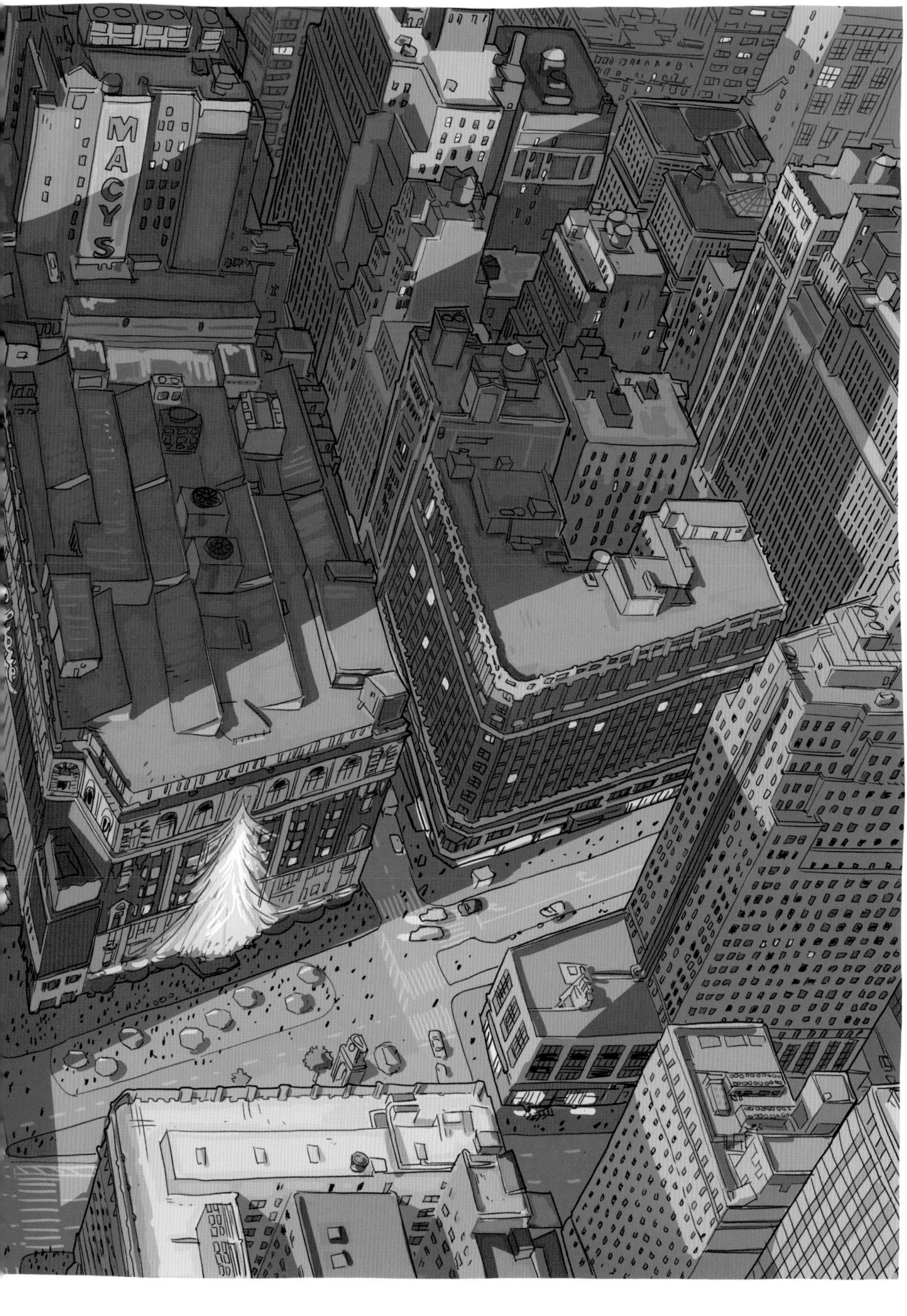
MACYS

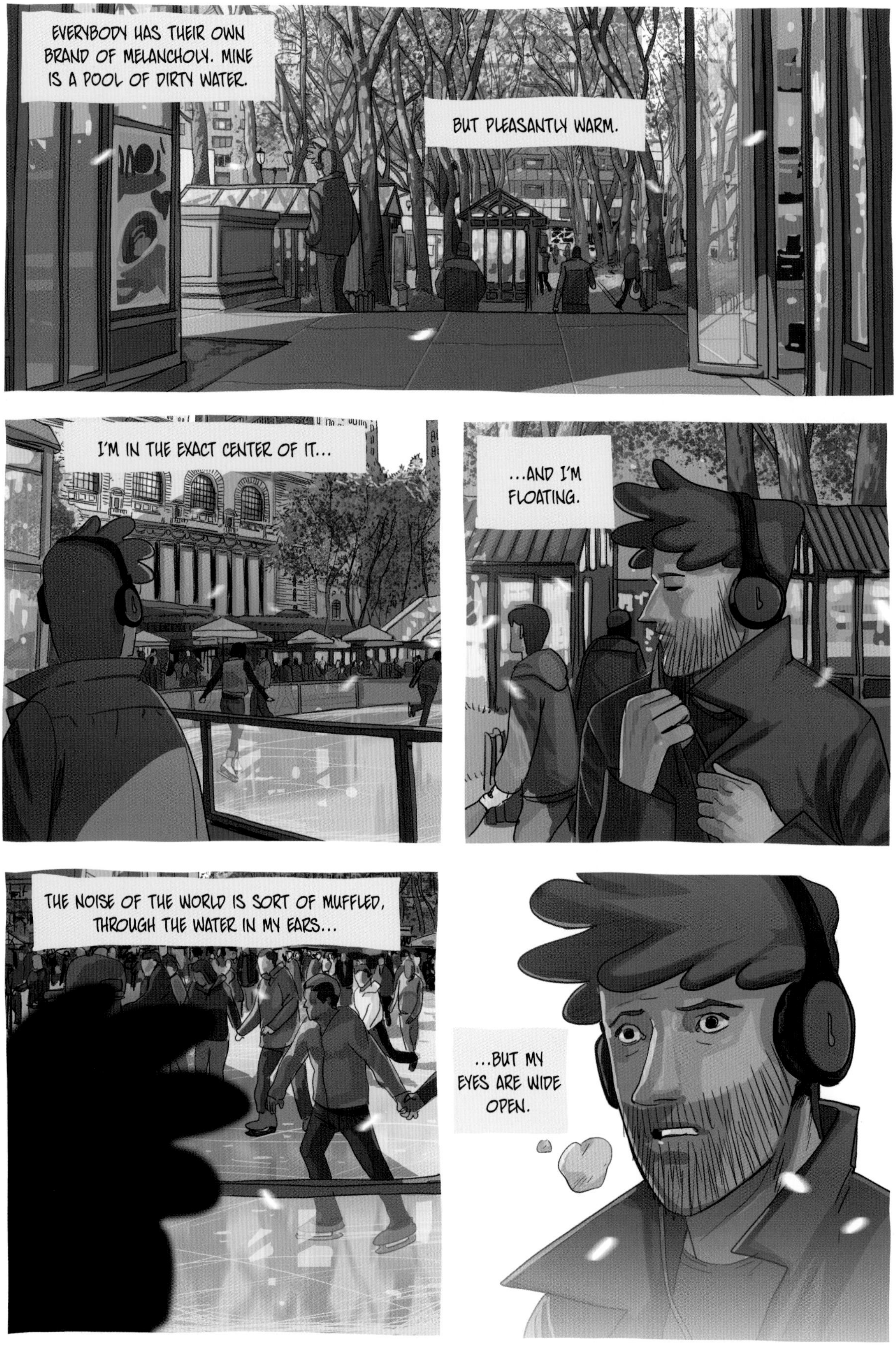
EVERYBODY HAS THEIR OWN BRAND OF MELANCHOLY. MINE IS A POOL OF DIRTY WATER.
BUT PLEASANTLY WARM.
I'M IN THE EXACT CENTER OF IT...
...AND I'M FLOATING.
THE NOISE OF THE WORLD IS SORT OF MUFFLED, THROUGH THE WATER IN MY EARS...
...BUT MY EYES ARE WIDE OPEN.

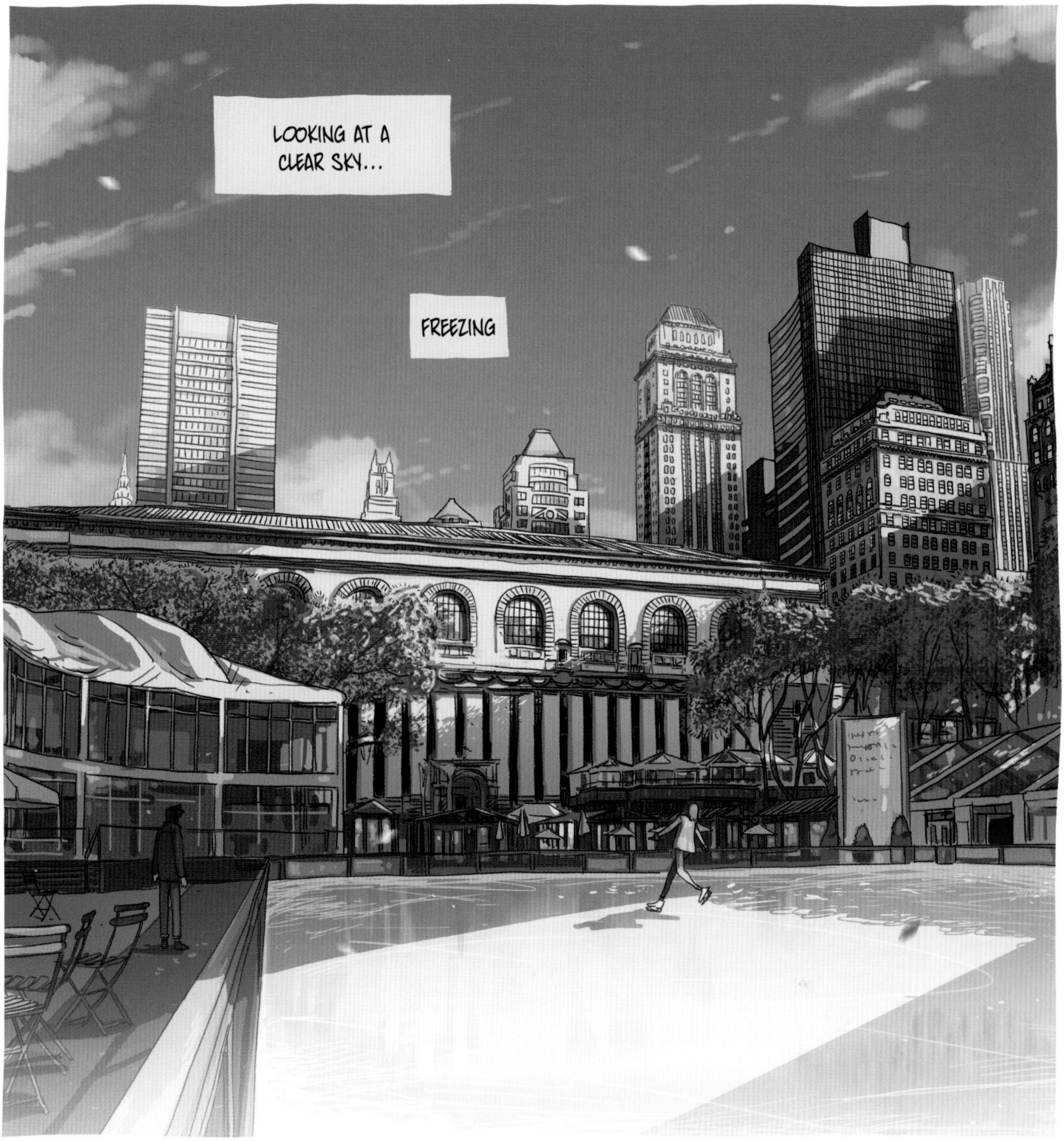
LOOKING AT A CLEAR SKY...
FREEZING

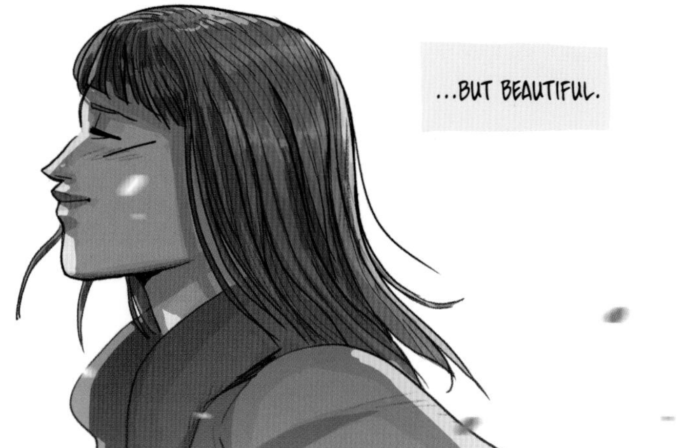
...BUT BEAUTIFUL.

DECEMBER 4ᵀᴴ

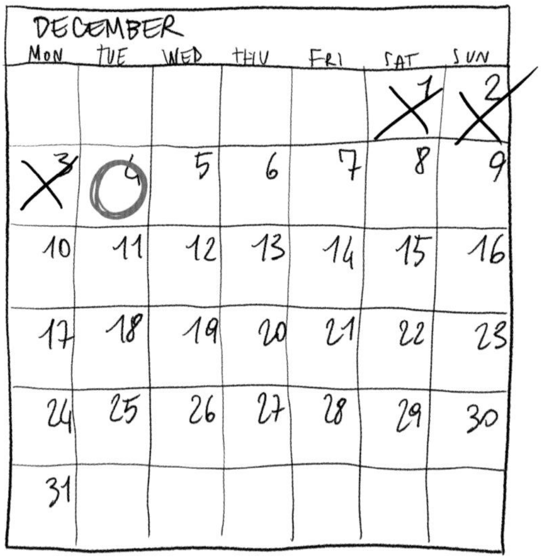

DECEMBER

MON	TUE	WED	THU	FRI	SAT	SUN
					~~1~~	~~2~~
~~3~~	④	5	6	7	8	9
10	11	12	13	14	15	16
17	18	19	20	21	22	23
24	25	26	27	28	29	30
31						

(...) THERE ARE PEOPLE WHO LOOK FOR, AND JUDGE, THEIR IDEAL PARTNER ACCORDING TO ASTROLOGICAL RULES, STAR CHARTS, PLANETARY ALIGNMENTS, AND GRAVITATIONAL INFLUENCES.

I HAVE NO REASON TO CLAIM ANY OF THAT IS SHEER NONSENSE, BUT I'M PERSONALLY MORE OF A "SEEING IS BELIEVING" KIND OF GUY. (MAYBE THAT'S WHY I BECAME A PHOTOGRAPHER, WHO KNOWS.)

STILL, I THINK THE ONLY STAR WE CAN RELY ON WHERE LOVE IS CONCERNED IS THE STAR WE CAN ALL SEE, WHICH, IN MY HUMBLE OPINION, DIVIDES THE WORLD INTO TWO KEY GROUPS:

- THOSE WHO PREFER TO WATCH IT RISE AT DAWN

- THOSE WHO PREFER TO WATCH IT SET IN THE EVENING

IN MY OPINION, THE IDEAL PARTNER IS ONE IN YOUR SAME CATEGORY.

SIMPLE AS THAT.

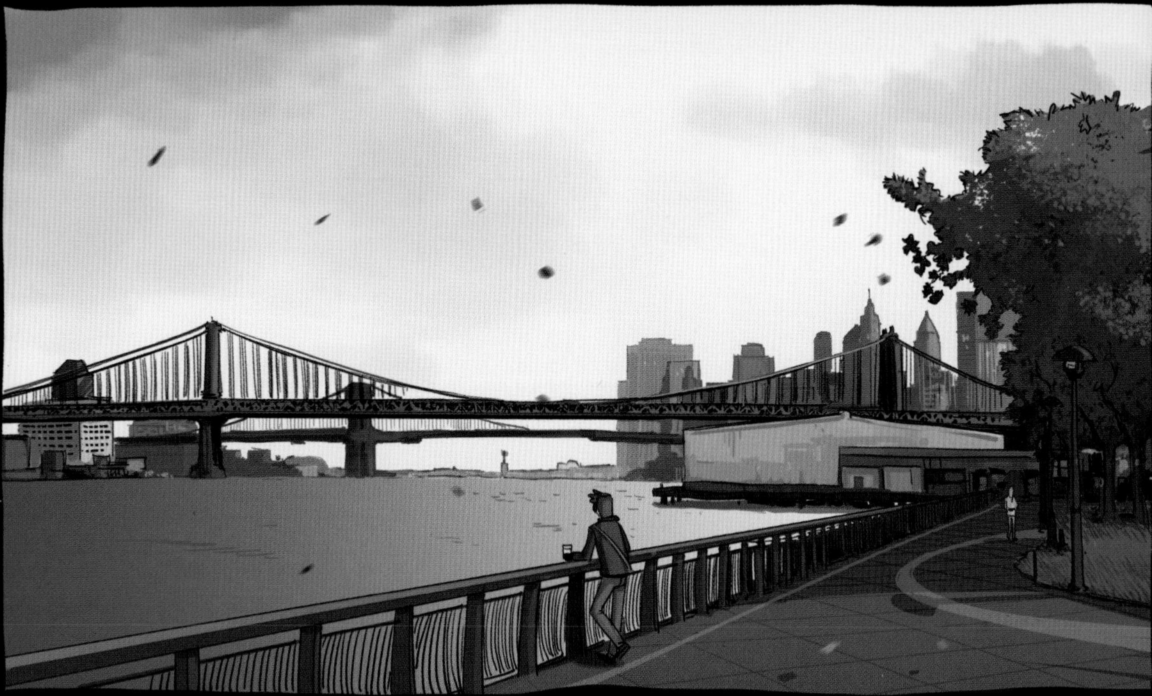

DECEMBER 8TH

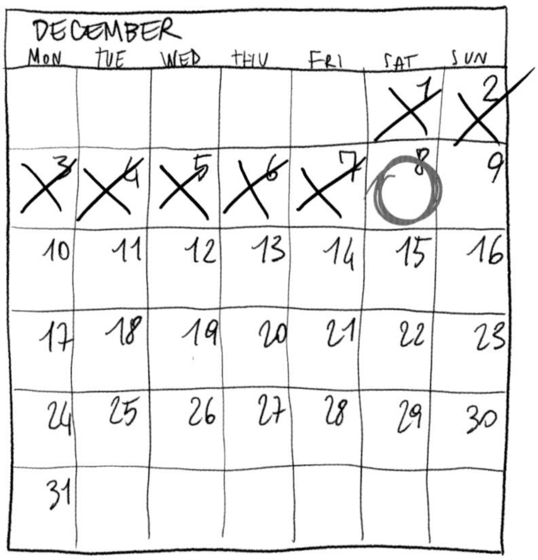

DECEMBER						
MON	TUE	WED	THU	FRI	SAT	SUN
					~~1~~	~~2~~
~~3~~	~~4~~	~~5~~	~~6~~	~~7~~	(8)	9
10	11	12	13	14	15	16
17	18	19	20	21	22	23
24	25	26	27	28	29	30
31						

(...) NOT MANY PEOPLE CAN HEAR IT, I'M SURE.

BUT I CAN. I'M ONE OF THOSE PEOPLE.

IT'S THERE, IT ALMOST NEVER GOES AWAY, A CONSTANT PRESENCE
YOU SLOWLY GET USED TO IT BEFORE IT NEARLY DISAPPEARS, BUT THE MINUTE YOU REMEMBER IT,
IT'S BACK AND LOUDER THAN EVER.

A BACKGROUND NOISE, A MURMUR, A FIXED AND CONSTANT VIBRATION
UNDERLYING THE SOUL OF THE CITY ITSELF.

IT'S LIKE THERE ARE PERPETUALLY CHURNING
UNDERGROUND MACHINES, SLOWLY AND TIRELESSLY HUMMING.

MACHINES WITH MASSIVE WHEELS, HEAVY, BUT WELL-OILED, THAT NEVER
CREAK. THEY JUST TRANSMIT THEIR POWERFUL VIBRATIONS THROUGH EVERY WALL,
EVERY PLANK, EVERY STEEL COLUMN. AND YOU CAN ALMOST SEE THEM SHAKE.

"MANHATTAN MURMURS."

THAT WOULD MAKE A GOOD SONG TITLE.
A SONG WHERE THE BASS IS MORE POWERFUL THAN THE MELODY.

TO BE PLAYED A MAXIMUM VOLUME,
WITH THE SPEAKERS FACING THE FLOOR.

SO YOU CAN IGNORE THE MUSIC AND MELODY...

...AND JUST FEEL THE VIBRATIONS.

AND THE RHYTHM.

DECEMBER 12TH

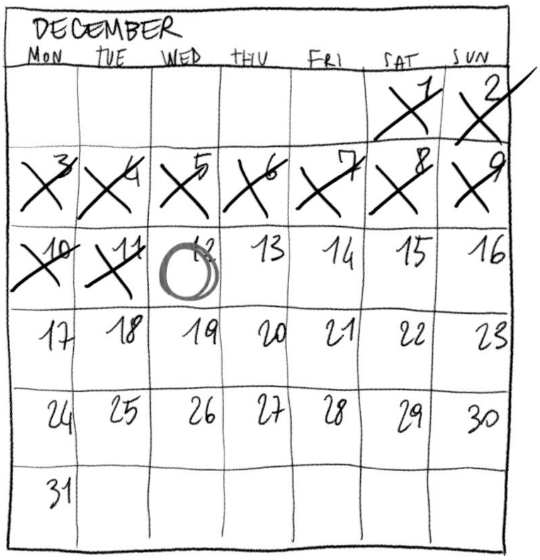

DECEMBER

MON	TUE	WED	THU	FRI	SAT	SUN
					~~1~~	~~2~~
~~3~~	~~4~~	~~5~~	~~6~~	~~7~~	~~8~~	~~9~~
~~10~~	~~11~~	(12)	13	14	15	16
17	18	19	20	21	22	23
24	25	26	27	28	29	30
31						

- HEY, WHAT SIGN DID YOU SAY YOU WERE AGAIN?

- SUNSET.

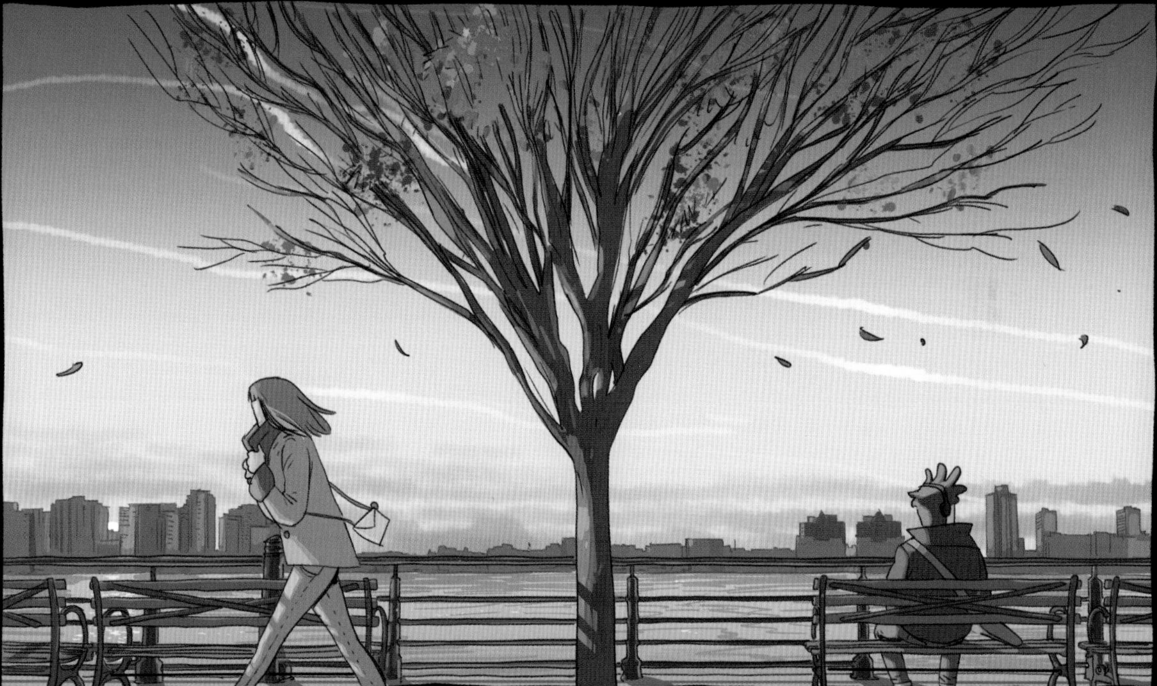

DECEMBER 14TH

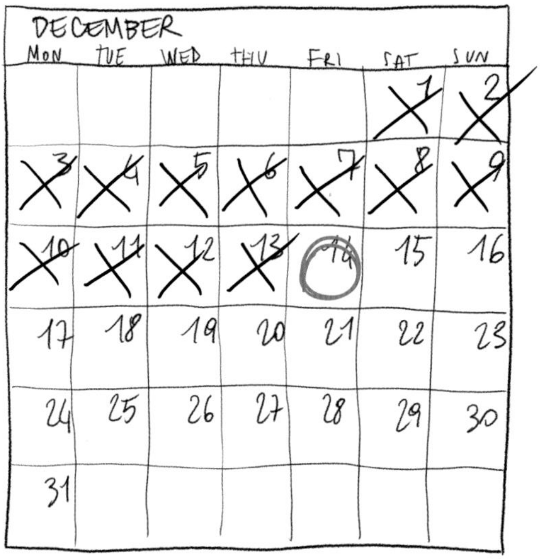

DECEMBER

MON	TUE	WED	THU	FRI	SAT	SUN
					~~1~~	~~2~~
~~3~~	~~4~~	~~5~~	~~6~~	~~7~~	~~8~~	~~9~~
~~10~~	~~11~~	~~12~~	~~13~~	(14)	15	16
17	18	19	20	21	22	23
24	25	26	27	28	29	30
31						

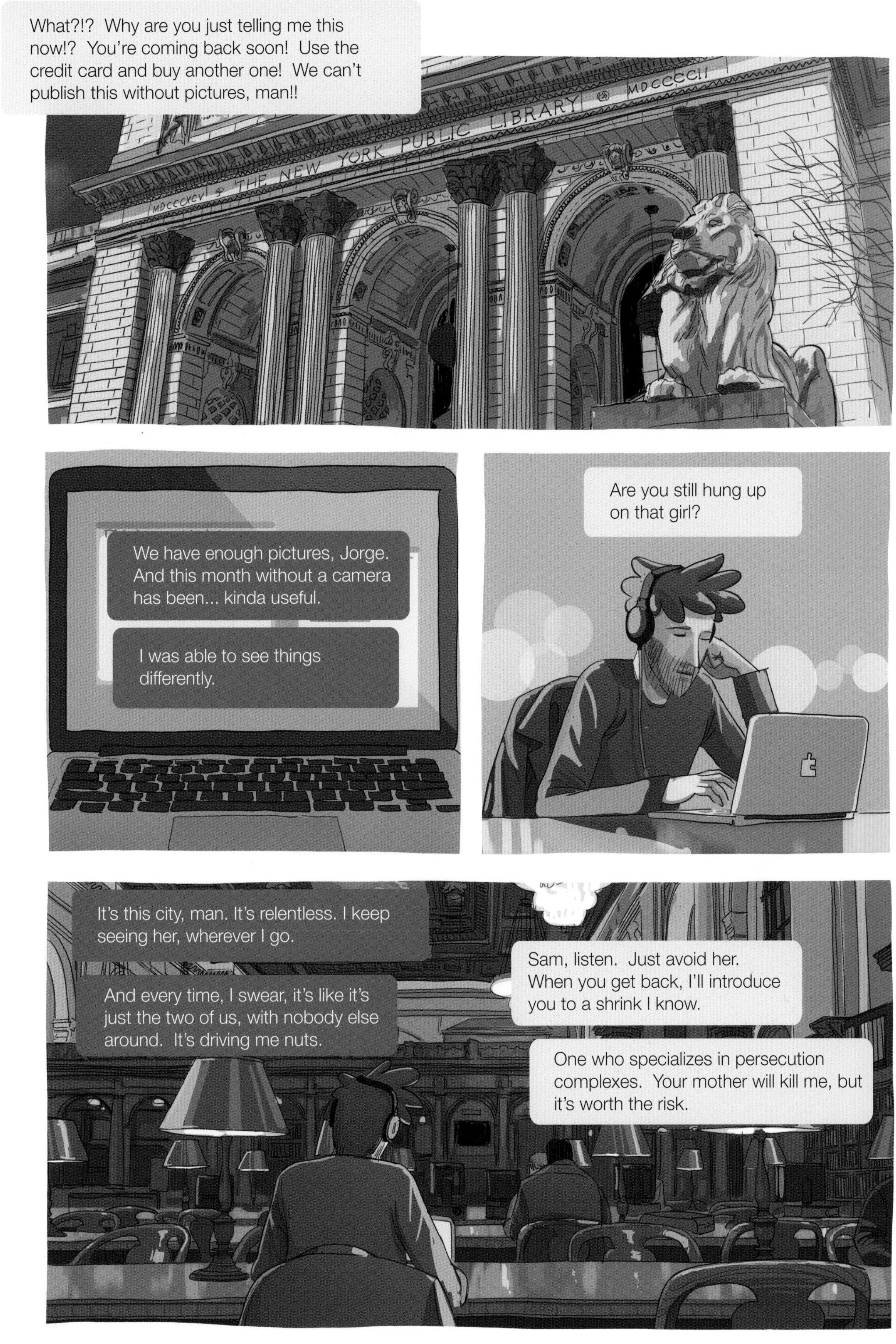
What?!? Why are you just telling me this now!? You're coming back soon! Use the credit card and buy another one! We can't publish this without pictures, man!!
THE NEW YORK PUBLIC LIBRARY
MDCCCXCV
MDCCCCII
We have enough pictures, Jorge. And this month without a camera has been... kinda useful.
I was able to see things differently.
Are you still hung up on that girl?
It's this city, man. It's relentless. I keep seeing her, wherever I go.
And every time, I swear, it's like it's just the two of us, with nobody else around. It's driving me nuts.
Sam, listen. Just avoid her. When you get back, I'll introduce you to a shrink I know.
One who specializes in persecution complexes. Your mother will kill me, but it's worth the risk.

As much as I try to avoid her, she's always there.

Hey, listen...

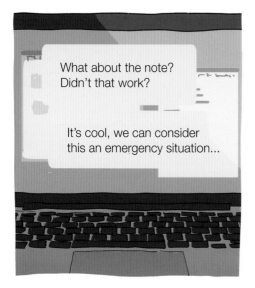

What about the note?
Didn't that work?

It's cool, we can consider
this an emergency situation...

The note?

Why are you
bringing that up
now?

Oh, come on...

We agreed on this
contingency plan.

If you need to sleep with someone to get over Sophie, it's cool.

Do you want to? Seriously, do it!
I'd love to know how you make
that happen without talking...
that could be another article!

We could sell it to Vice, LOL.
Otherwise, just forget the challenge,
it's over, you're over Sophie, it's fine.
Get it out of your system, dude.

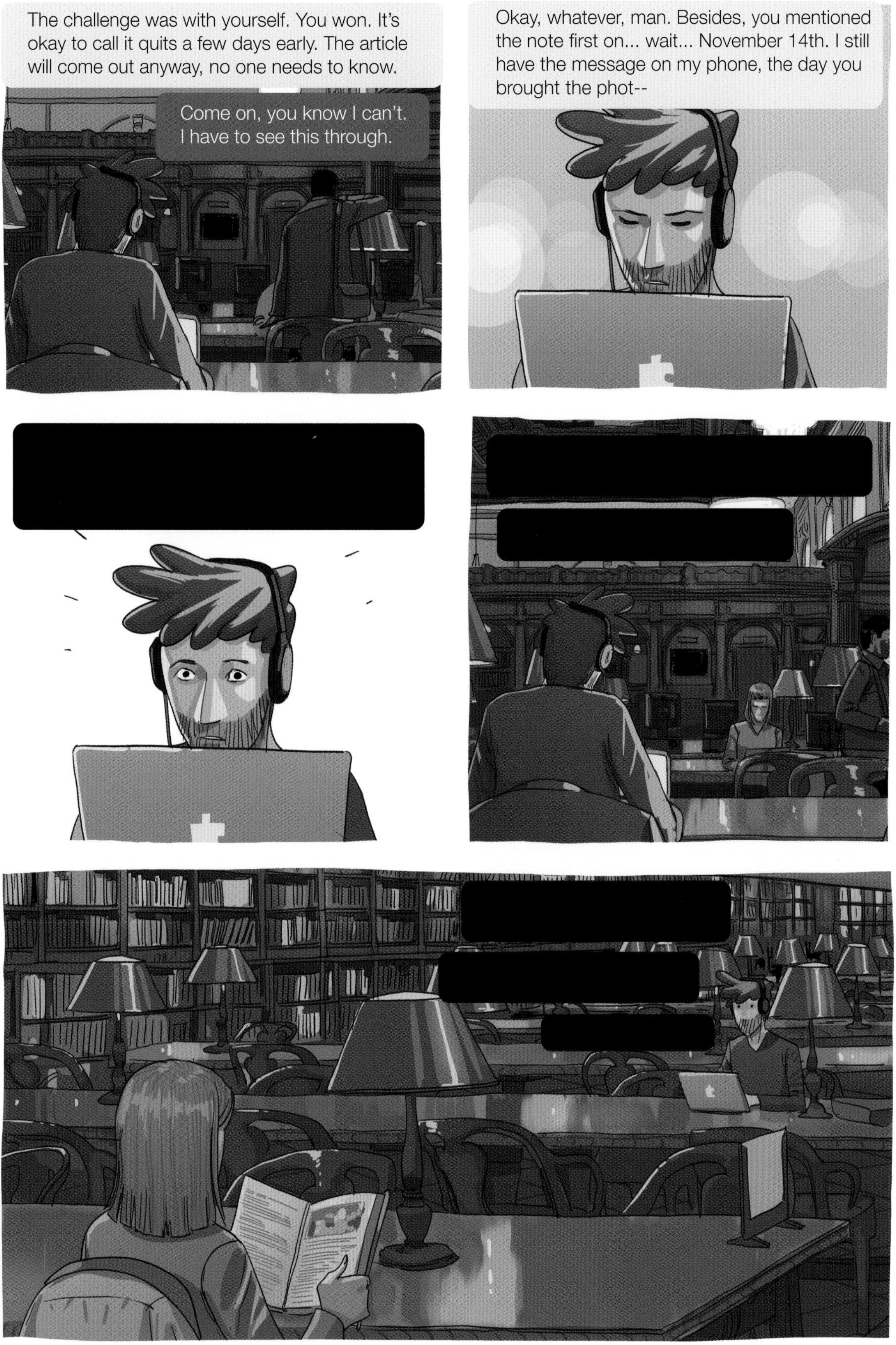
The challenge was with yourself. You won. It's okay to call it quits a few days early. The article will come out anyway, no one needs to know.
Come on, you know I can't. I have to see this through.
Okay, whatever, man. Besides, you mentioned the note first on... wait... November 14th. I still have the message on my phone, the day you brought the phot--
[redacted]
[redacted]
[redacted]
[redacted]
[redacted]
[redacted]

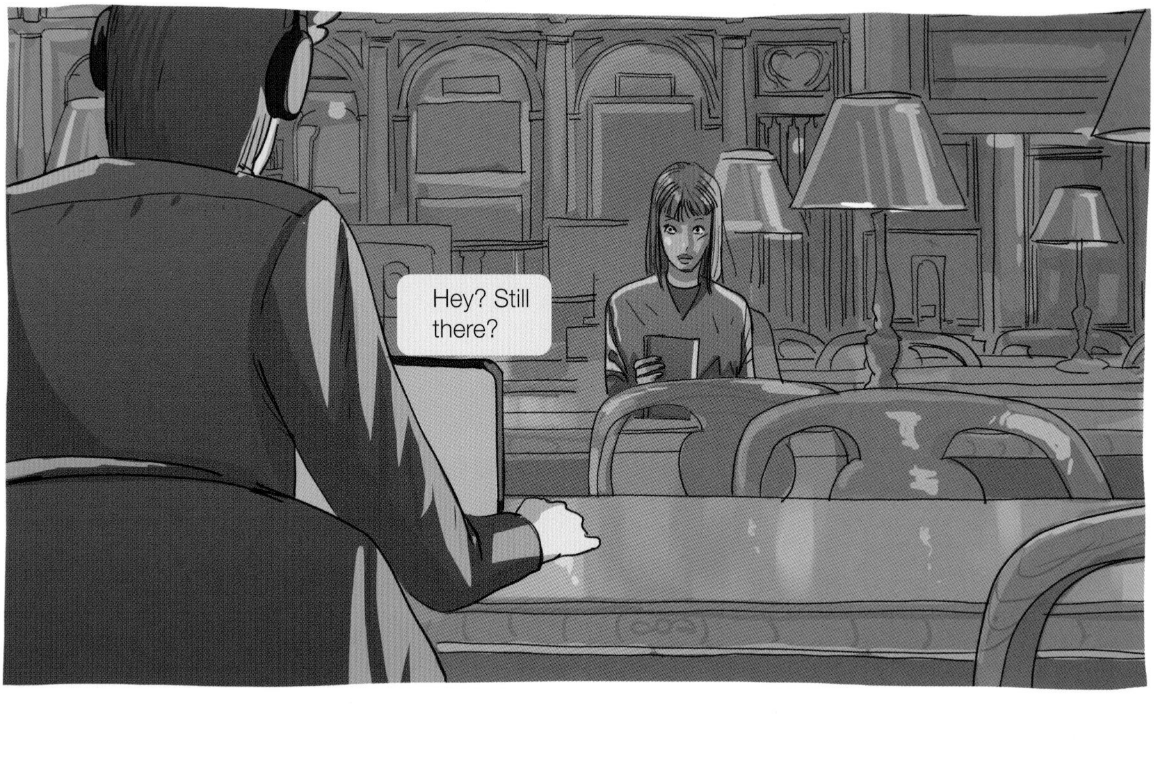
Hey? Still there?

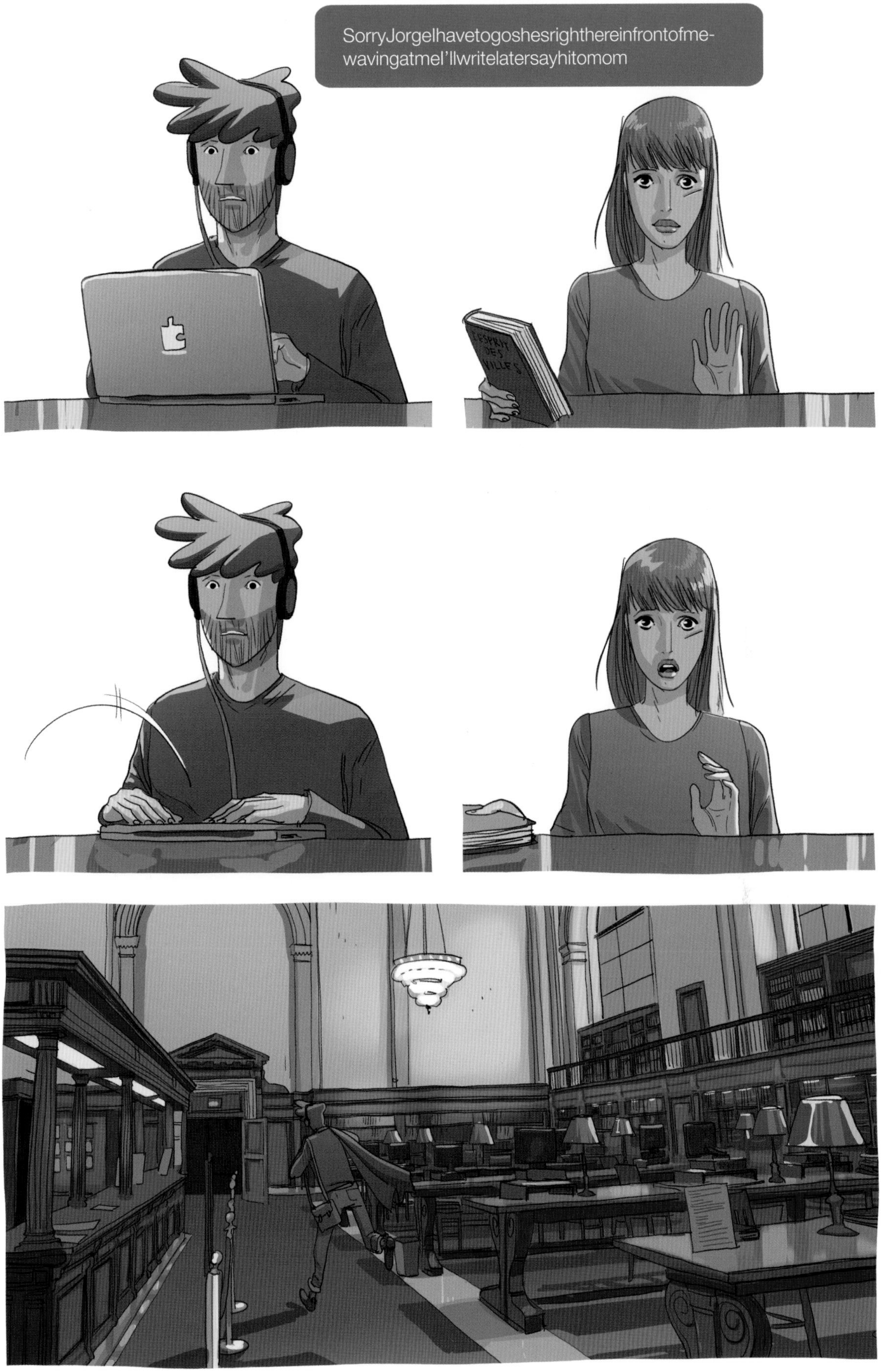
SorryJorgeIhavetogoshesrighthereinfrontofme-wavingatmeI'llwritelatersayhitomom
LESPRIT DES VILLES

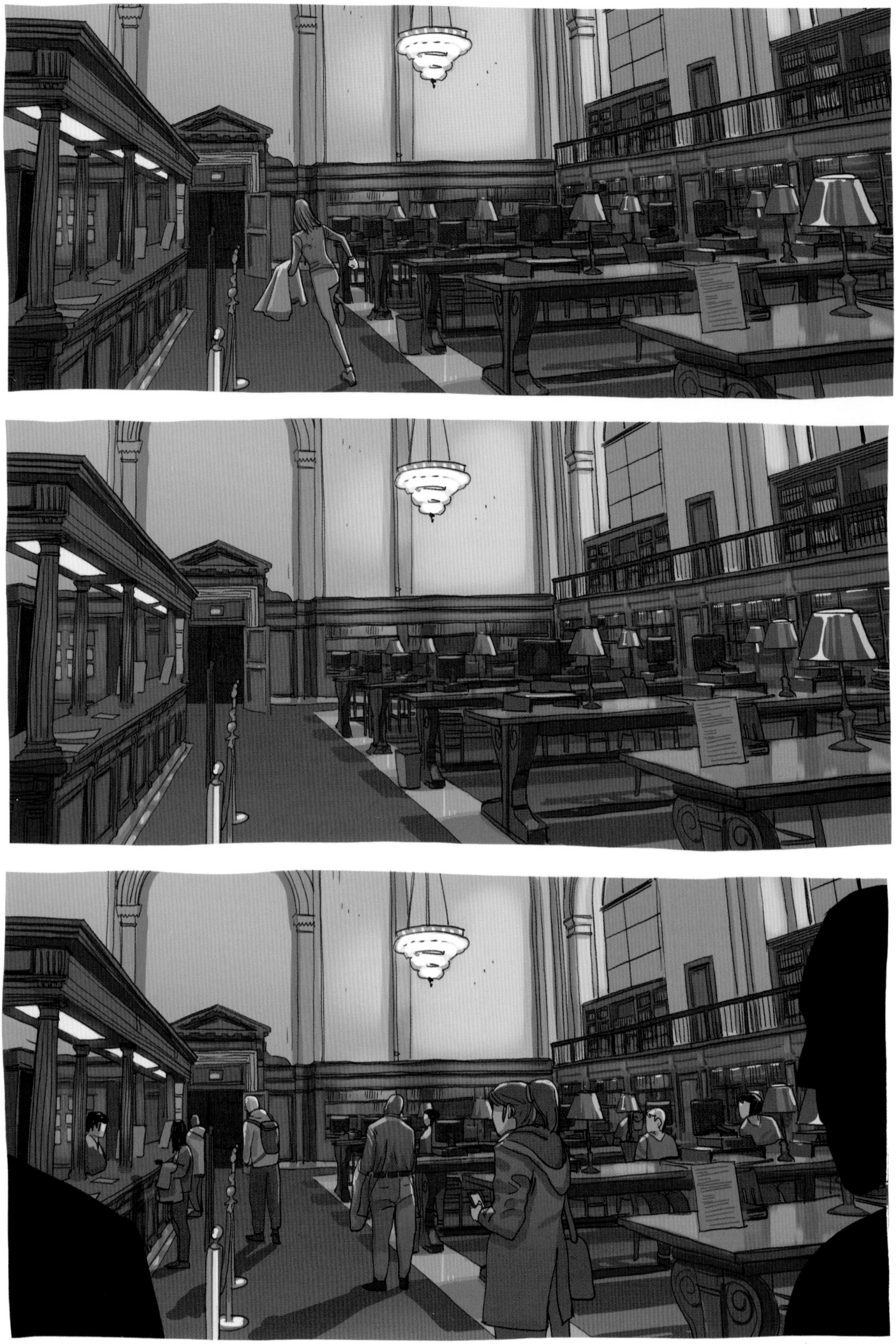

SO AS WE COME TO THE END OF
THIS STORY, LET ME ASK YOU THE SAME
QUESTION SAM ASKED IN HIS ARTICLE:

WHAT'S YOUR EARLIEST MEMORY?

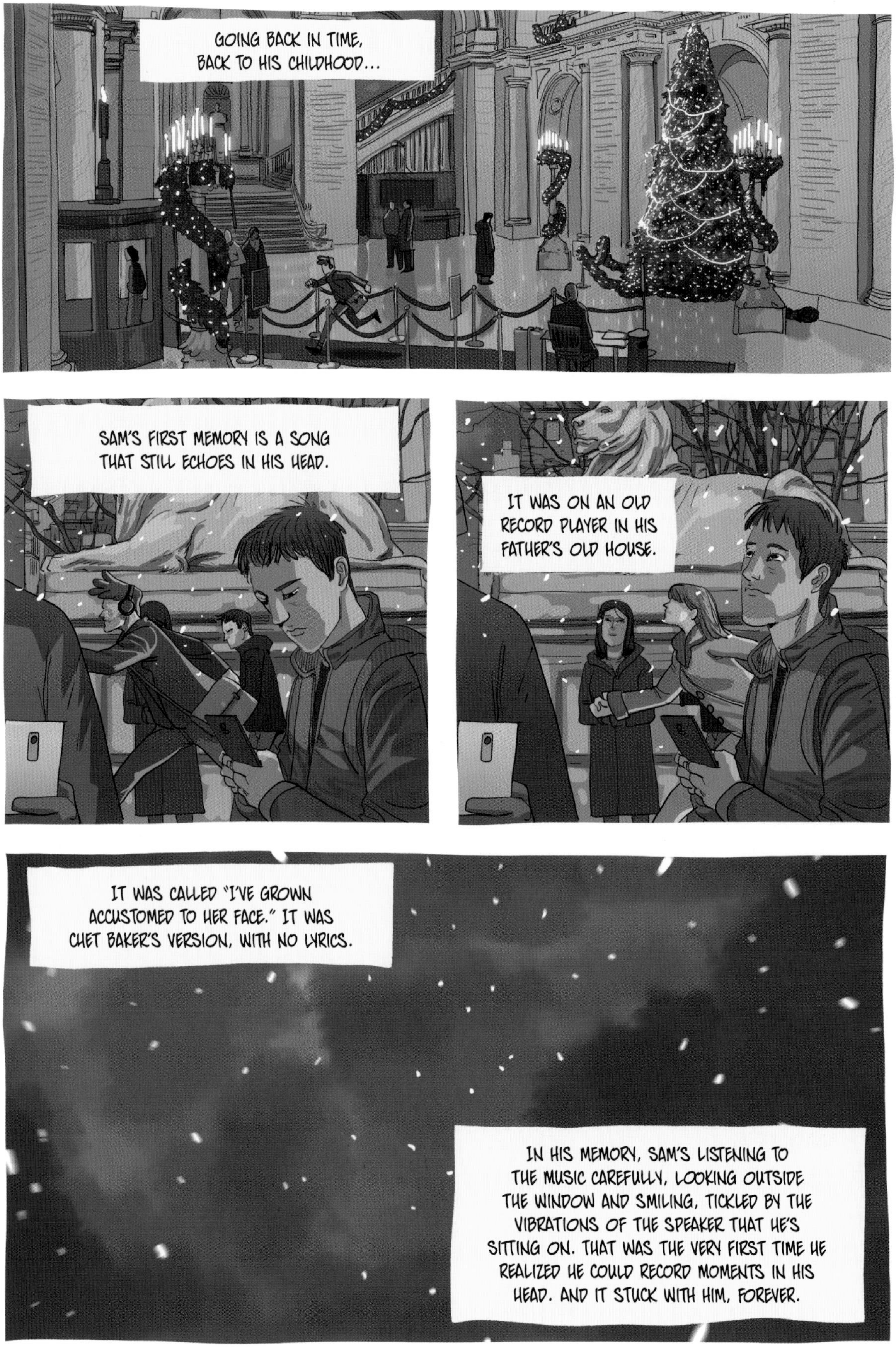
GOING BACK IN TIME, BACK TO HIS CHILDHOOD...
SAM'S FIRST MEMORY IS A SONG THAT STILL ECHOES IN HIS HEAD.
IT WAS ON AN OLD RECORD PLAYER IN HIS FATHER'S OLD HOUSE.
IT WAS CALLED "I'VE GROWN ACCUSTOMED TO HER FACE." IT WAS CHET BAKER'S VERSION, WITH NO LYRICS.
IN HIS MEMORY, SAM'S LISTENING TO THE MUSIC CAREFULLY, LOOKING OUTSIDE THE WINDOW AND SMILING, TICKLED BY THE VIBRATIONS OF THE SPEAKER THAT HE'S SITTING ON. THAT WAS THE VERY FIRST TIME HE REALIZED HE COULD RECORD MOMENTS IN HIS HEAD. AND IT STUCK WITH HIM, FOREVER.

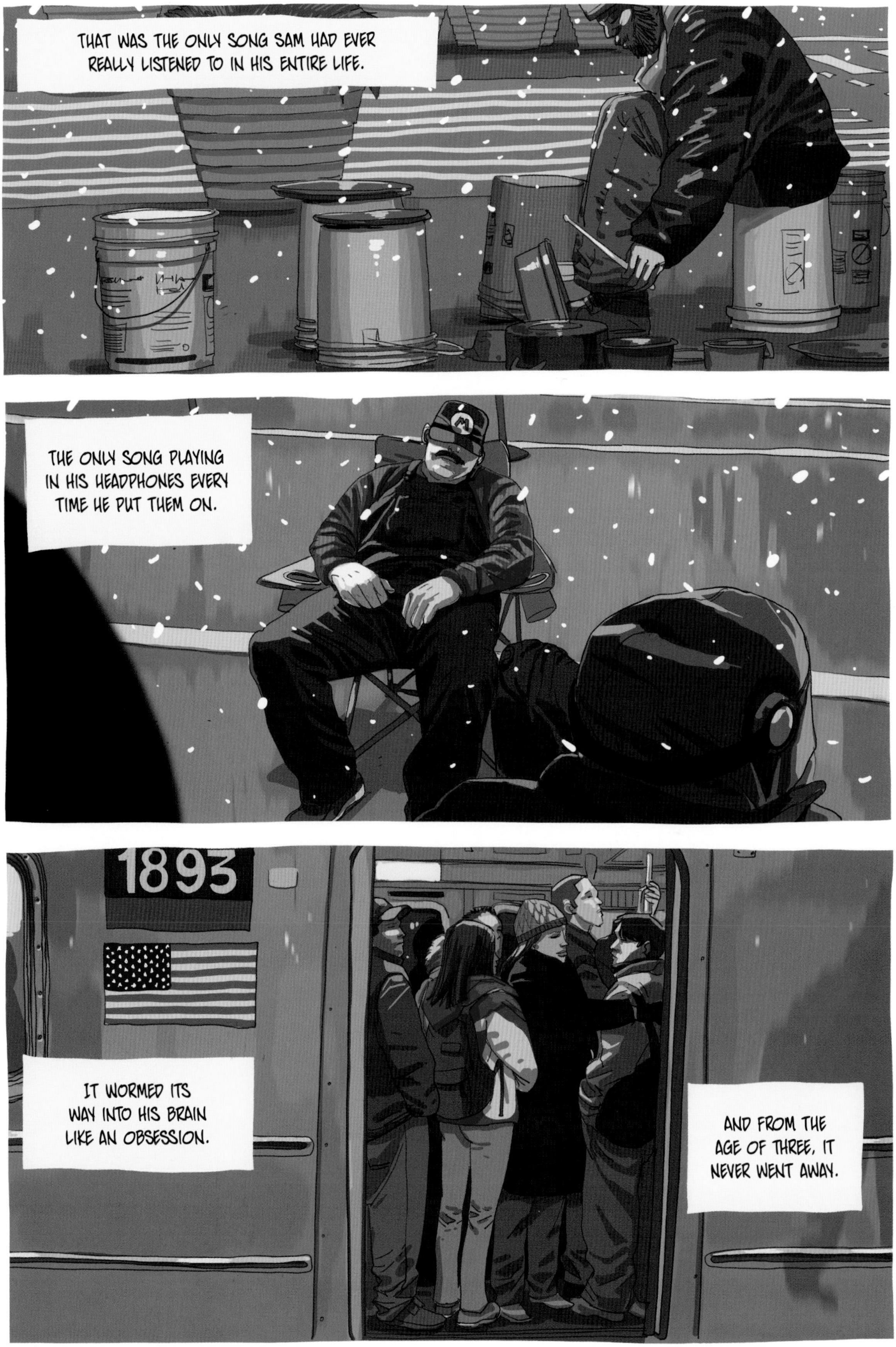
THAT WAS THE ONLY SONG SAM HAD EVER REALLY LISTENED TO IN HIS ENTIRE LIFE.
THE ONLY SONG PLAYING IN HIS HEADPHONES EVERY TIME HE PUT THEM ON.
1893
IT WORMED ITS WAY INTO HIS BRAIN LIKE AN OBSESSION.
AND FROM THE AGE OF THREE, IT NEVER WENT AWAY.

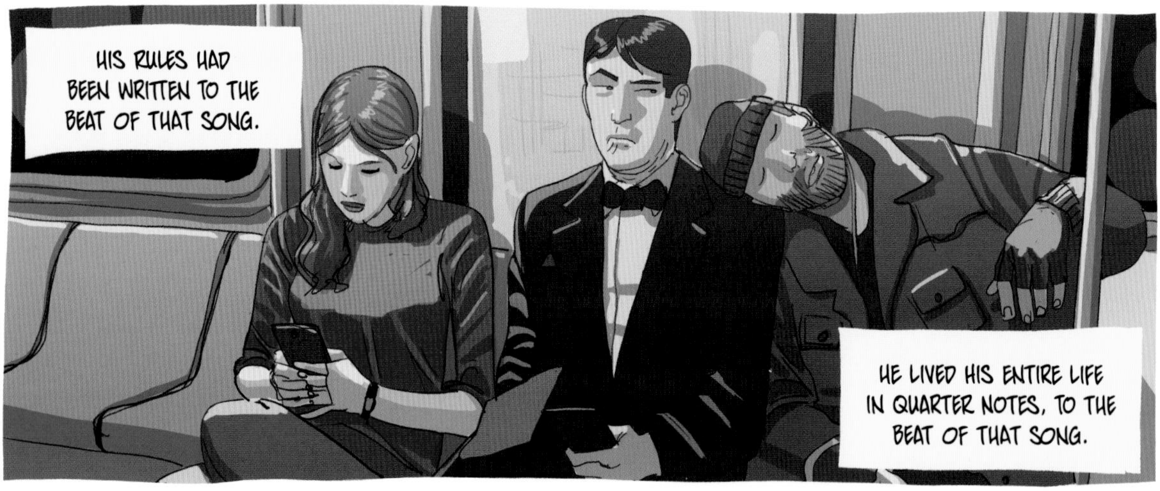
HIS RULES HAD BEEN WRITTEN TO THE BEAT OF THAT SONG.
HE LIVED HIS ENTIRE LIFE IN QUARTER NOTES, TO THE BEAT OF THAT SONG.

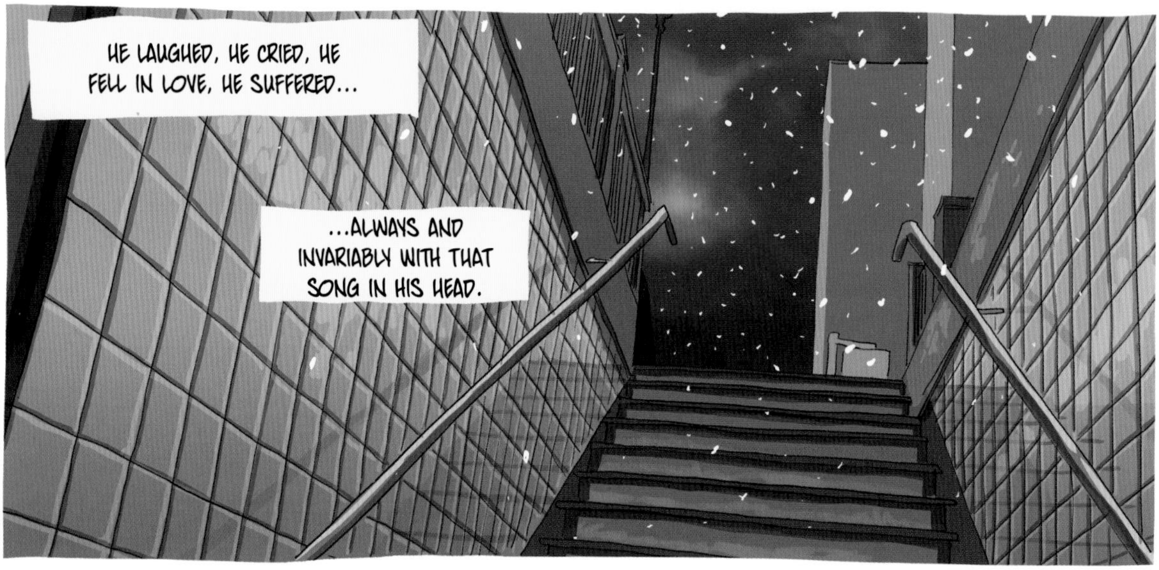
HE LAUGHED, HE CRIED, HE FELL IN LOVE, HE SUFFERED...
...ALWAYS AND INVARIABLY WITH THAT SONG IN HIS HEAD.

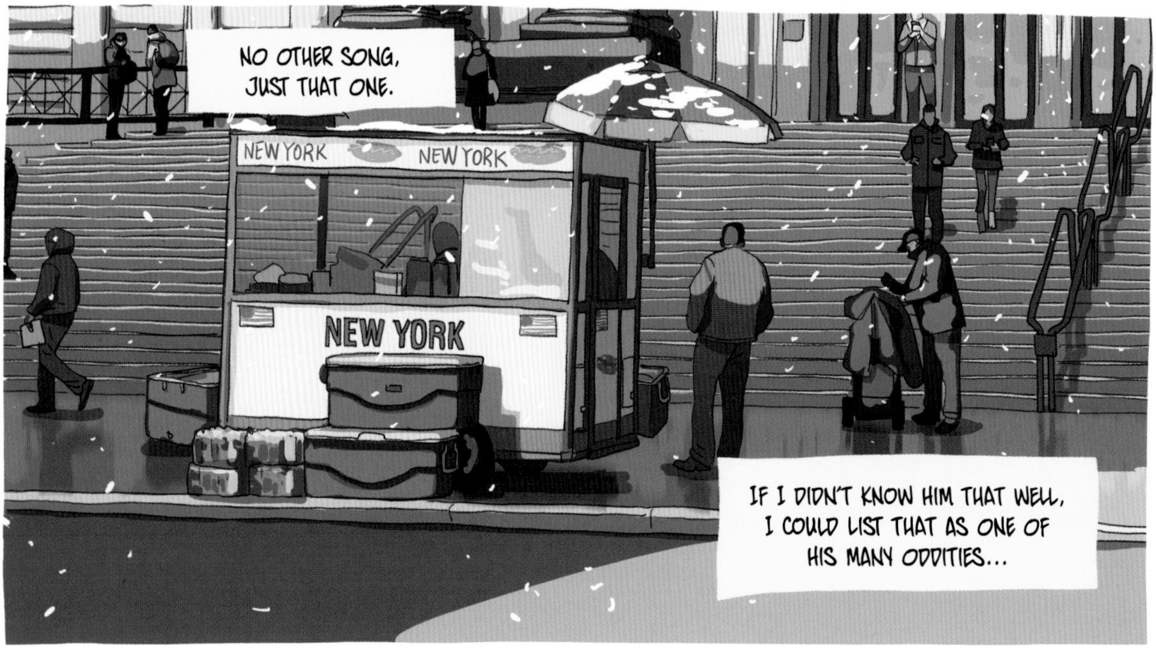
NO OTHER SONG, JUST THAT ONE.
NEW YORK
NEW YORK
NEW YORK
IF I DIDN'T KNOW HIM THAT WELL, I COULD LIST THAT AS ONE OF HIS MANY ODDITIES...

...BUT THE SONG WAS PLAYING IN HIS HEADPHONES AND IN HIS HEAD EVEN AT THAT MOMENT HE ENTERED THE MUSEUM.

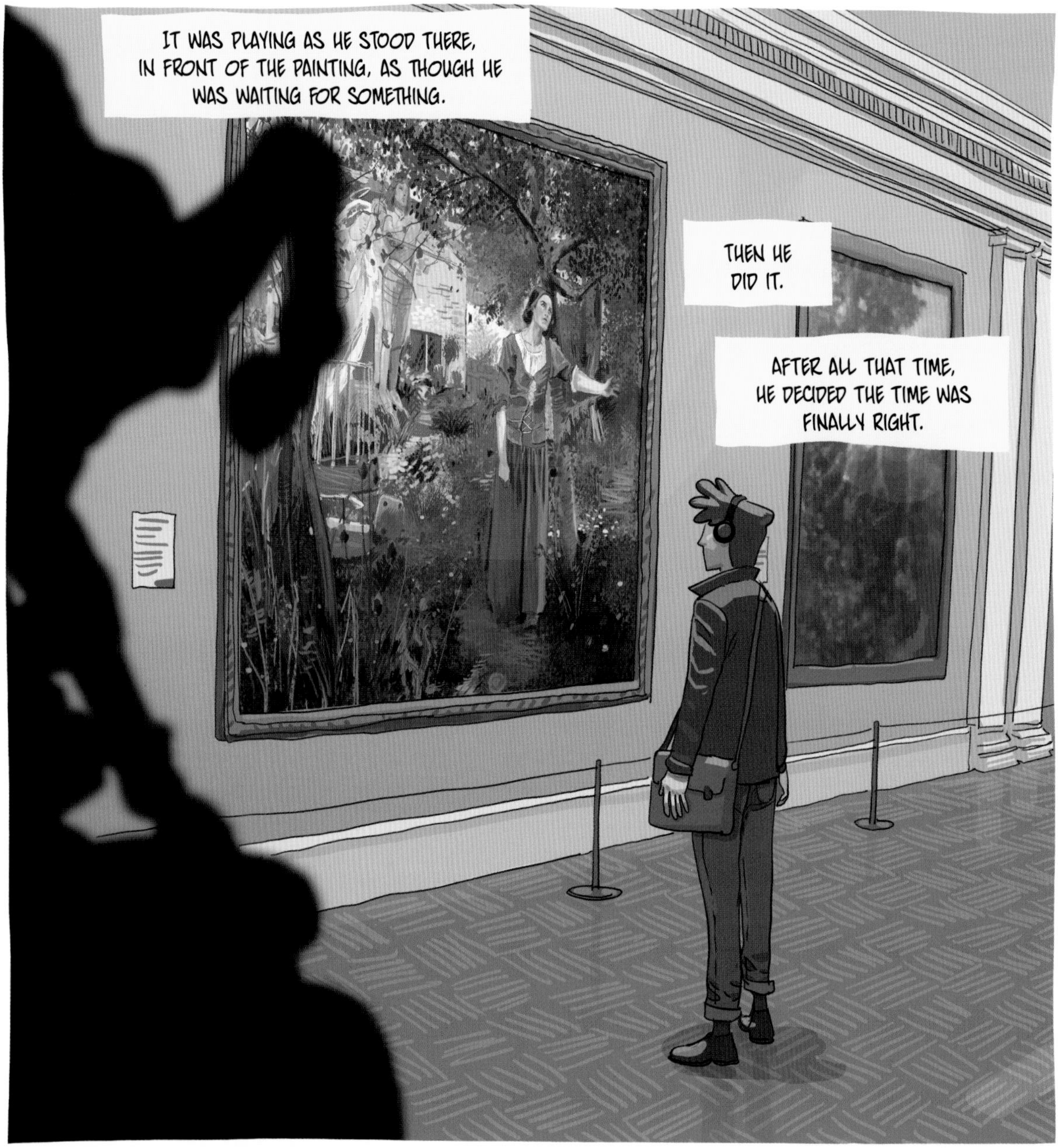
IT WAS PLAYING AS HE STOOD THERE, IN FRONT OF THE PAINTING, AS THOUGH HE WAS WAITING FOR SOMETHING.
THEN HE DID IT.
AFTER ALL THAT TIME, HE DECIDED THE TIME WAS FINALLY RIGHT.

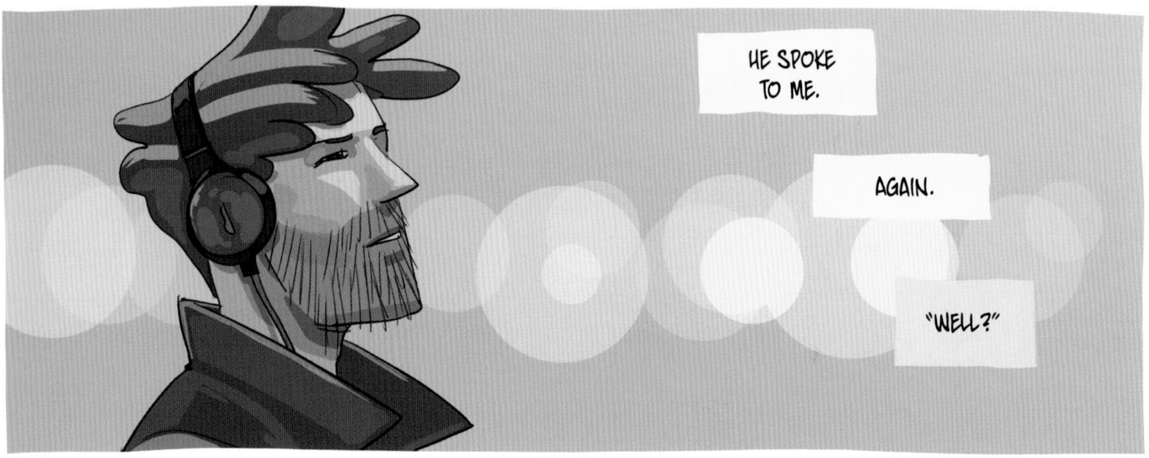
HE SPOKE TO ME.
AGAIN.
"WELL?"

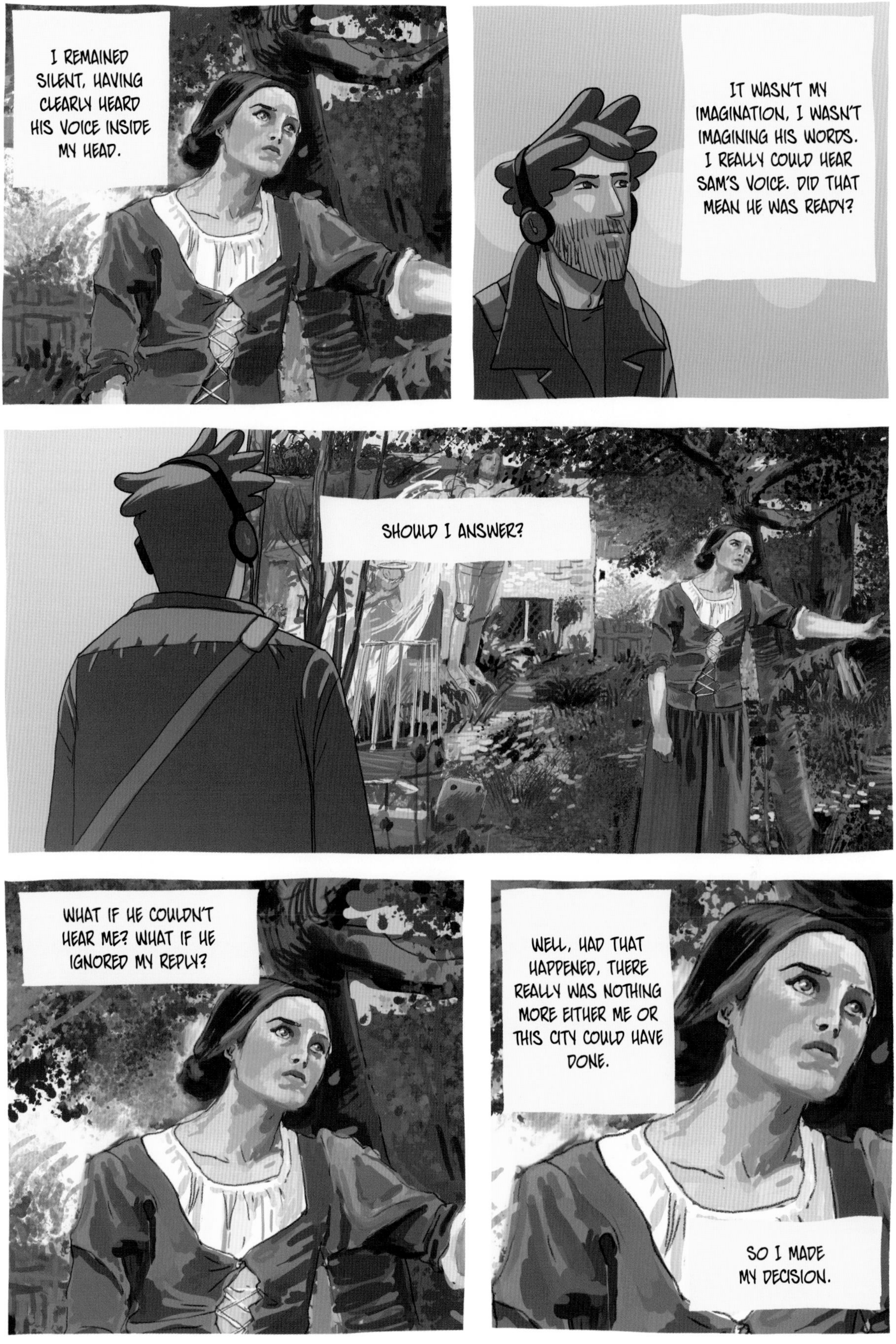
I REMAINED SILENT, HAVING CLEARLY HEARD HIS VOICE INSIDE MY HEAD.
IT WASN'T MY IMAGINATION, I WASN'T IMAGINING HIS WORDS. I REALLY COULD HEAR SAM'S VOICE. DID THAT MEAN HE WAS READY?
SHOULD I ANSWER?
WHAT IF HE COULDN'T HEAR ME? WHAT IF HE IGNORED MY REPLY?
WELL, HAD THAT HAPPENED, THERE REALLY WAS NOTHING MORE EITHER ME OR THIS CITY COULD HAVE DONE.
SO I MADE MY DECISION.

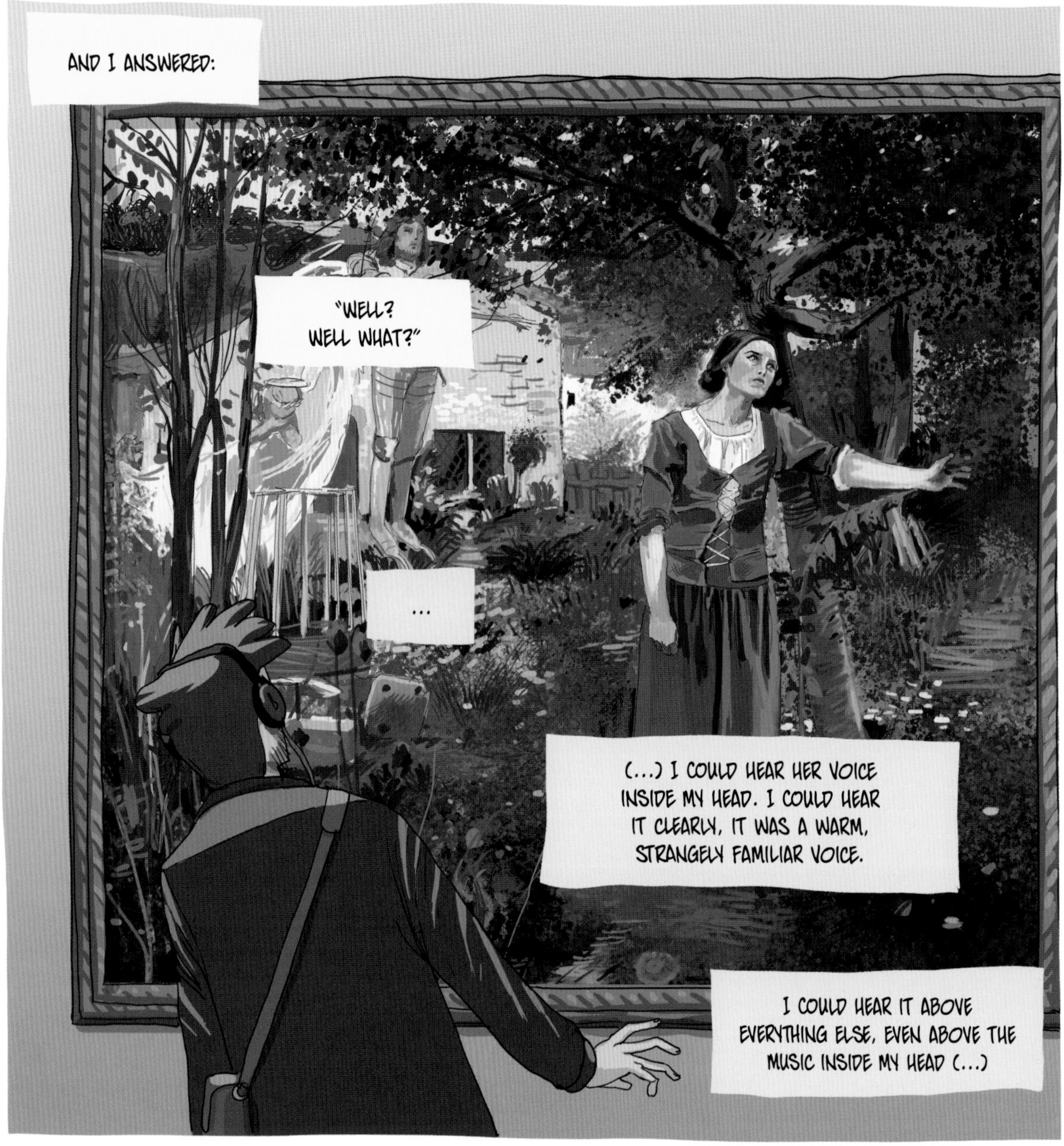
AND I ANSWERED:
"WELL?
WELL WHAT?"
...
(...) I COULD HEAR HER VOICE INSIDE MY HEAD. I COULD HEAR IT CLEARLY, IT WAS A WARM, STRANGELY FAMILIAR VOICE.
I COULD HEAR IT ABOVE EVERYTHING ELSE, EVEN ABOVE THE MUSIC INSIDE MY HEAD (...)

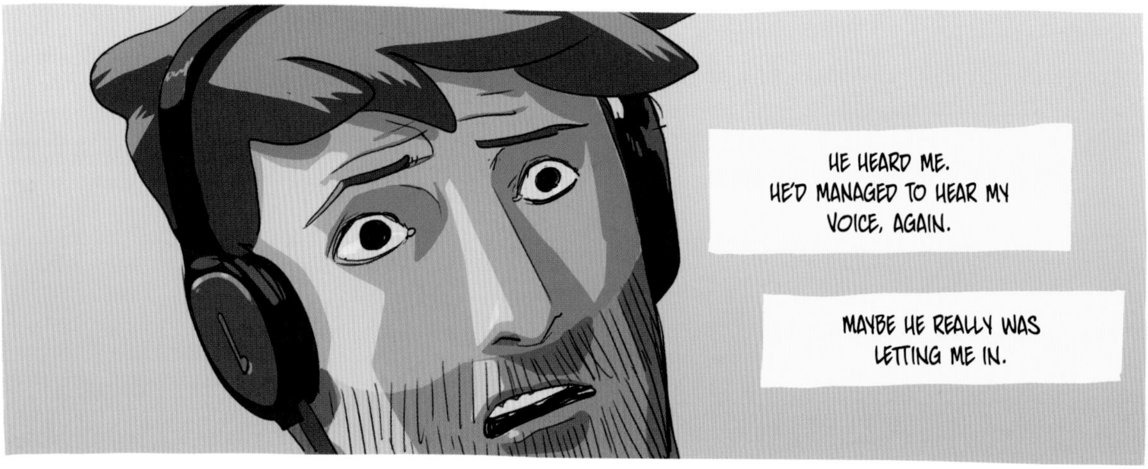
HE HEARD ME.
HE'D MANAGED TO HEAR MY VOICE, AGAIN.
MAYBE HE REALLY WAS LETTING ME IN.

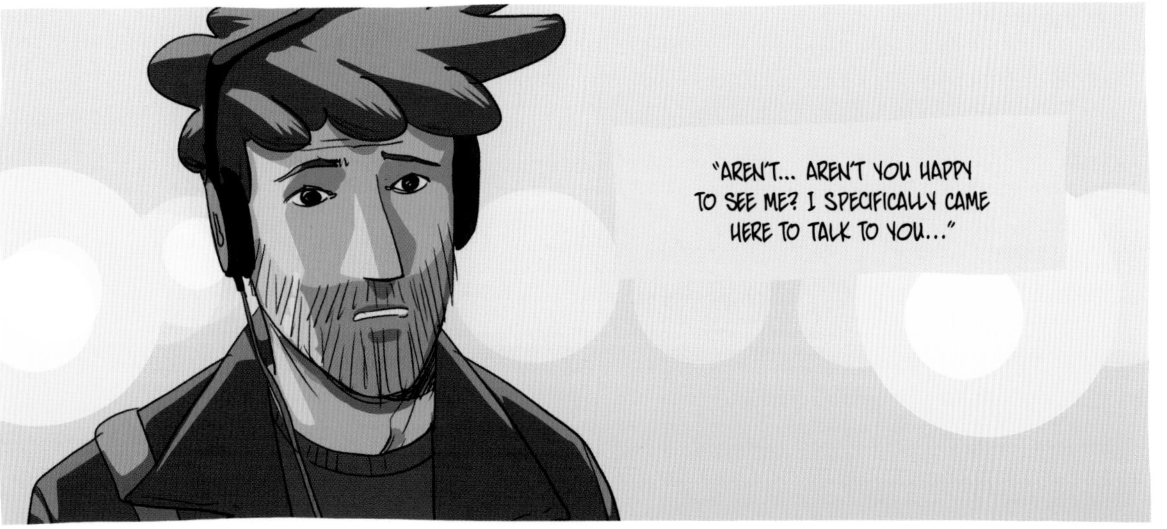
"AREN'T... AREN'T YOU HAPPY TO SEE ME? I SPECIFICALLY CAME HERE TO TALK TO YOU..."

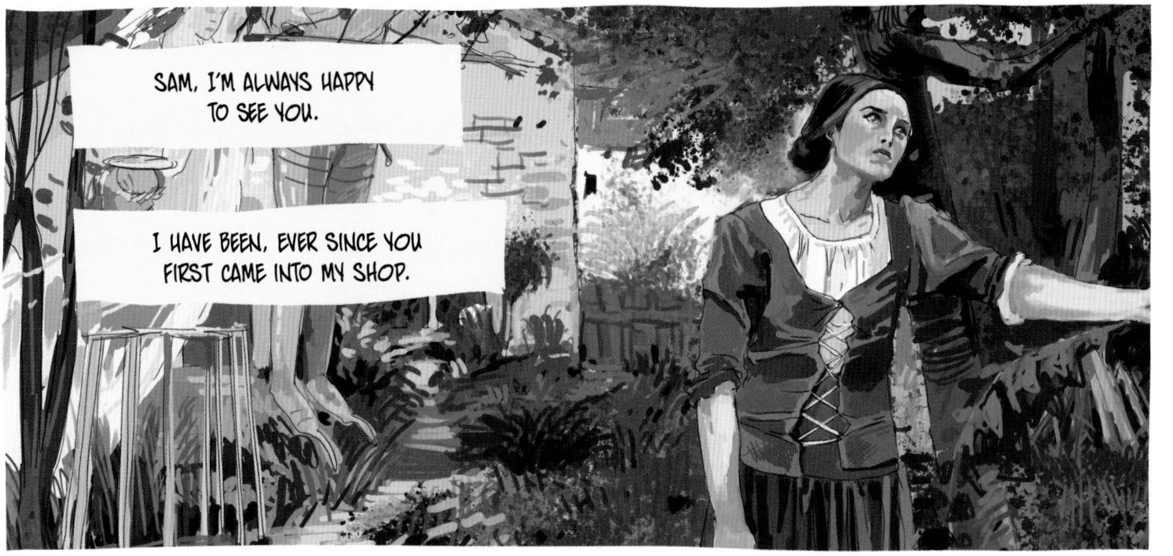
SAM, I'M ALWAYS HAPPY TO SEE YOU.
I HAVE BEEN, EVER SINCE YOU FIRST CAME INTO MY SHOP.

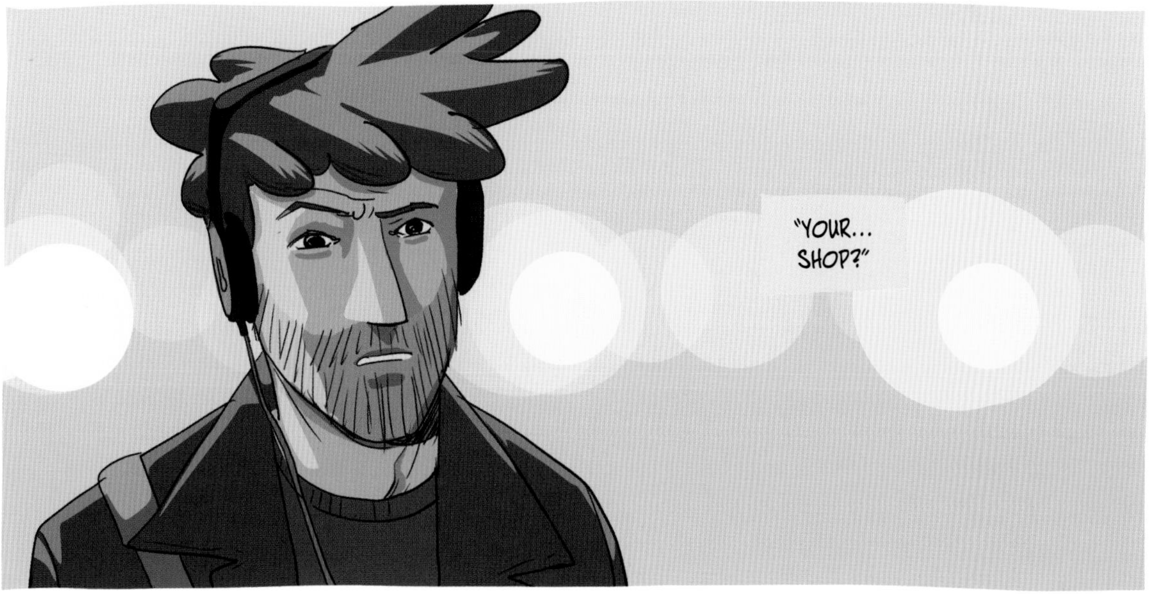
"YOUR... SHOP?"

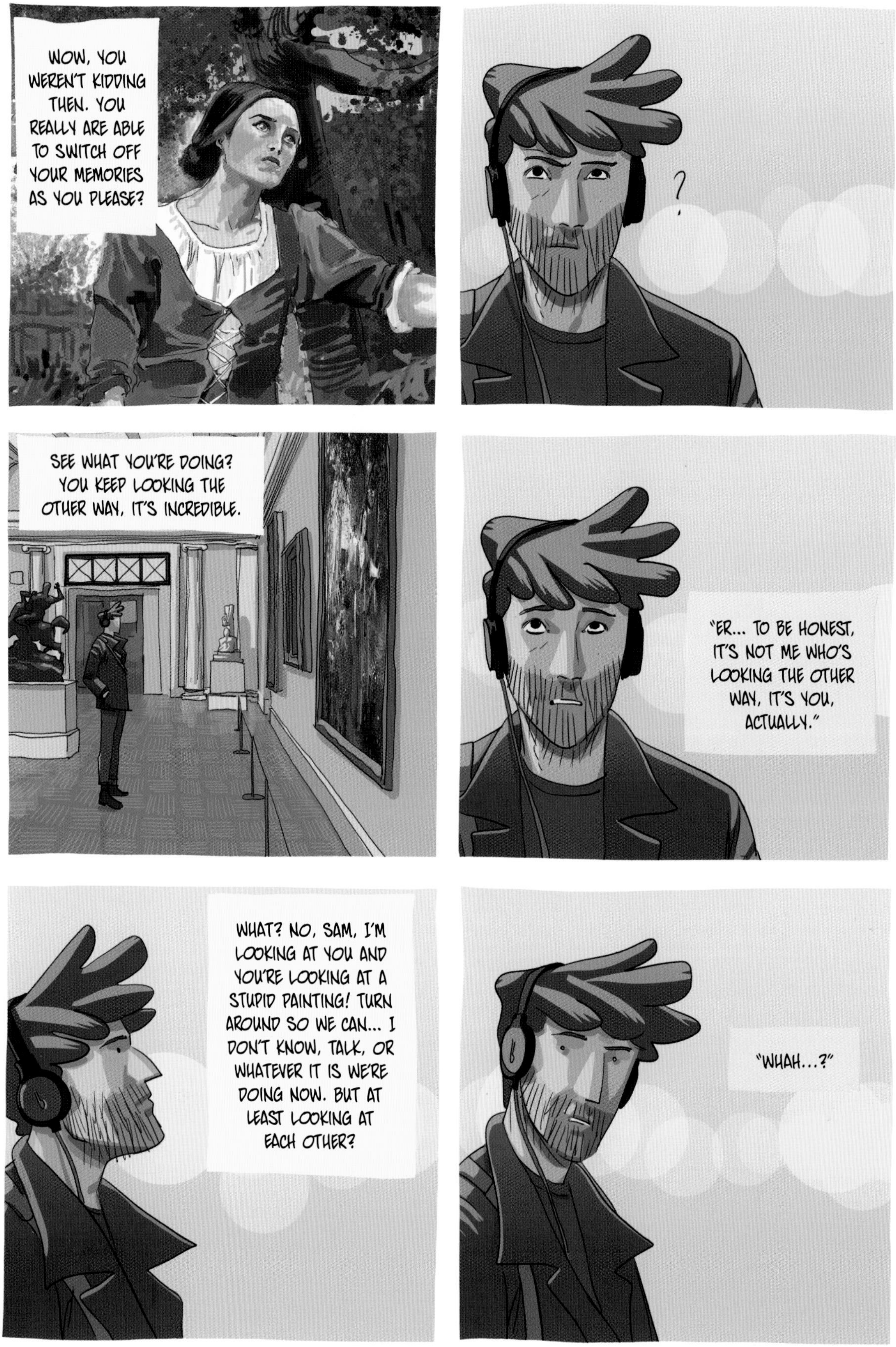
WOW, YOU WEREN'T KIDDING THEN. YOU REALLY ARE ABLE TO SWITCH OFF YOUR MEMORIES AS YOU PLEASE?
?
SEE WHAT YOU'RE DOING? YOU KEEP LOOKING THE OTHER WAY, IT'S INCREDIBLE.
"ER... TO BE HONEST, IT'S NOT ME WHO'S LOOKING THE OTHER WAY, IT'S YOU, ACTUALLY."
WHAT? NO, SAM, I'M LOOKING AT YOU AND YOU'RE LOOKING AT A STUPID PAINTING! TURN AROUND SO WE CAN... I DON'T KNOW, TALK, OR WHATEVER IT IS WE'RE DOING NOW. BUT AT LEAST LOOKING AT EACH OTHER?
"WHAH...?"

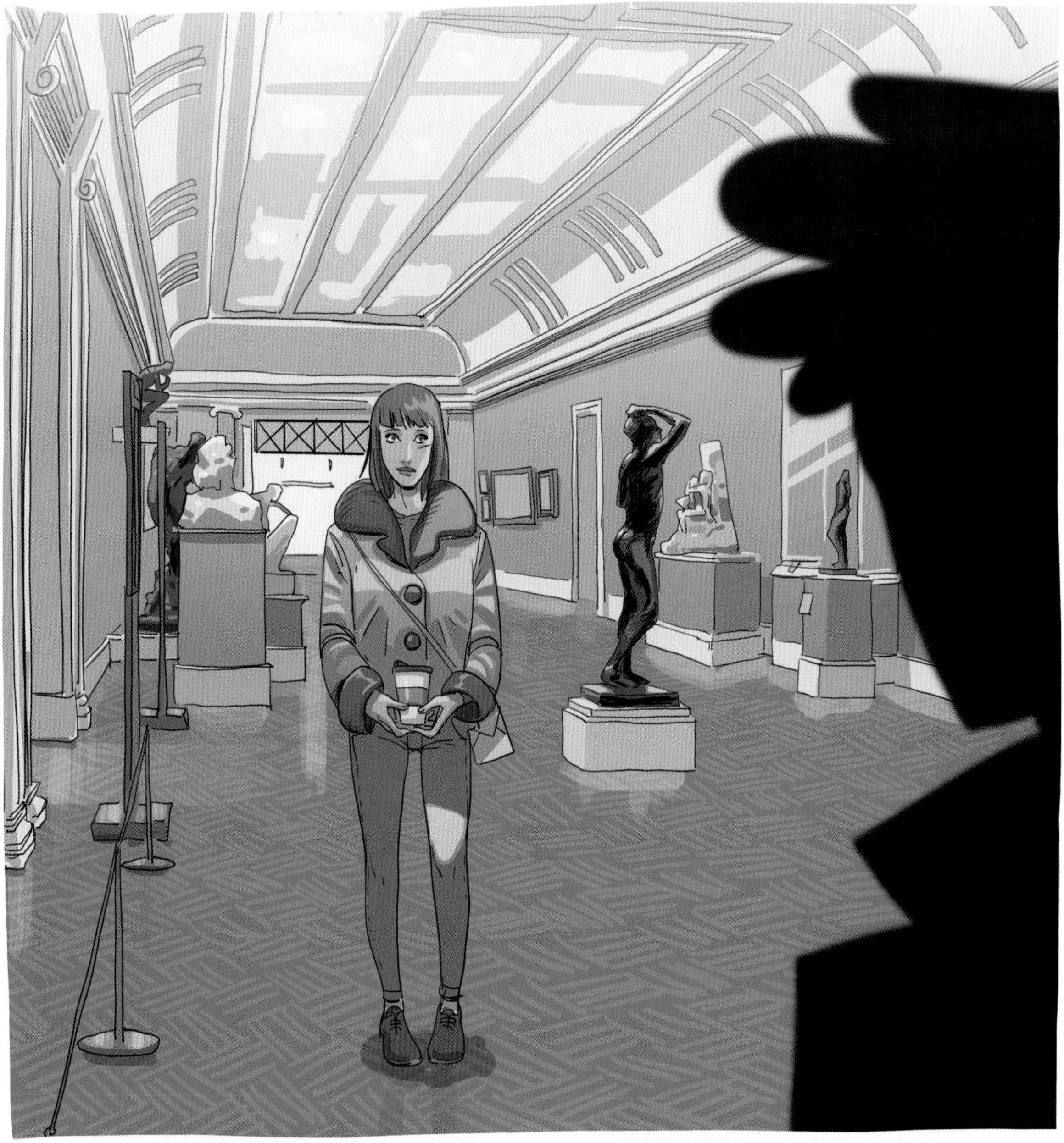

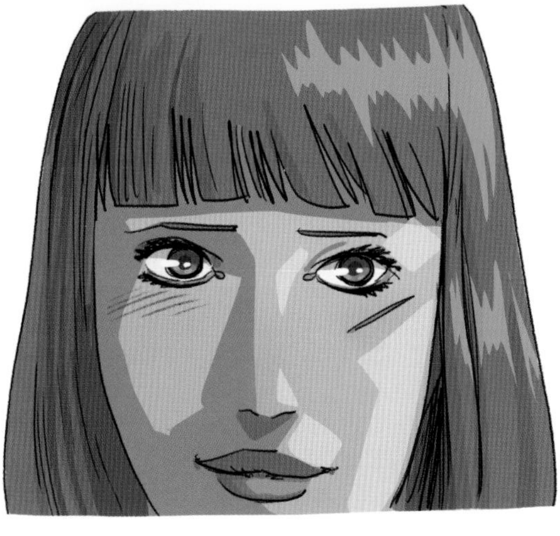

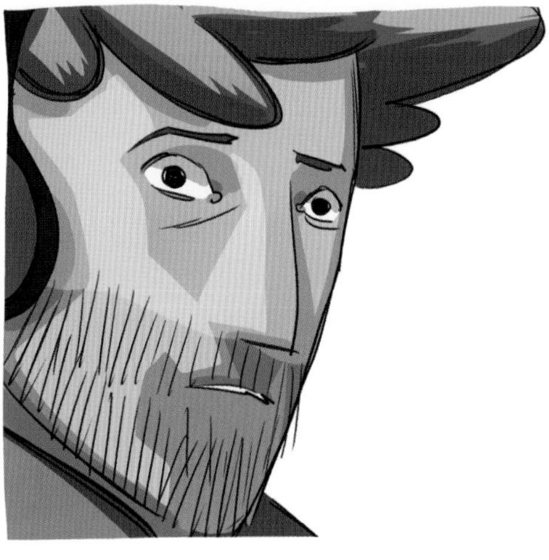

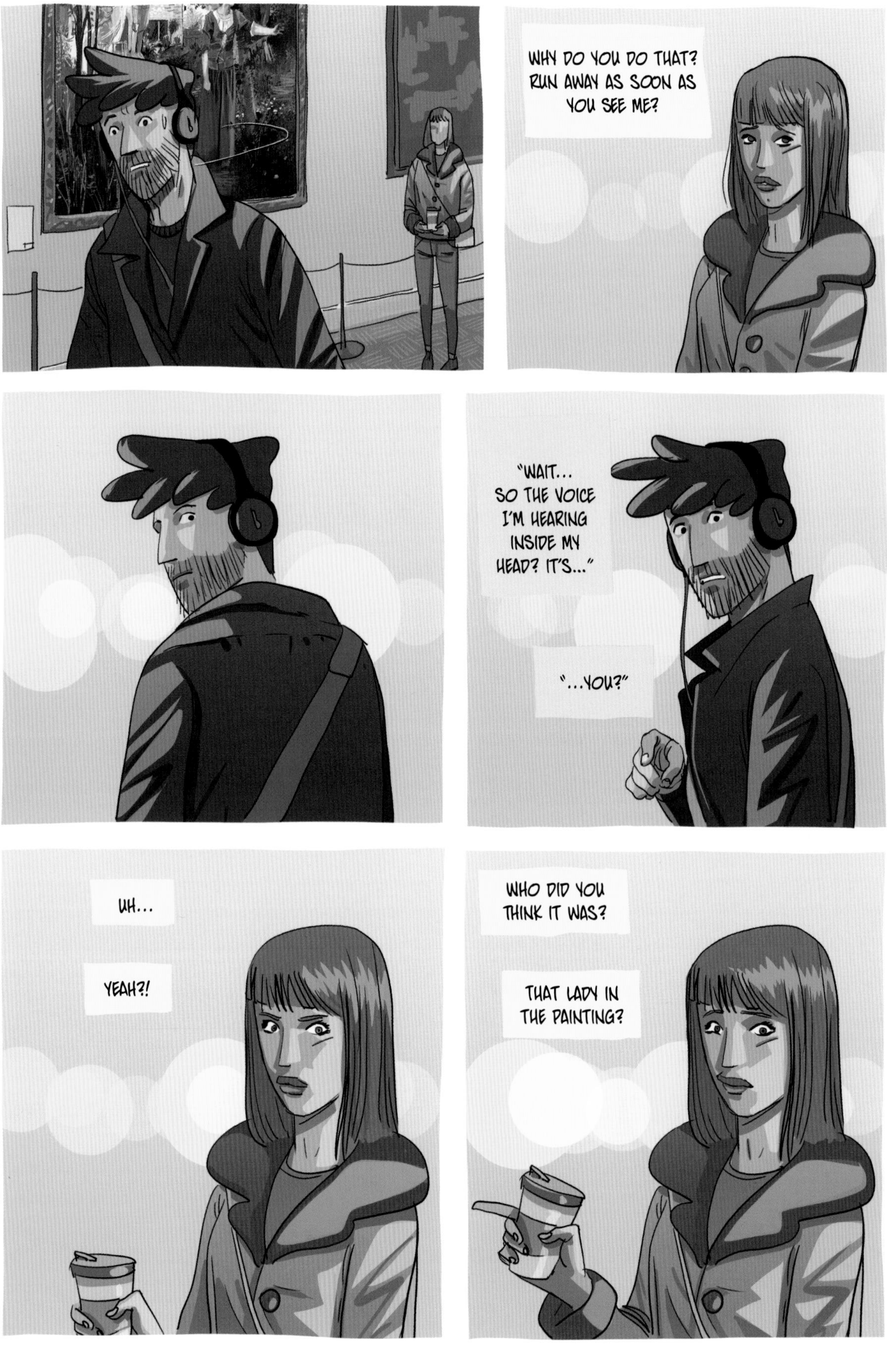
WHY DO YOU DO THAT? RUN AWAY AS SOON AS YOU SEE ME?
"WAIT... SO THE VOICE I'M HEARING INSIDE MY HEAD? IT'S..."
"...YOU?"
UH...
YEAH?!
WHO DID YOU THINK IT WAS?
THAT LADY IN THE PAINTING?

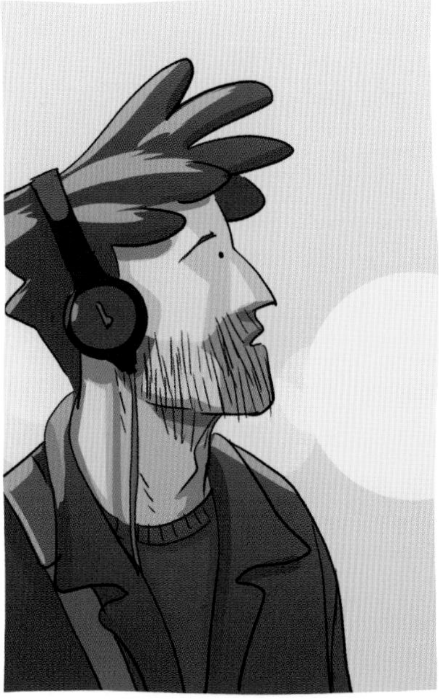

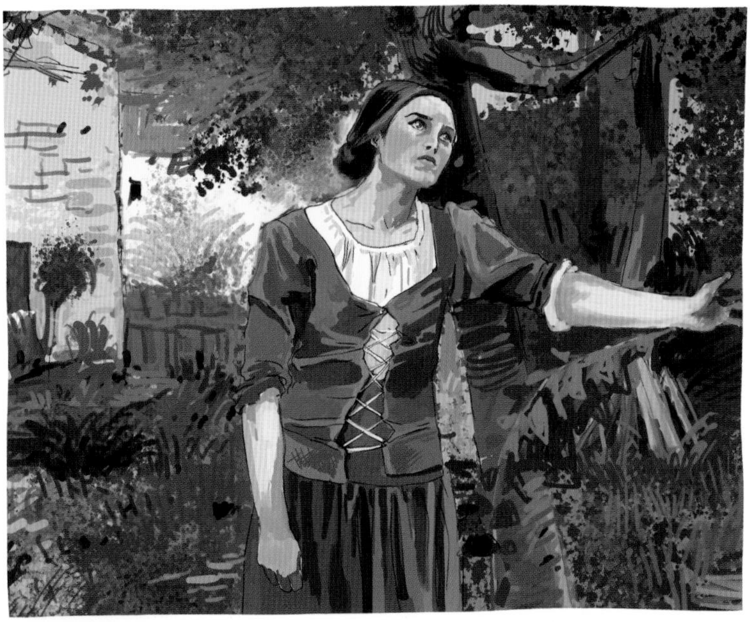

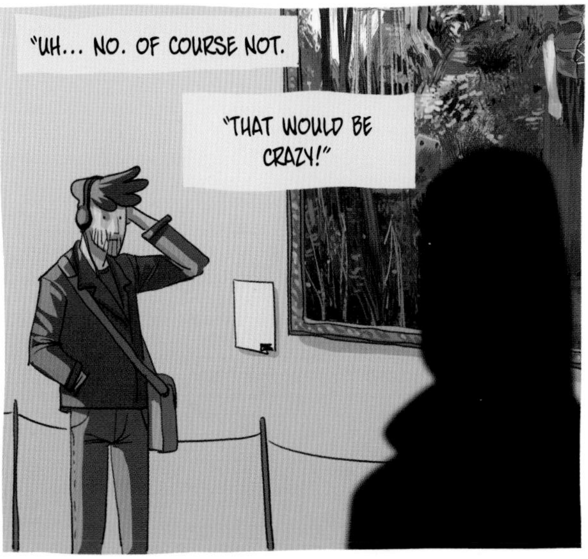
"UH... NO. OF COURSE NOT.
"THAT WOULD BE CRAZY!"

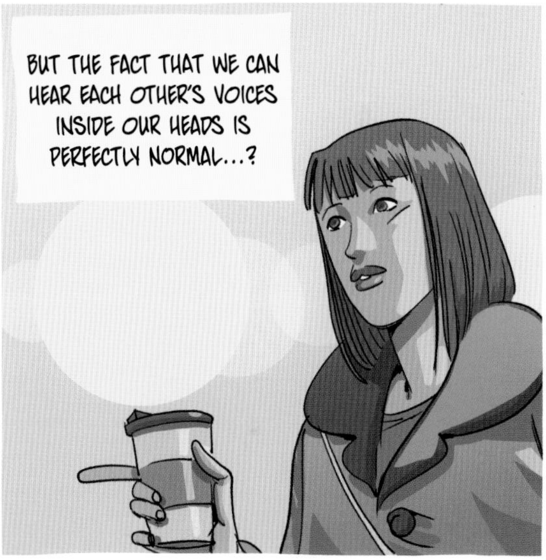
BUT THE FACT THAT WE CAN HEAR EACH OTHER'S VOICES INSIDE OUR HEADS IS PERFECTLY NORMAL...?

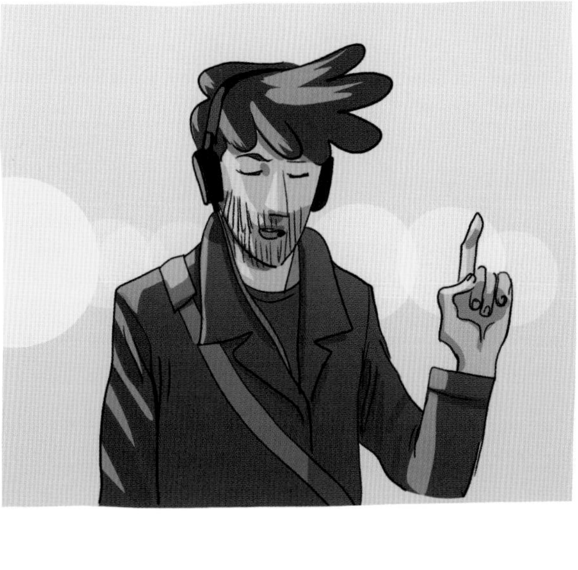

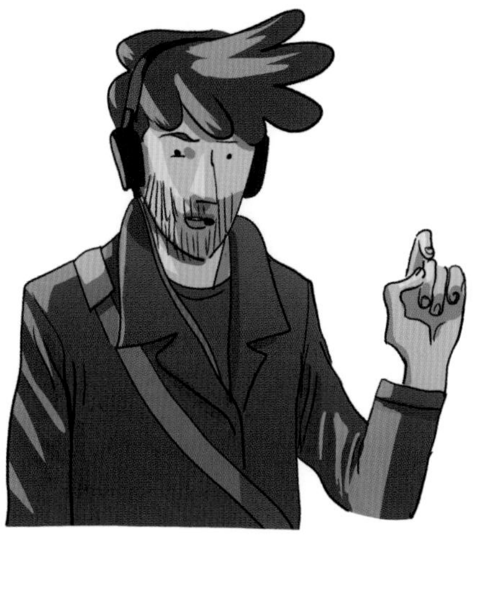

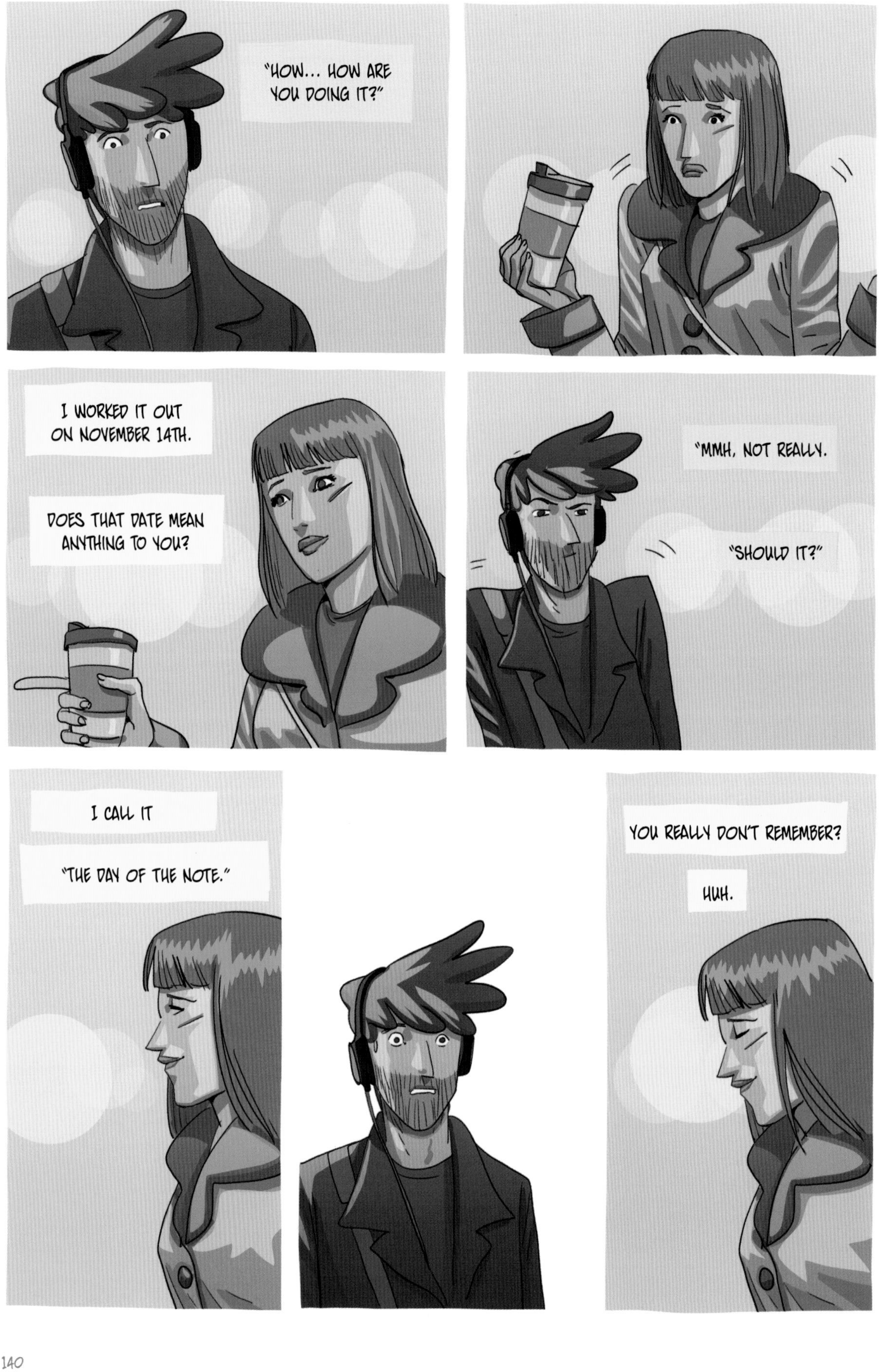
"HOW… HOW ARE YOU DOING IT?"
I WORKED IT OUT ON NOVEMBER 14TH.
DOES THAT DATE MEAN ANYTHING TO YOU?
"MMH, NOT REALLY.
"SHOULD IT?"
I CALL IT
"THE DAY OF THE NOTE."
YOU REALLY DON'T REMEMBER?
HUH.

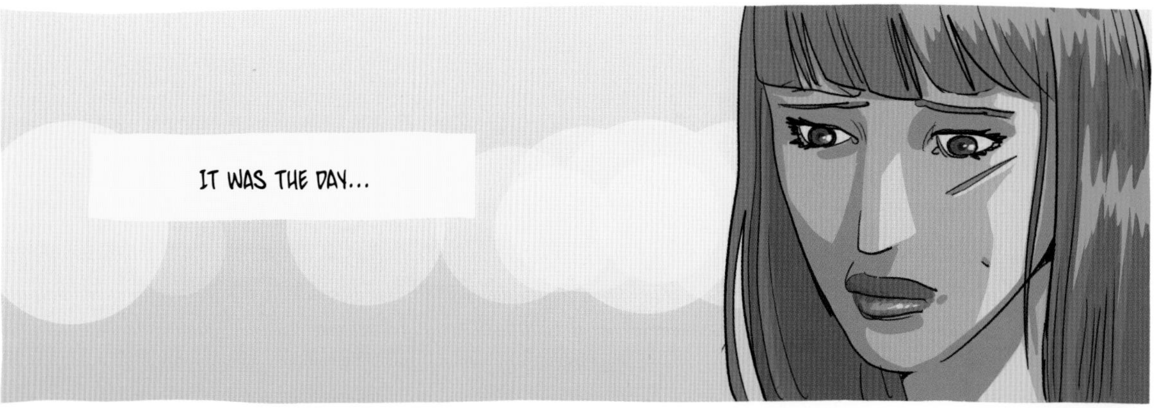
IT WAS THE DAY...

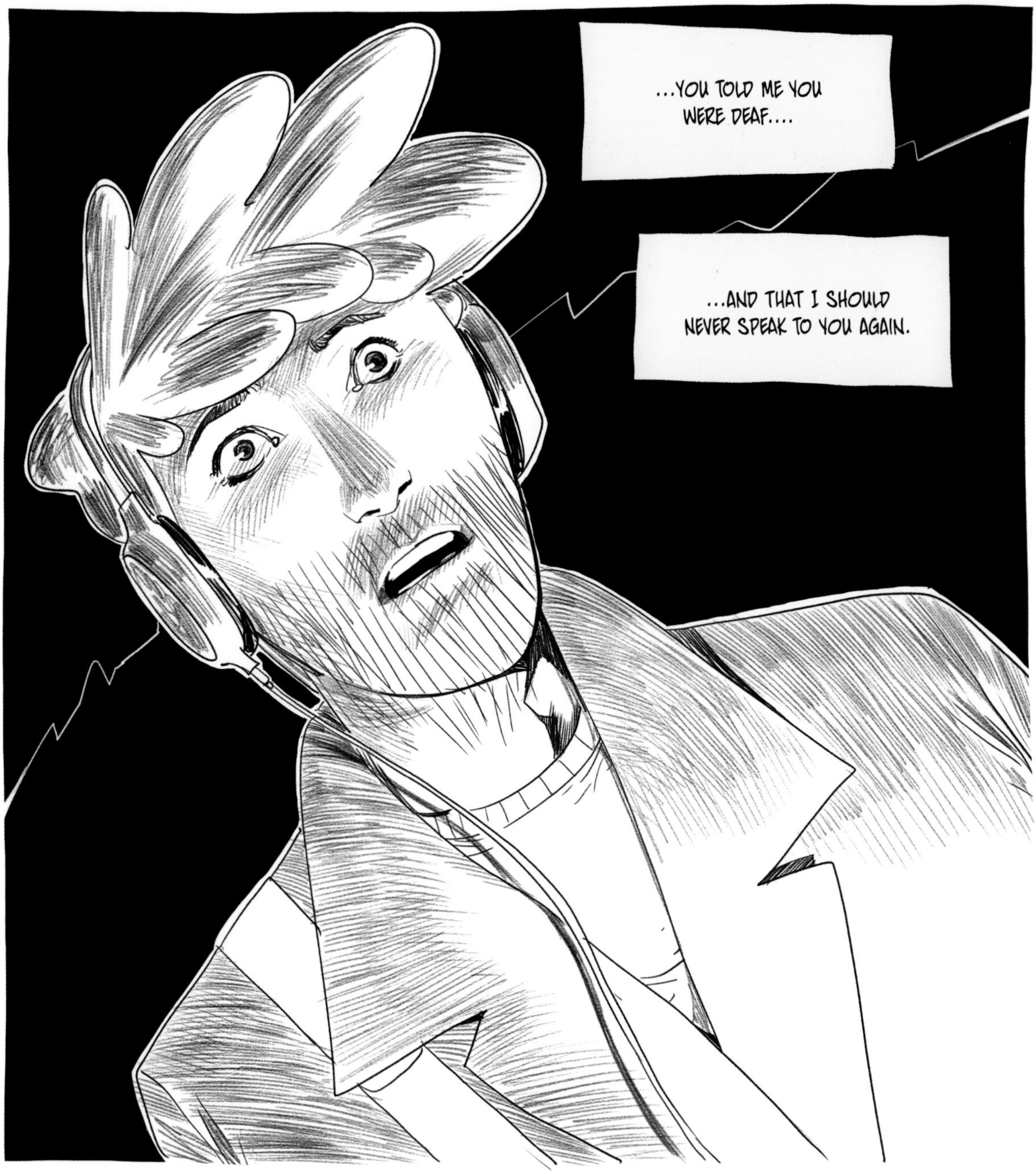
...YOU TOLD ME YOU WERE DEAF....
...AND THAT I SHOULD NEVER SPEAK TO YOU AGAIN.

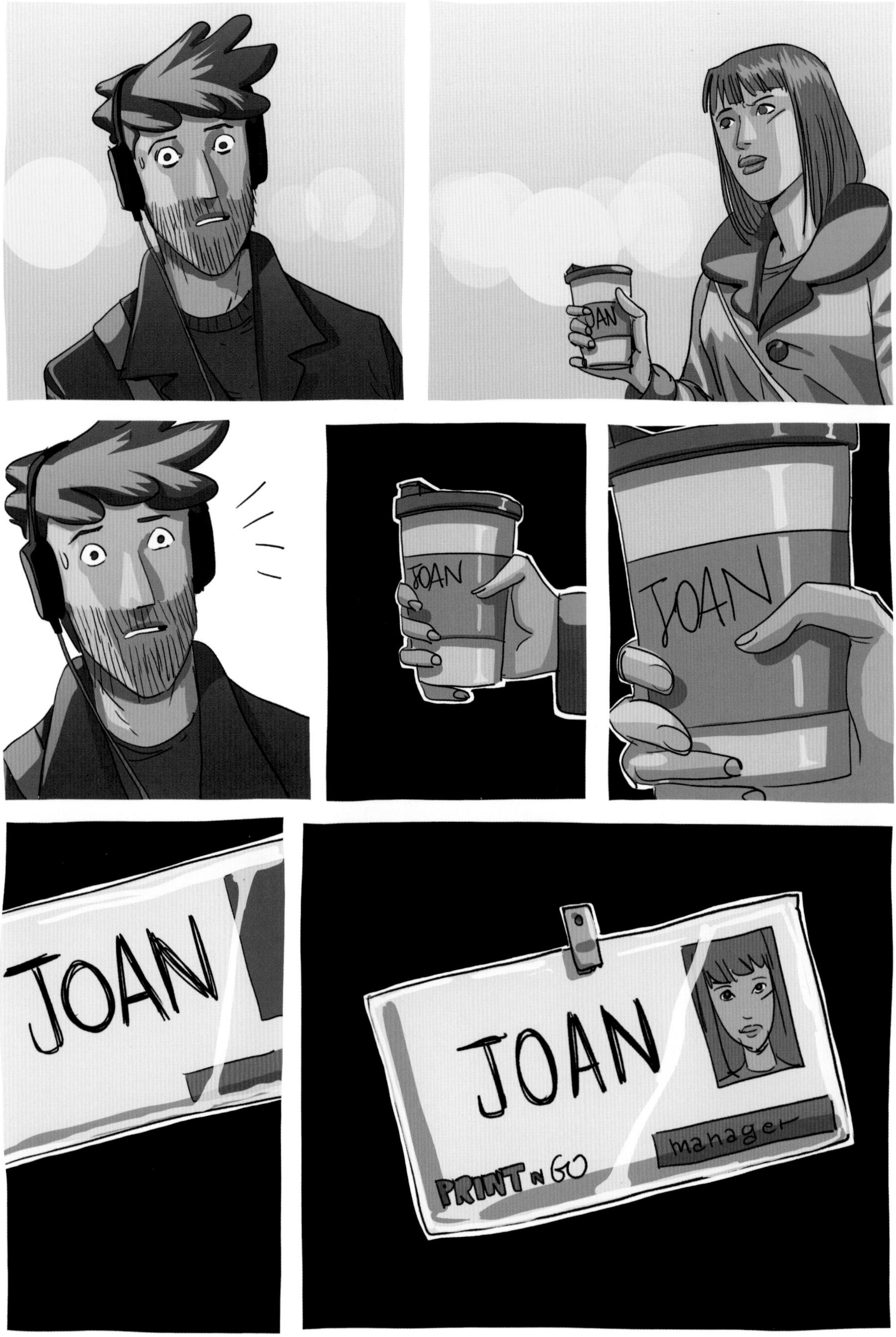
JAN
JOAN
JOAN
JOAN
JOAN
manager
PRINT N GO

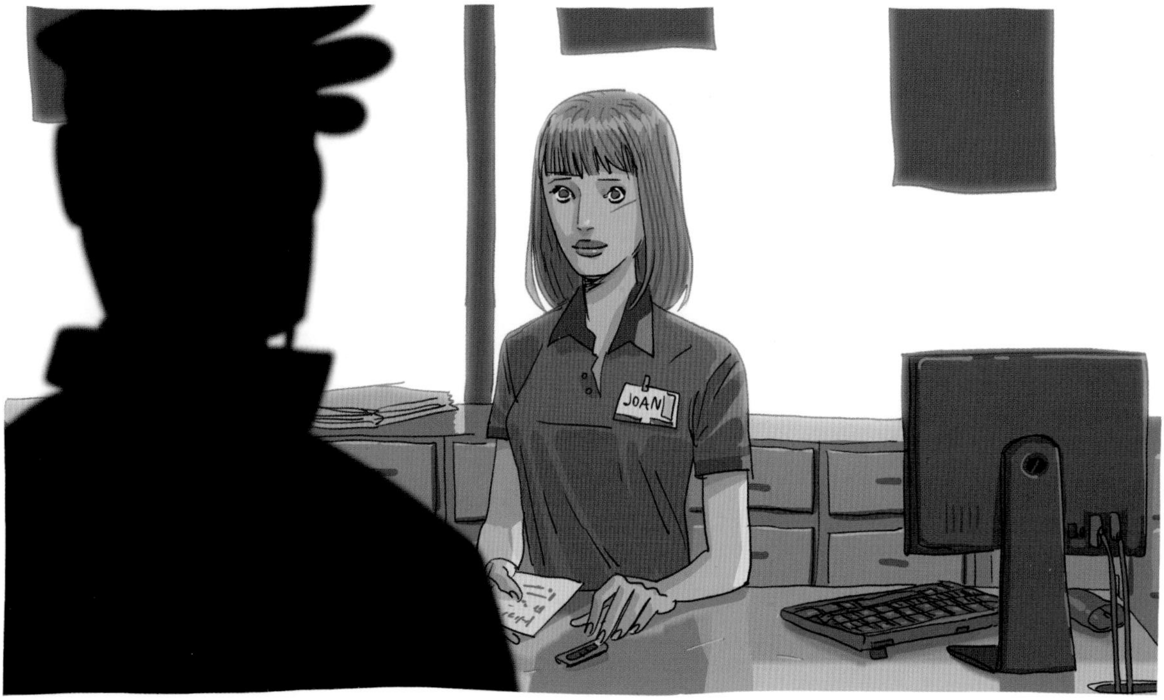
JOAN

NOVEMBER 14TH

NOVEMBER
MON TUE WED THU FRI SAT SUN
1 2 3 4
5 6 7 8 9 10 11
12 13 14 15 16 17 18
19 20 21 22 23 24 25
26 27 28 29 30

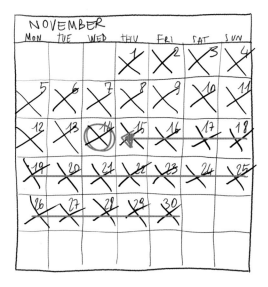

(OR, "THE MAN WHO DELETED MOMENTS")

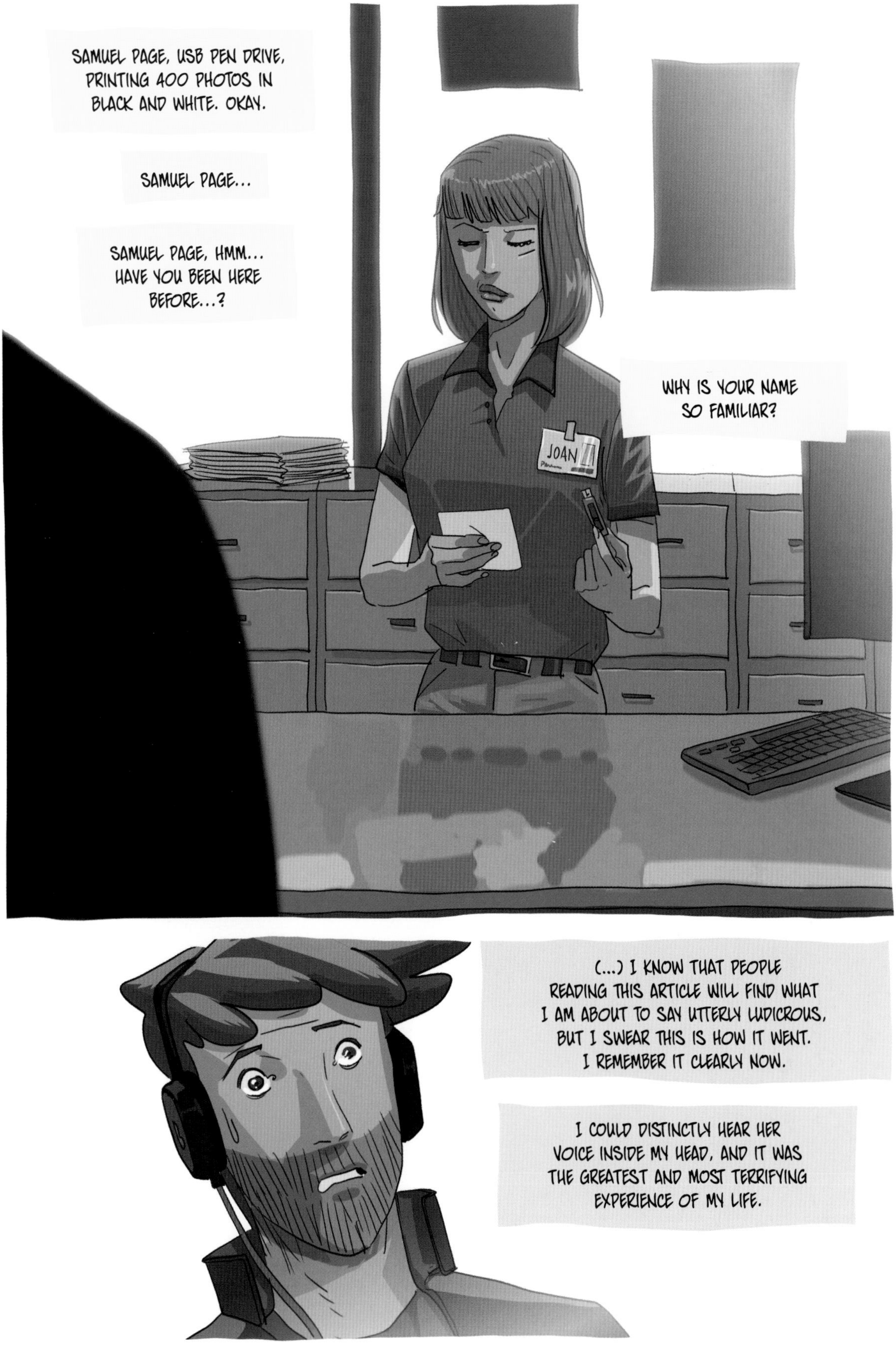
SAMUEL PAGE, USB PEN DRIVE, PRINTING 400 PHOTOS IN BLACK AND WHITE. OKAY.
SAMUEL PAGE...
SAMUEL PAGE, HMM... HAVE YOU BEEN HERE BEFORE...?
WHY IS YOUR NAME SO FAMILIAR?
JOAN
(...) I KNOW THAT PEOPLE READING THIS ARTICLE WILL FIND WHAT I AM ABOUT TO SAY UTTERLY LUDICROUS, BUT I SWEAR THIS IS HOW IT WENT. I REMEMBER IT CLEARLY NOW.
I COULD DISTINCTLY HEAR HER VOICE INSIDE MY HEAD, AND IT WAS THE GREATEST AND MOST TERRIFYING EXPERIENCE OF MY LIFE.

IT WAS WARM, LIKE A KNIFE LEFT OVER A FIRE, AND
IT CUT THROUGH MY PAIN AS IF IT WERE BUTTER.

EVERY BEAT OF MY HEART WAS THE SOUND OF THE BLADE HITTING THE CUTTING BOARD.

HAVE YOU EVER EXPERIENCED THAT FLOW OF CONNECTED THOUGHTS? WHERE THEY SEEM TO LAST AN ETERNITY, BUT WHEN THEY'RE OVER YOU REALIZE THEY ONLY LASTED A SPLIT SECOND? WELL, IT WAS DURING ONE OF THOSE MOMENTS THAT I CAUGHT MYSELF SMILING AT HER, TALKING TO HER, HOLDING HER, KISSING HER, AND, LAST BUT NOT LEAST, CRYING IN HER ARMS IN A WAY I HADN'T FOR QUITE SOME TIME.

IMMEDIATELY AFTERWARDS I REALIZED I WASN'T READY FOR THAT,
I WASN'T READY FOR ANY OF WHAT I HAD JUST SEEN A MOMENT EARLIER.
WEIRD, RIGHT?

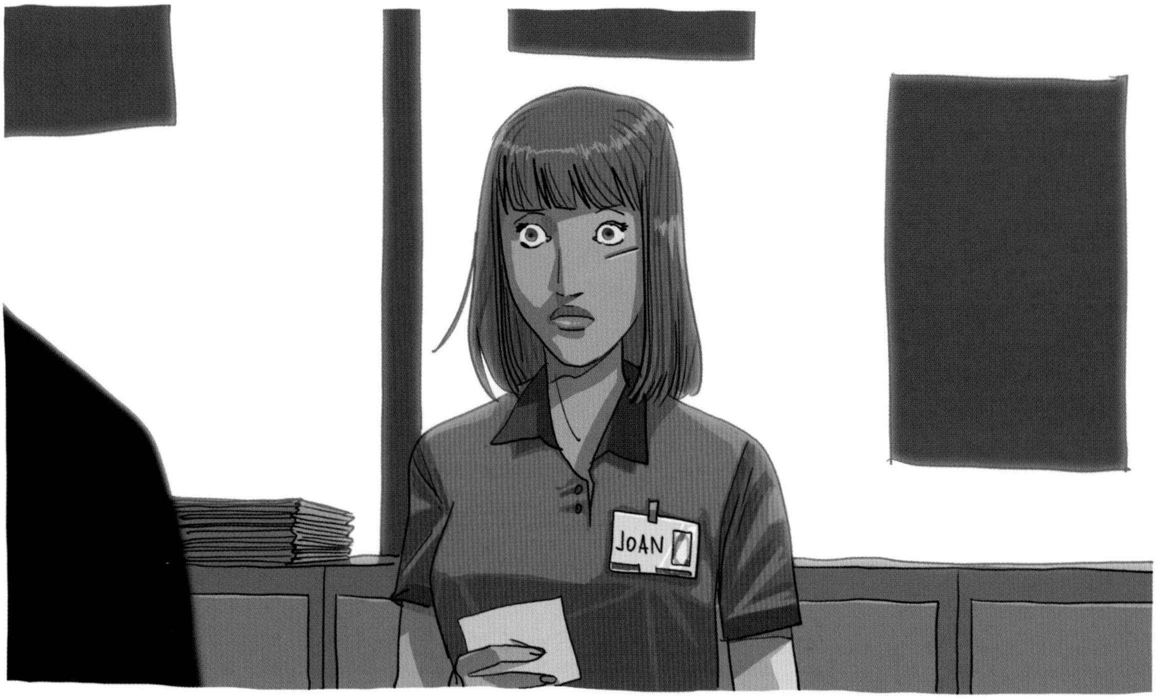
JOAN

BECAUSE YOU CAN'T JUST CUT OFF PAIN LIKE THAT.

IT WASN'T RIGHT.

NOT THAT KIND OF PAIN.

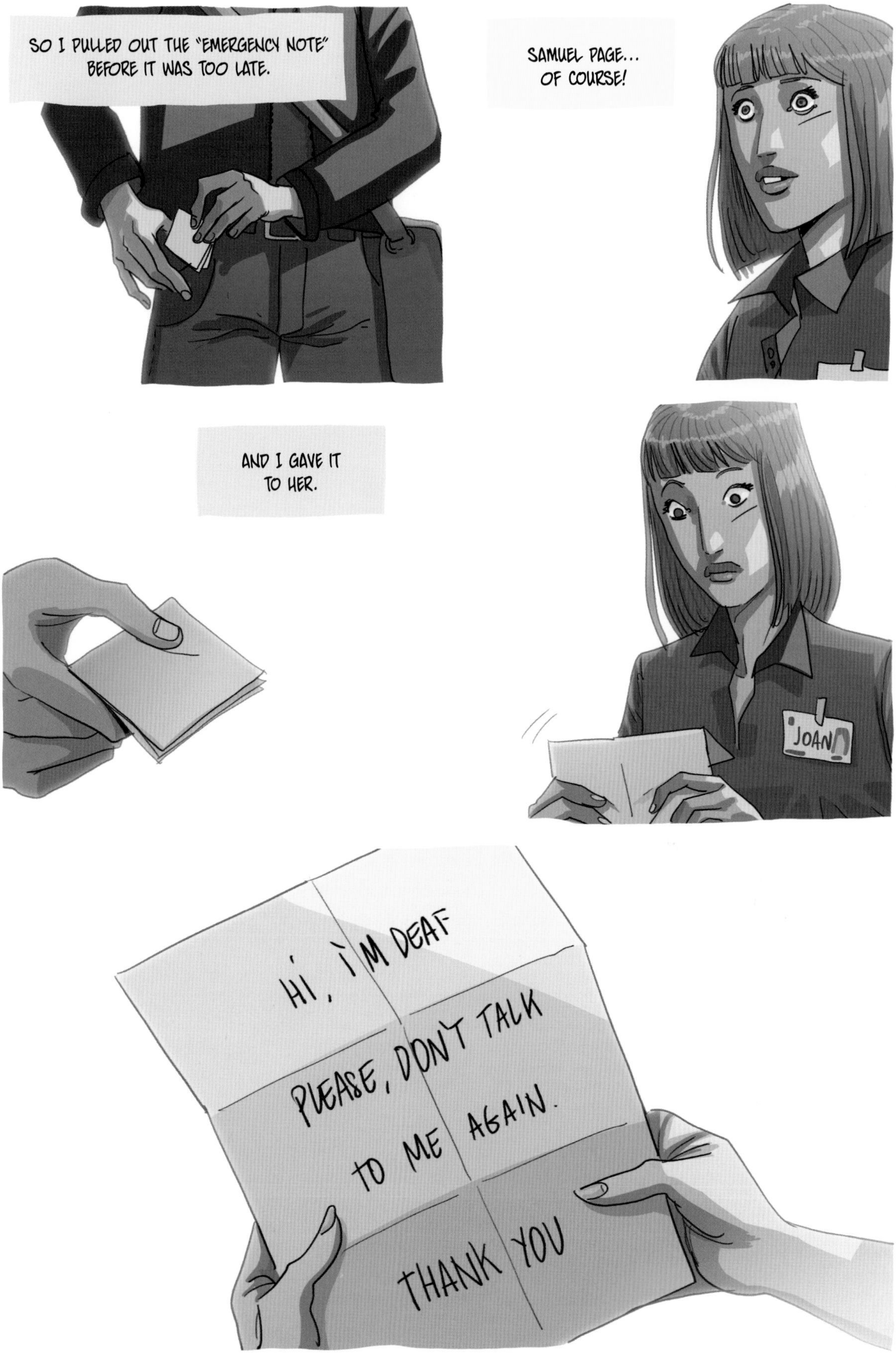
SO I PULLED OUT THE "EMERGENCY NOTE" BEFORE IT WAS TOO LATE.
SAMUEL PAGE... OF COURSE!
AND I GAVE IT TO HER.
JOAN
HI, I'M DEAF
PLEASE, DON'T TALK TO ME AGAIN.
THANK YOU

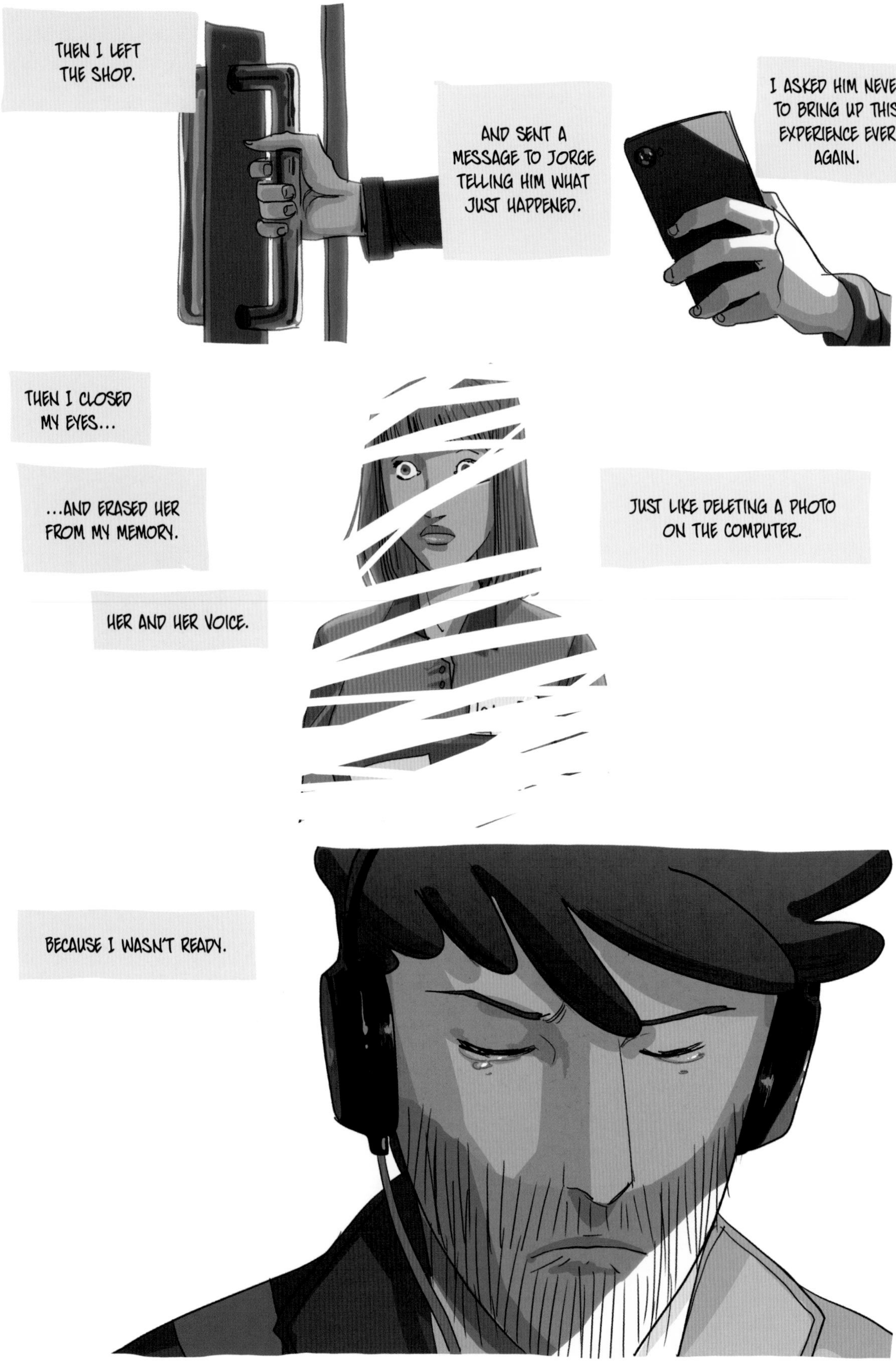
THEN I LEFT THE SHOP.
AND SENT A MESSAGE TO JORGE TELLING HIM WHAT JUST HAPPENED.
I ASKED HIM NEVER TO BRING UP THIS EXPERIENCE EVER AGAIN.
THEN I CLOSED MY EYES...
...AND ERASED HER FROM MY MEMORY.
JUST LIKE DELETING A PHOTO ON THE COMPUTER.
HER AND HER VOICE.
BECAUSE I WASN'T READY.

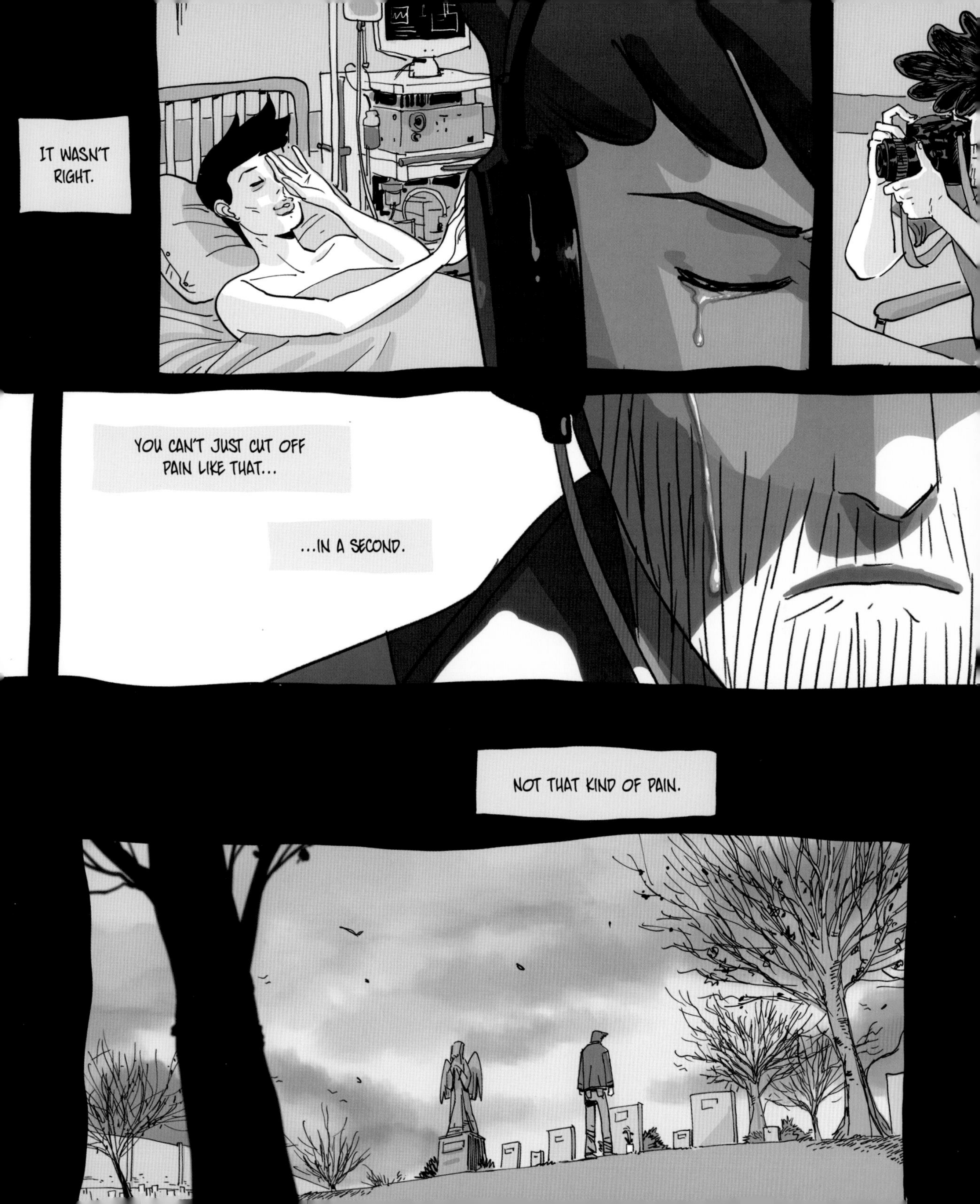
IT WASN'T RIGHT.
YOU CAN'T JUST CUT OFF PAIN LIKE THAT...
...IN A SECOND.
NOT THAT KIND OF PAIN.

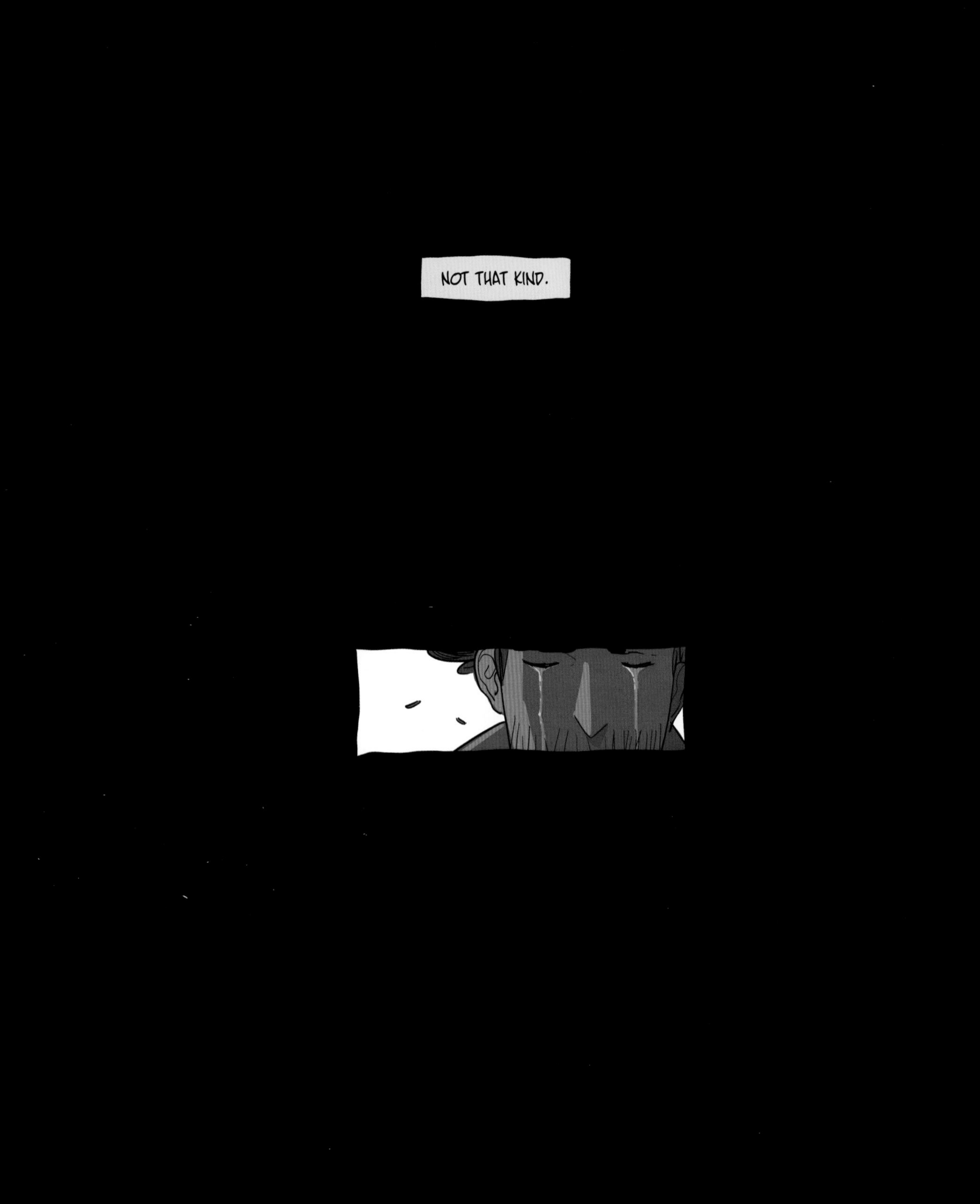
NOT THAT KIND.

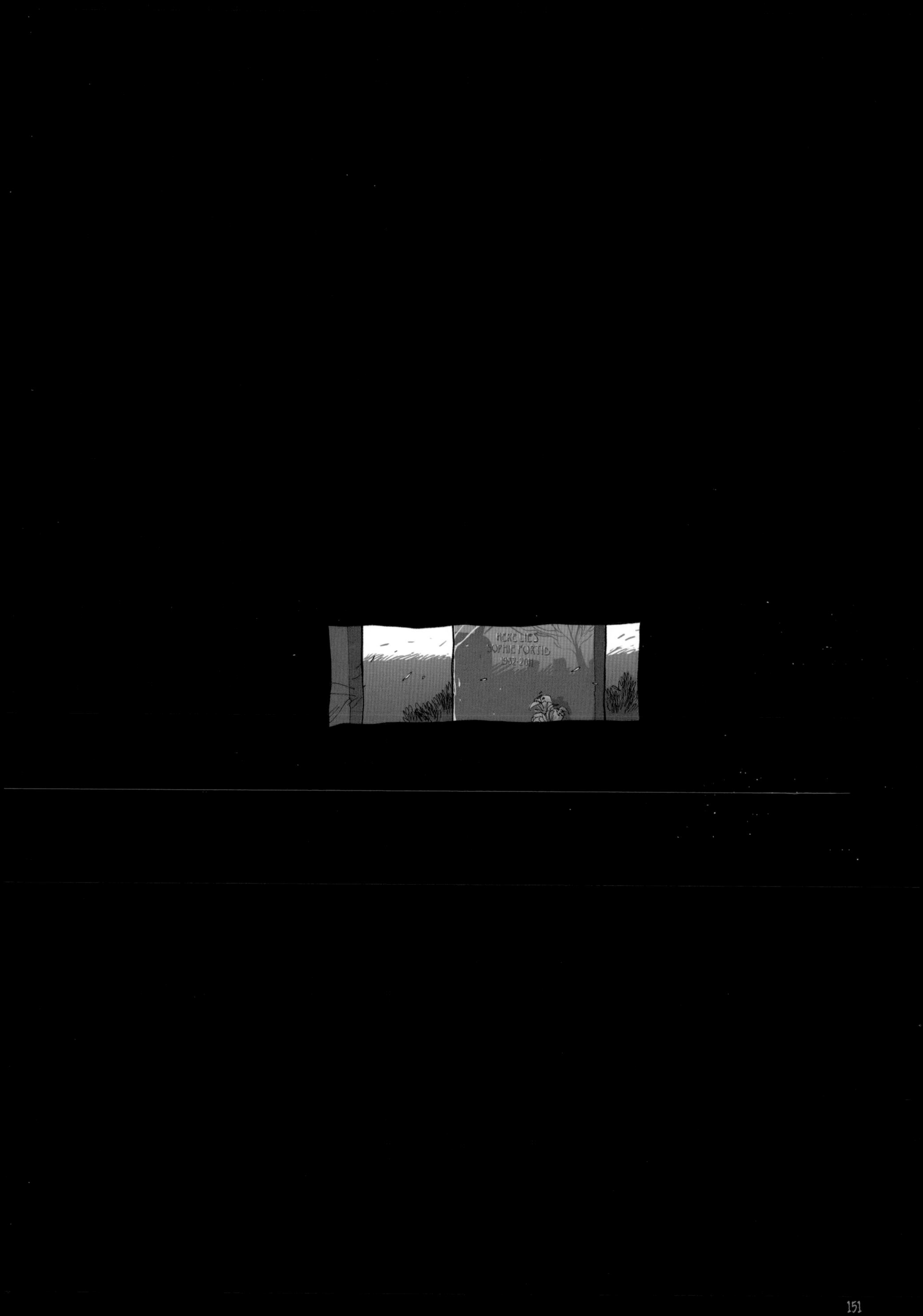
HERE LIES
SOPHIE FORTID
1982-2011

NOVEMBER 14TH

NOVEMBER
MON TUE WED THU FRI SAT SUN
1 2 3 4
5 6 7 8 9 10 11
12 13 14 15 16 17 18
19 20 21 22 23 24 25
26 27 28 29 30

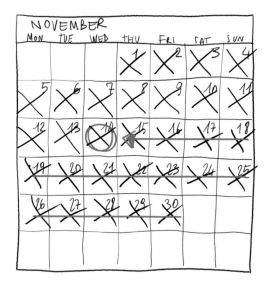

(OR, "THE JOAN WHO HEARD VOICES")

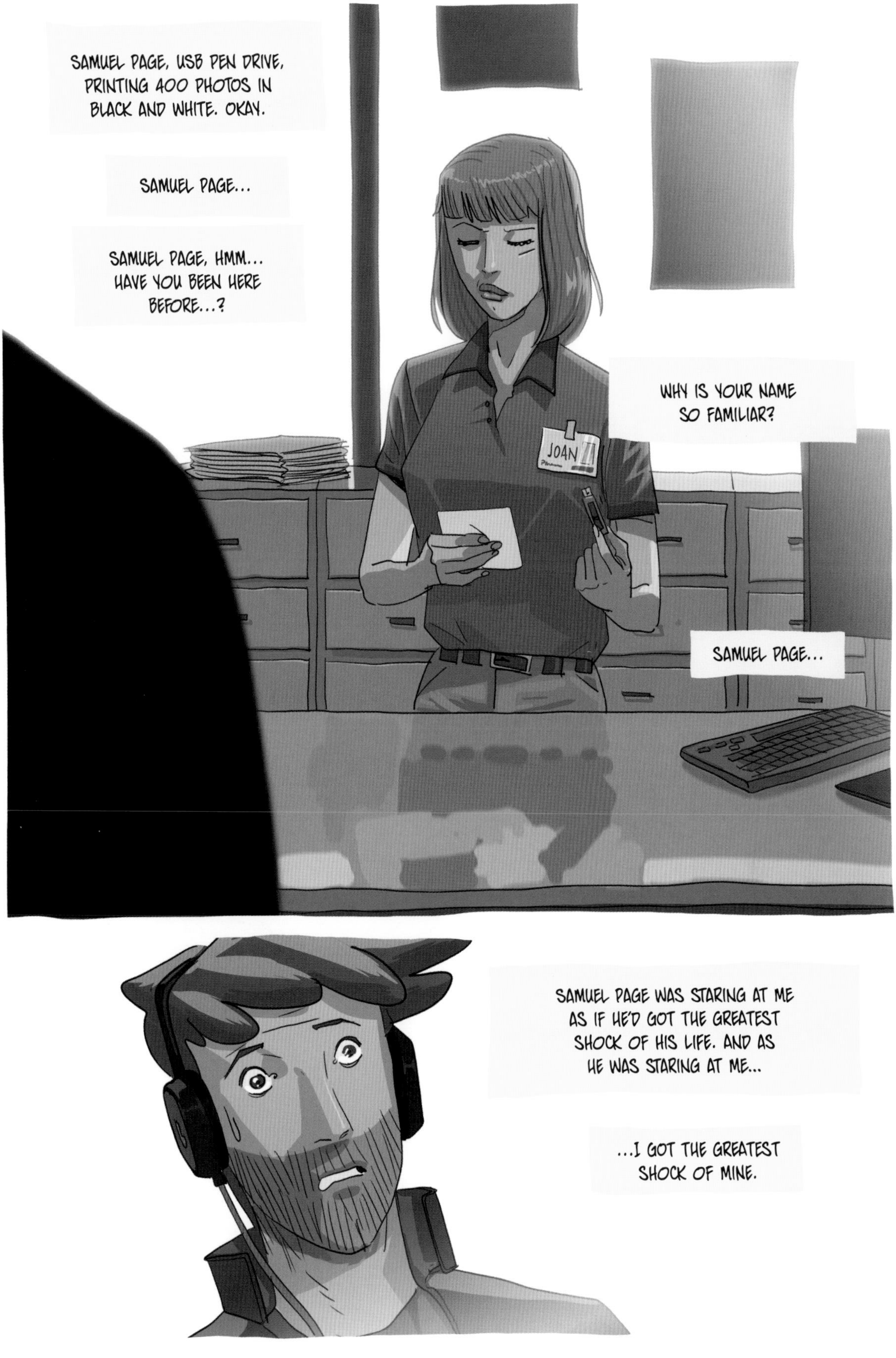
SAMUEL PAGE, USB PEN DRIVE, PRINTING 400 PHOTOS IN BLACK AND WHITE. OKAY.
SAMUEL PAGE...
SAMUEL PAGE, HMM... HAVE YOU BEEN HERE BEFORE...?
WHY IS YOUR NAME SO FAMILIAR?
JOAN
SAMUEL PAGE...
SAMUEL PAGE WAS STARING AT ME AS IF HE'D GOT THE GREATEST SHOCK OF HIS LIFE. AND AS HE WAS STARING AT ME...
...I GOT THE GREATEST SHOCK OF MINE.

"SHITSHITSHITSHITSHITSHITSHIT!"

I COULD HEAR HIS VOICE INSIDE MY HEAD. CRYSTAL CLEAR. I KNOW THAT THOSE WHO FOUND HIS ARTICLE RIDICULOUS WILL FEEL THE SAME ABOUT MY VERSION OF EVENTS, TOO, BUT I SWEAR THAT THIS IS EXACTLY HOW IT WENT. FOR ME, TOO.

I MEAN, IT'S NOT AS THOUGH HE WAS SAYING INTERESTING STUFF.

"SHIT FUCKSHIT WHERE DID I PUT IT, SHIT!"

BUT IT WAS ONE OF THE GREATEST AND MOST TERRIFYING EXPERIENCES OF MY LIFE.

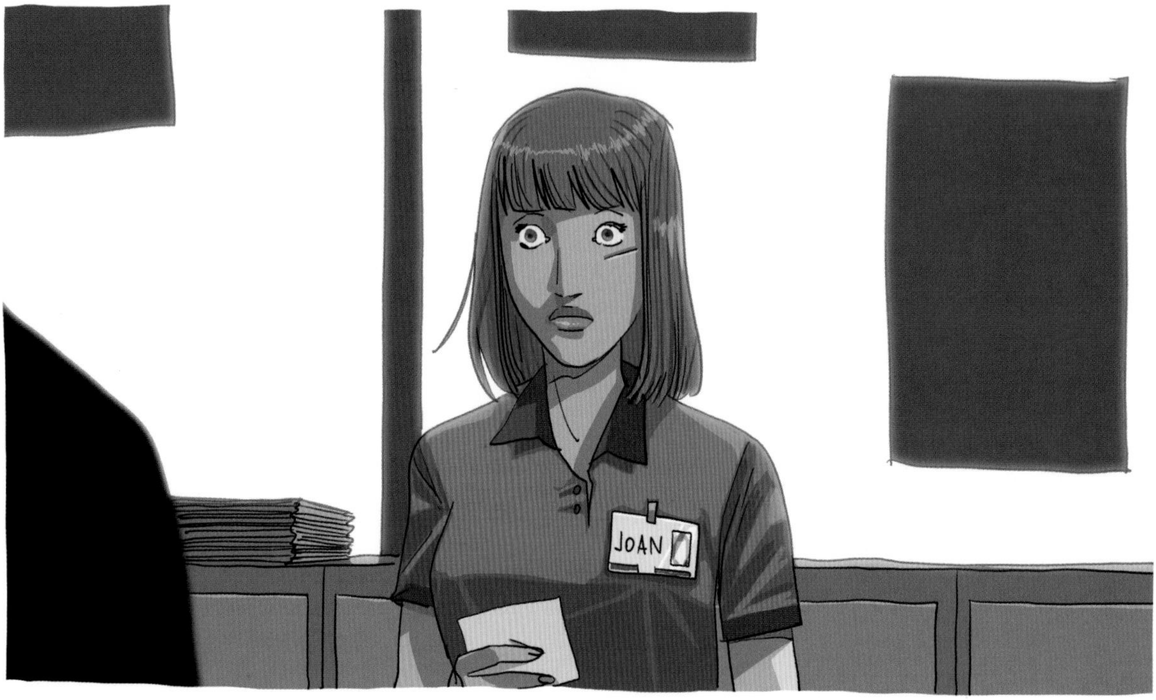
JOAN

THEN HE SAID SOMETHING UNDERSTANDABLE.

"CAN'T LET HER TALK, NOT ANYMORE, NOPE, CAN'T LET HER INSIDE MY HEAD"

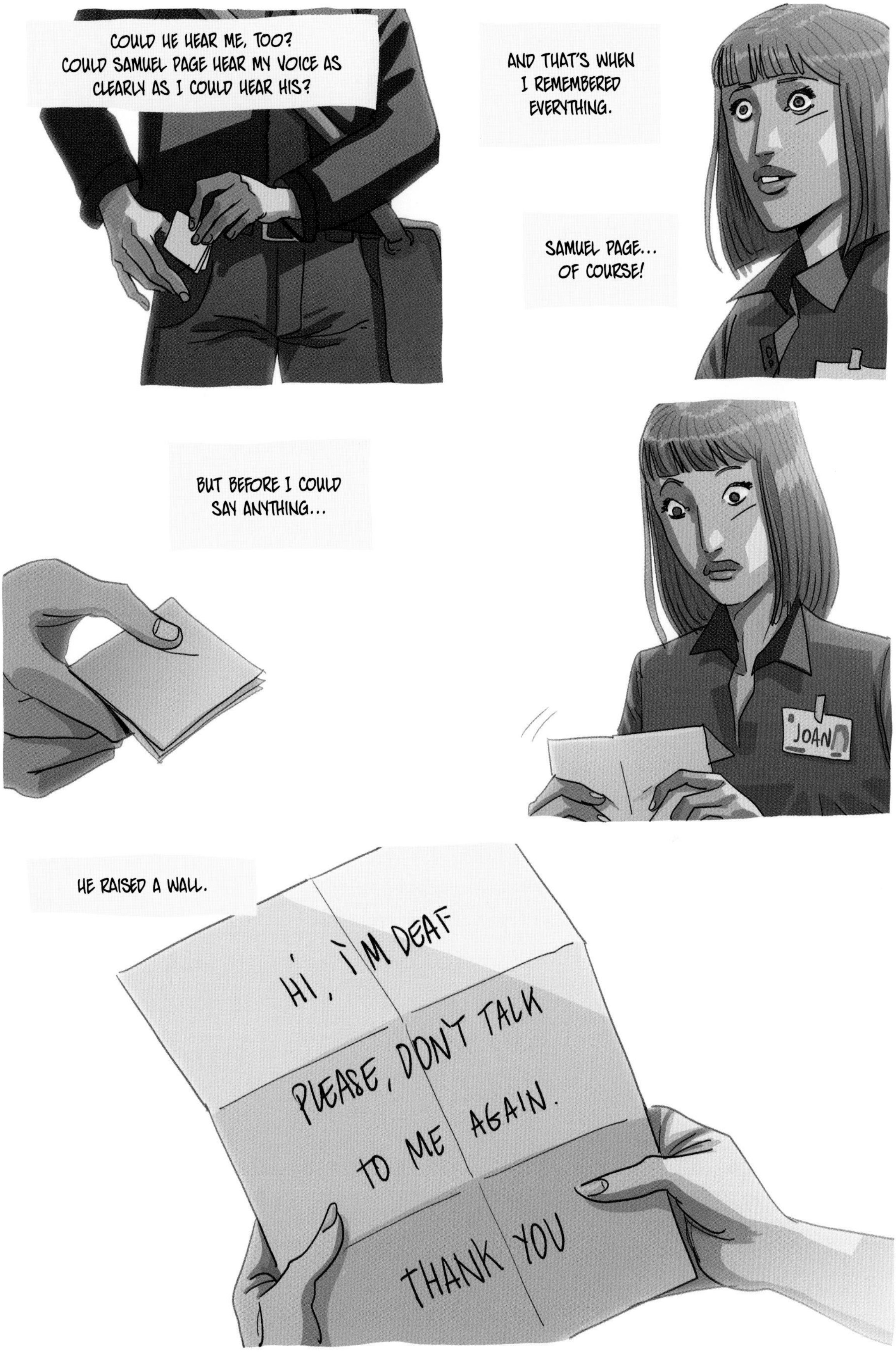

COULD HE HEAR ME, TOO?
COULD SAMUEL PAGE HEAR MY VOICE AS CLEARLY AS I COULD HEAR HIS?
AND THAT'S WHEN I REMEMBERED EVERYTHING.
SAMUEL PAGE... OF COURSE!
BUT BEFORE I COULD SAY ANYTHING...
JOAN
HE RAISED A WALL.
HI, I'M DEAF
PLEASE, DON'T TALK TO ME AGAIN.
THANK YOU

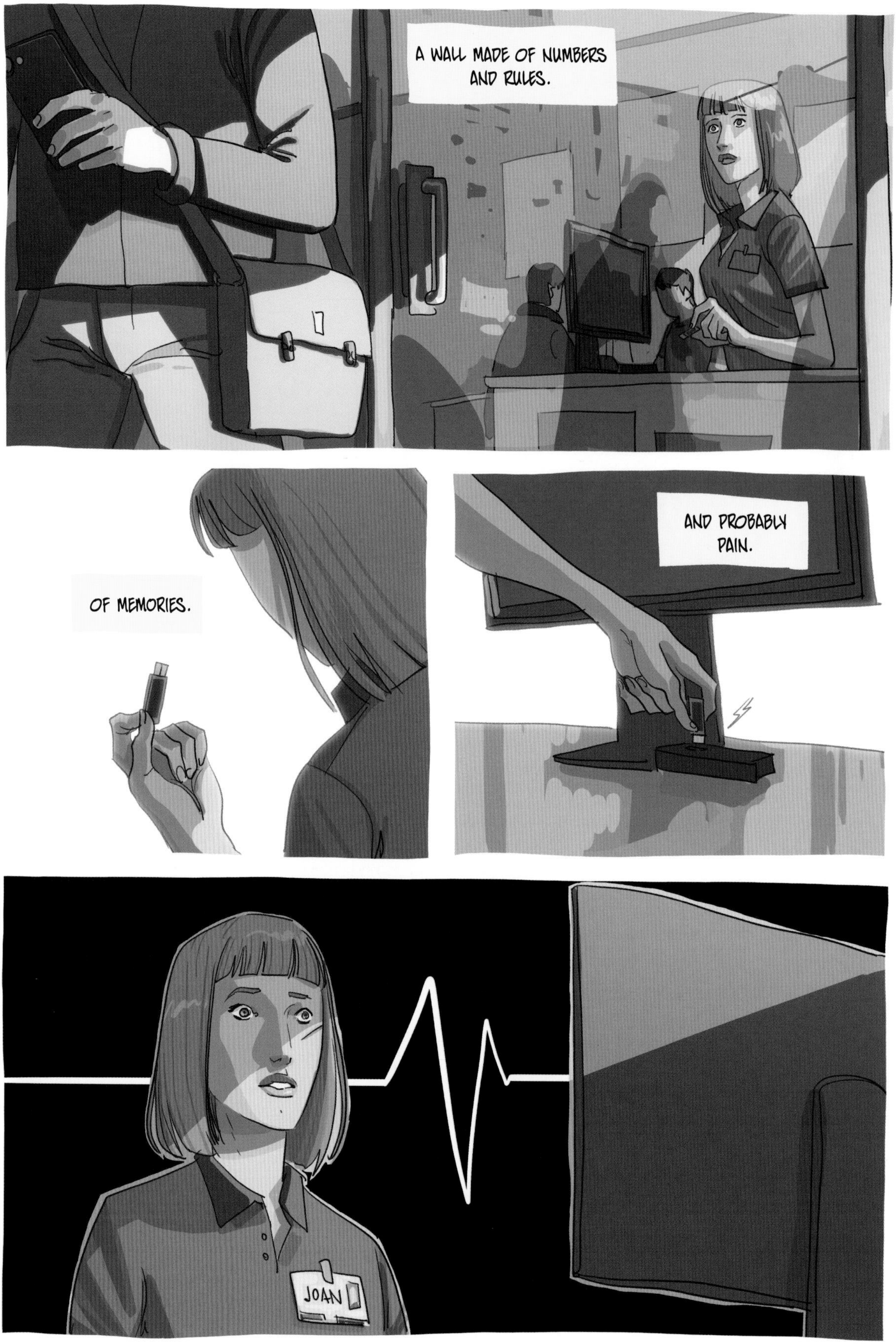
A WALL MADE OF NUMBERS AND RULES.
OF MEMORIES.
AND PROBABLY PAIN.
JOAN

A WALL, HOWEVER, THAT THIS CITY HAD ALREADY STARTED TO CARVE THROUGH.

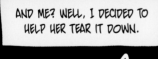

AND ME? WELL, I DECIDED TO HELP HER TEAR IT DOWN.

QUITE HAPPILY.

THE ELBOW

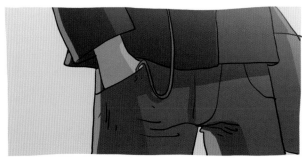
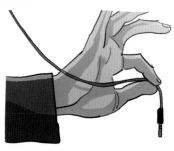

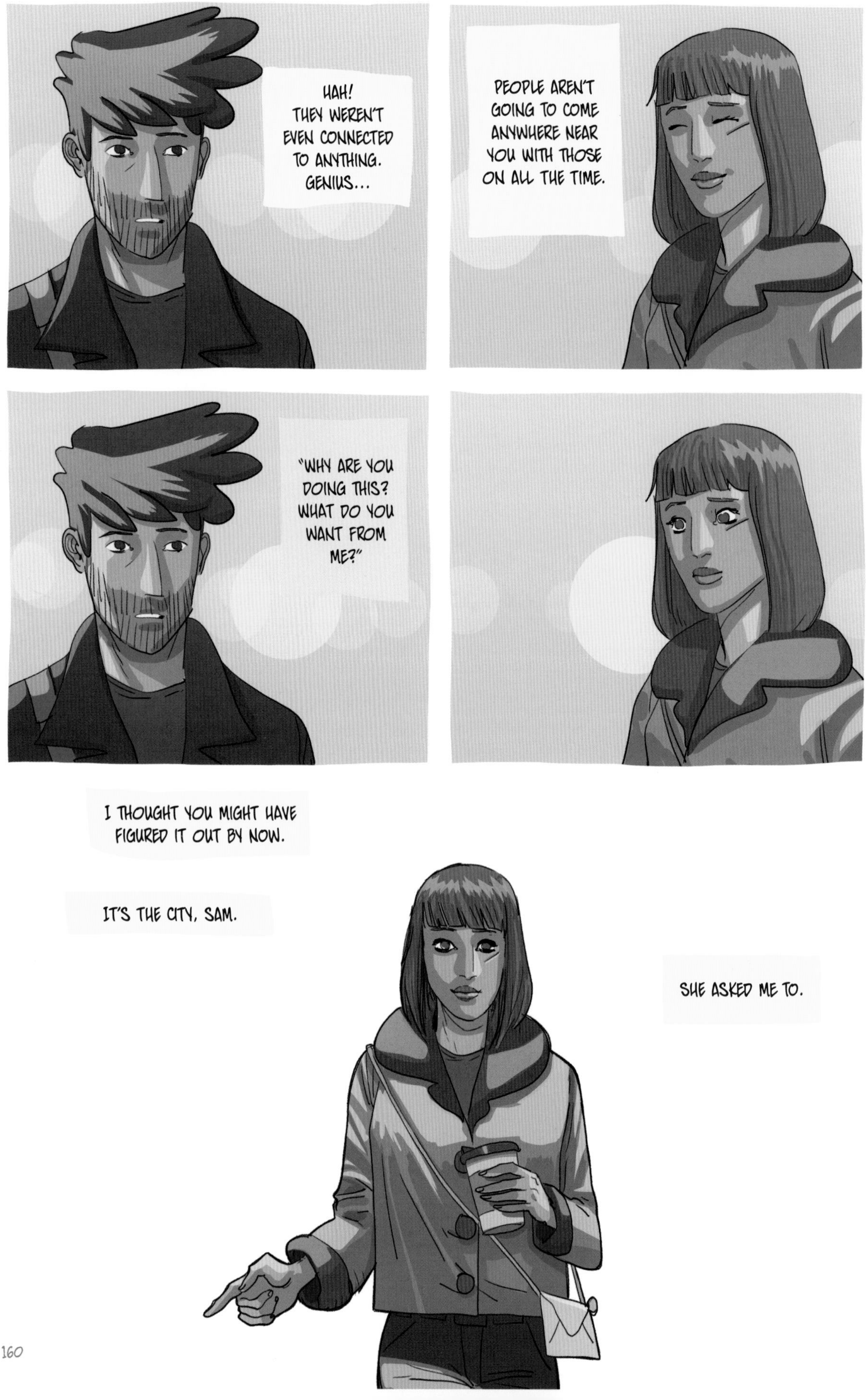
HAH! THEY WEREN'T EVEN CONNECTED TO ANYTHING. GENIUS...
PEOPLE AREN'T GOING TO COME ANYWHERE NEAR YOU WITH THOSE ON ALL THE TIME.
"WHY ARE YOU DOING THIS? WHAT DO YOU WANT FROM ME?"
I THOUGHT YOU MIGHT HAVE FIGURED IT OUT BY NOW.
IT'S THE CITY, SAM.
SHE ASKED ME TO.

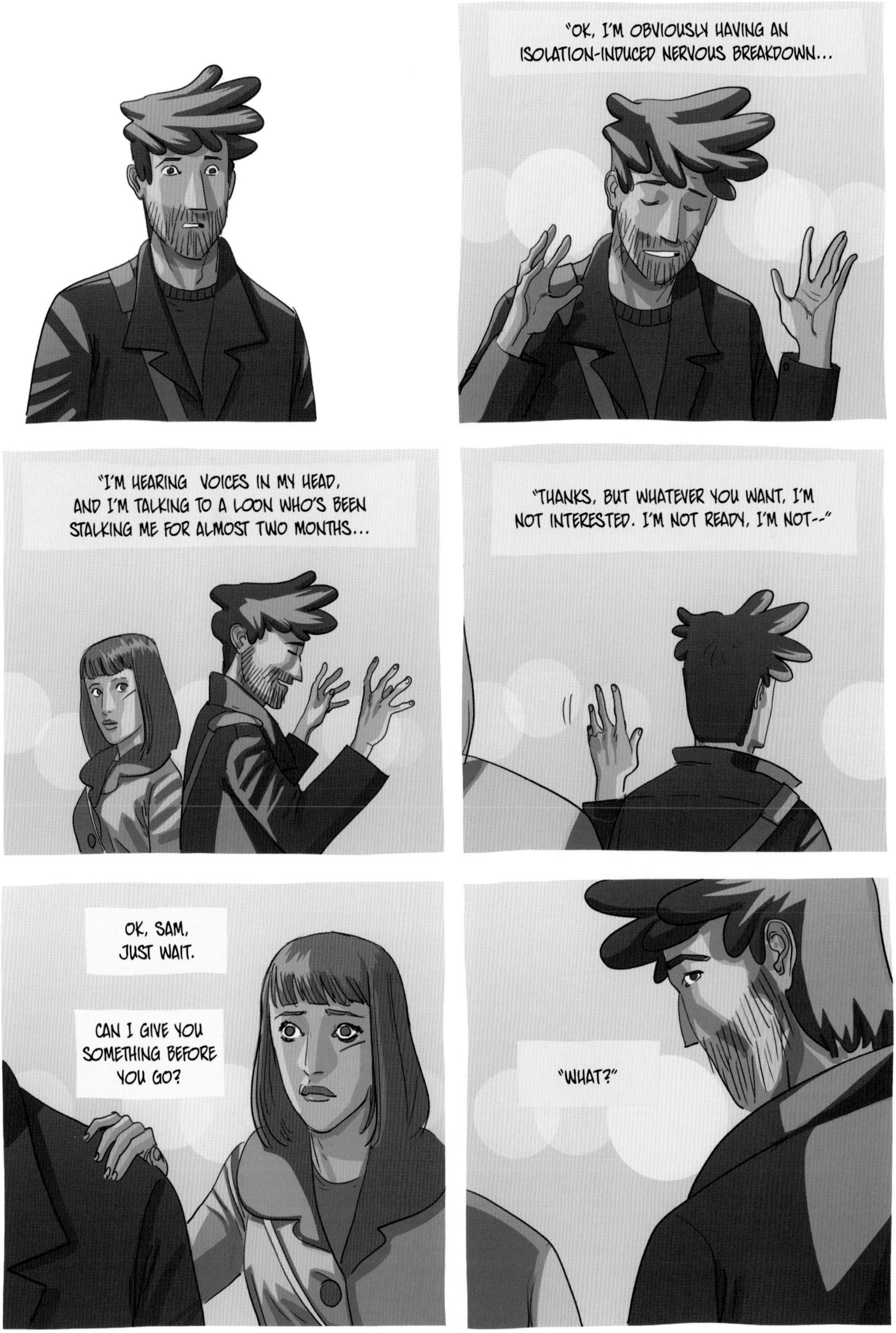
"OK, I'M OBVIOUSLY HAVING AN ISOLATION-INDUCED NERVOUS BREAKDOWN...
"I'M HEARING VOICES IN MY HEAD, AND I'M TALKING TO A LOON WHO'S BEEN STALKING ME FOR ALMOST TWO MONTHS...
"THANKS, BUT WHATEVER YOU WANT, I'M NOT INTERESTED. I'M NOT READY, I'M NOT--"
OK, SAM, JUST WAIT.
CAN I GIVE YOU SOMETHING BEFORE YOU GO?
"WHAT?"

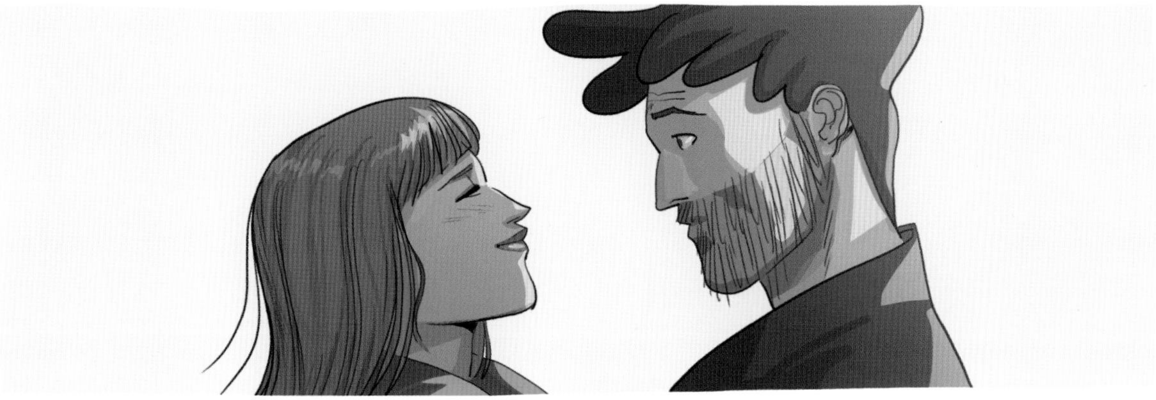

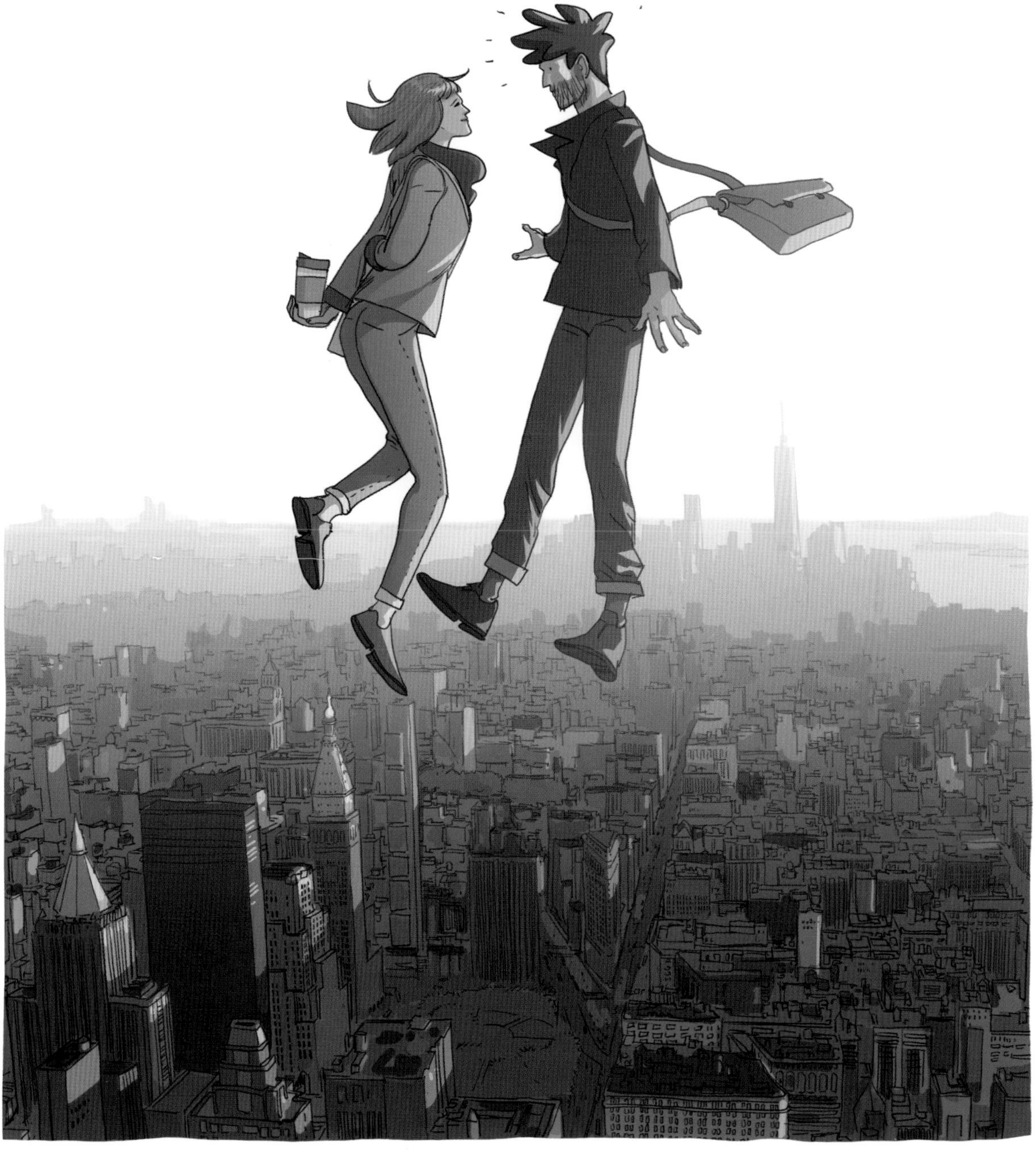

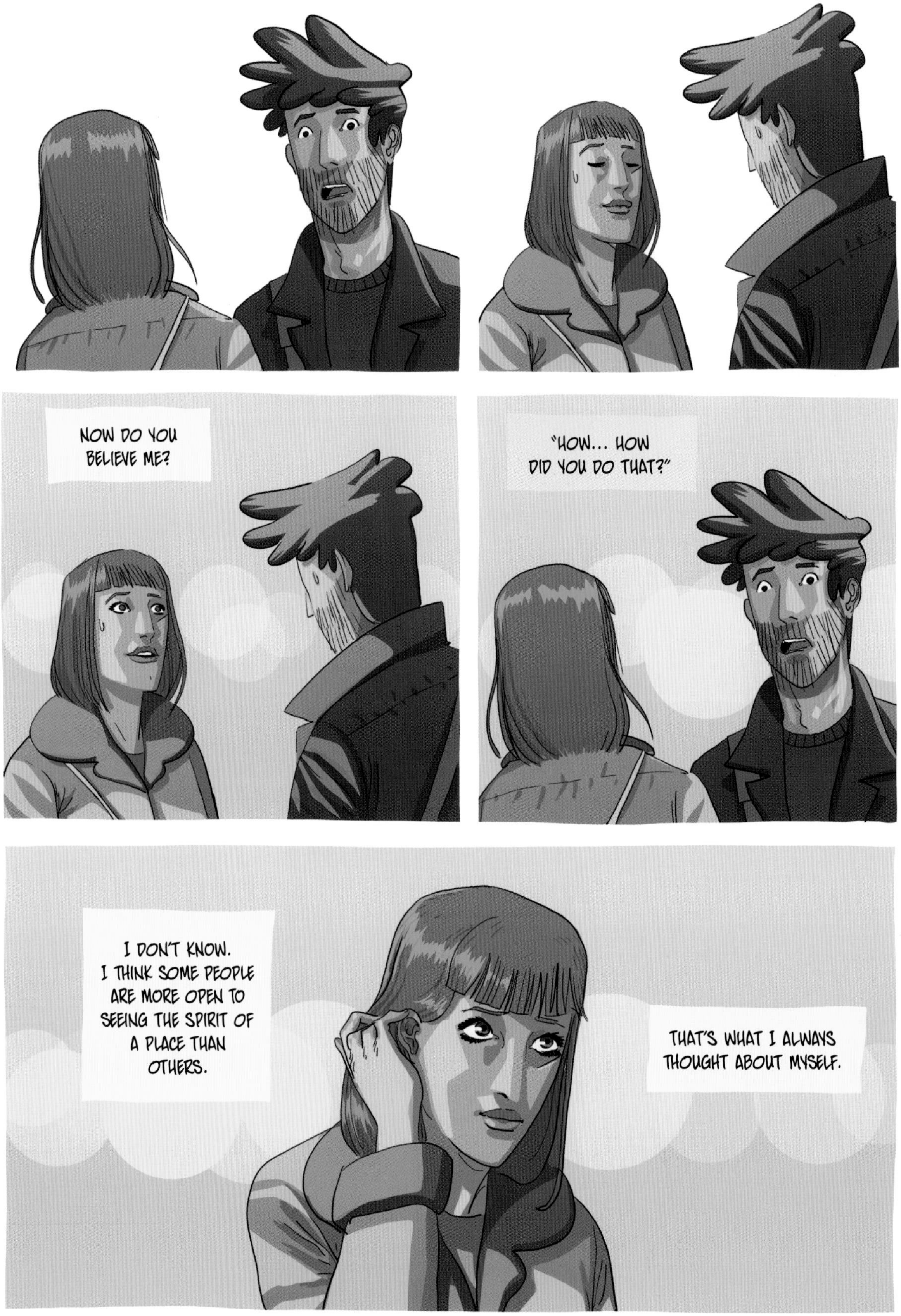
NOW DO YOU BELIEVE ME?
"HOW... HOW DID YOU DO THAT?"
I DON'T KNOW. I THINK SOME PEOPLE ARE MORE OPEN TO SEEING THE SPIRIT OF A PLACE THAN OTHERS.
THAT'S WHAT I ALWAYS THOUGHT ABOUT MYSELF.

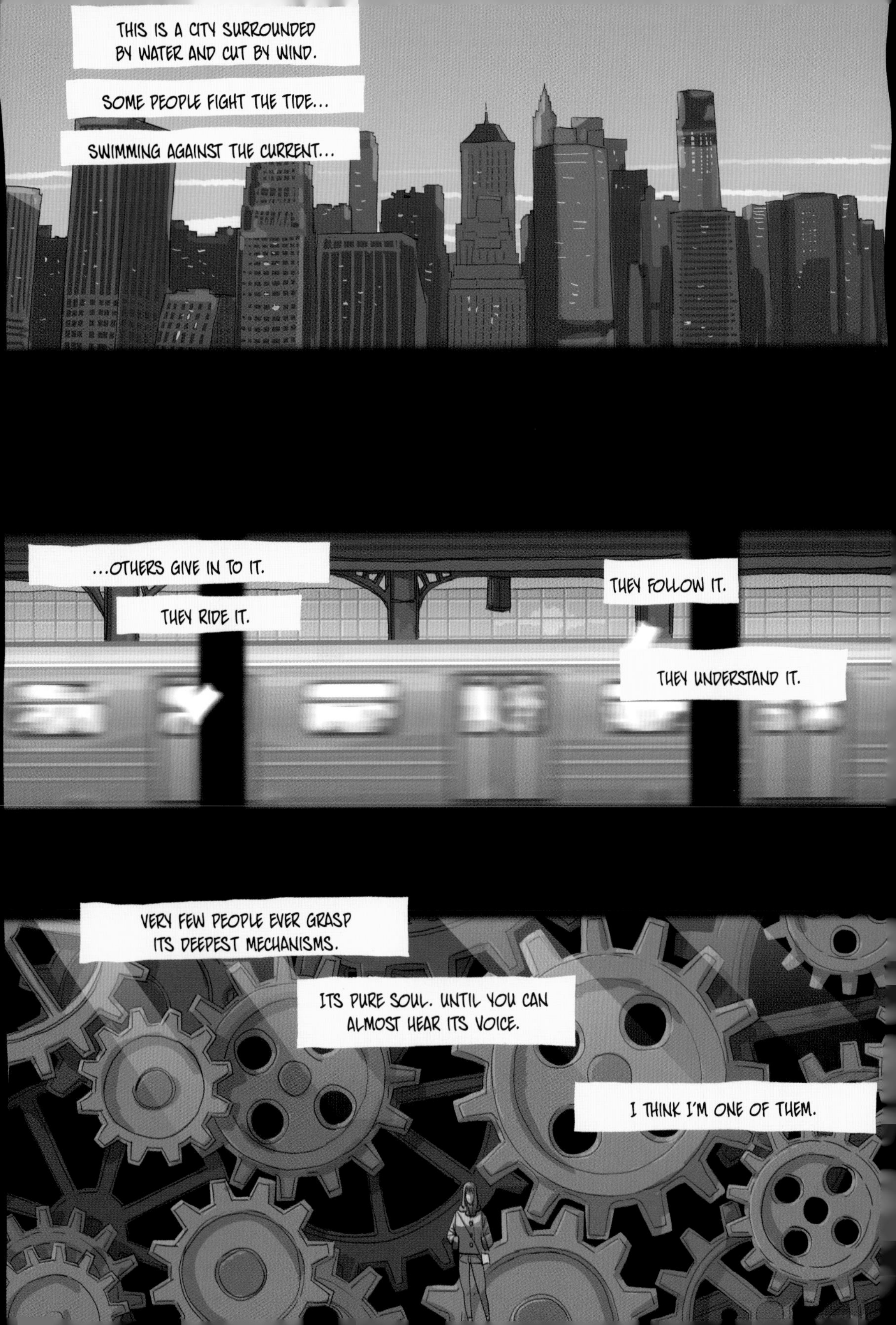
THIS IS A CITY SURROUNDED BY WATER AND CUT BY WIND.
SOME PEOPLE FIGHT THE TIDE...
SWIMMING AGAINST THE CURRENT...
...OTHERS GIVE IN TO IT.
THEY RIDE IT.
THEY FOLLOW IT.
THEY UNDERSTAND IT.
VERY FEW PEOPLE EVER GRASP ITS DEEPEST MECHANISMS.
ITS PURE SOUL. UNTIL YOU CAN ALMOST HEAR ITS VOICE.
I THINK I'M ONE OF THEM.

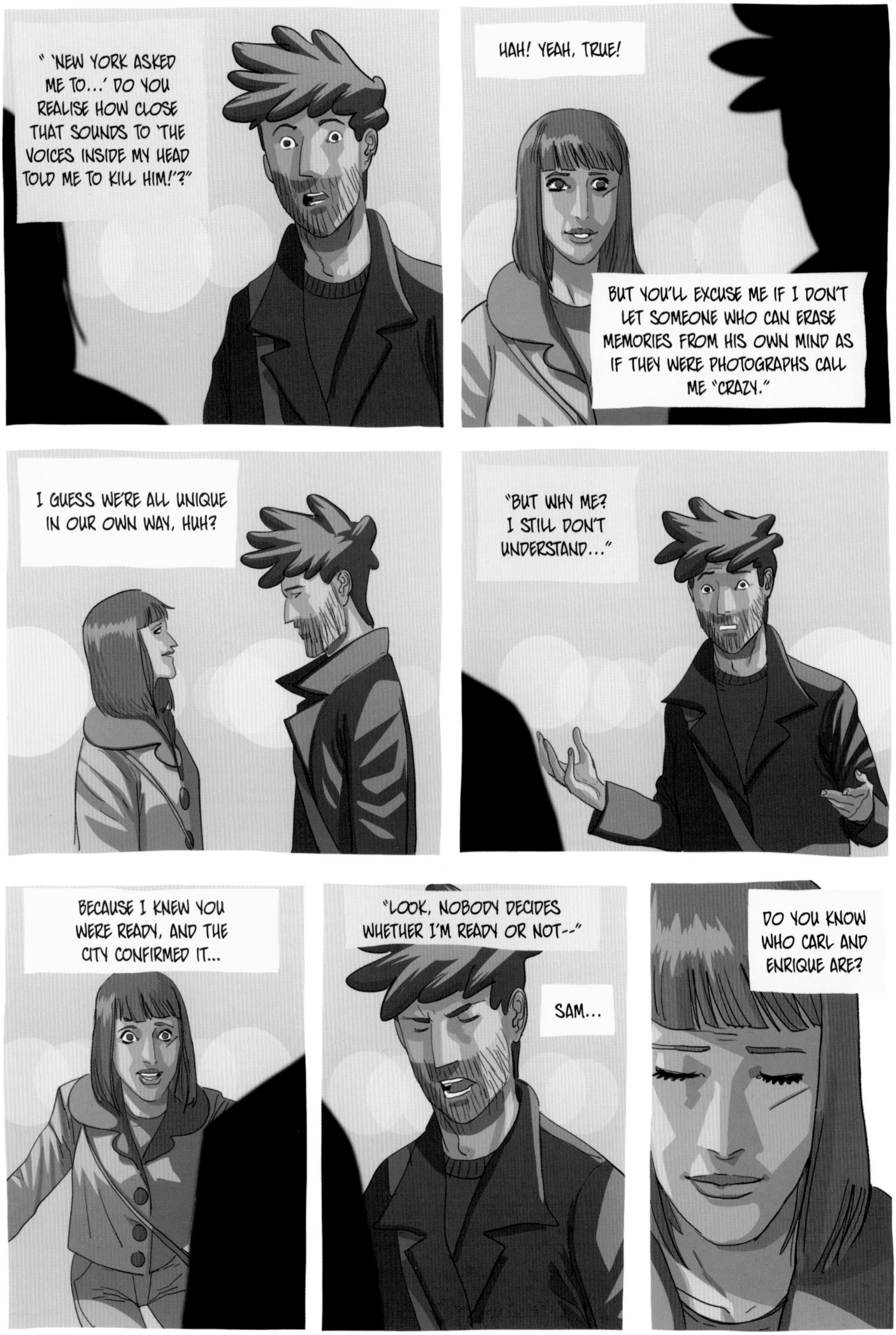
" 'NEW YORK ASKED ME TO...' DO YOU REALISE HOW CLOSE THAT SOUNDS TO 'THE VOICES INSIDE MY HEAD TOLD ME TO KILL HIM!'?"
HAH! YEAH, TRUE!
BUT YOU'LL EXCUSE ME IF I DON'T LET SOMEONE WHO CAN ERASE MEMORIES FROM HIS OWN MIND AS IF THEY WERE PHOTOGRAPHS CALL ME "CRAZY."
I GUESS WE'RE ALL UNIQUE IN OUR OWN WAY, HUH?
"BUT WHY ME? I STILL DON'T UNDERSTAND..."
BECAUSE I KNEW YOU WERE READY, AND THE CITY CONFIRMED IT...
"LOOK, NOBODY DECIDES WHETHER I'M READY OR NOT--"
SAM...
DO YOU KNOW WHO CARL AND ENRIQUE ARE?

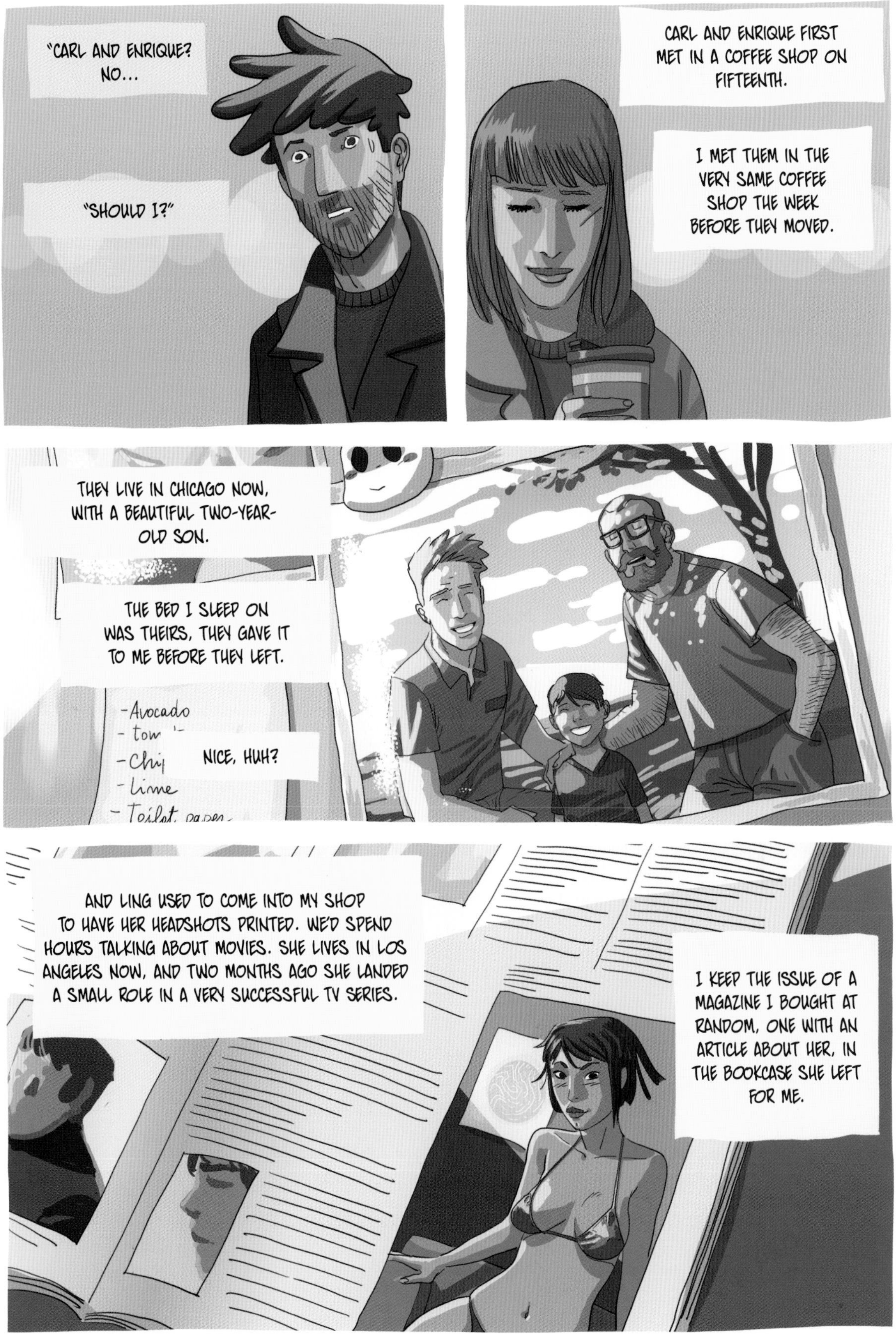
"CARL AND ENRIQUE? NO...
"SHOULD I?"
CARL AND ENRIQUE FIRST MET IN A COFFEE SHOP ON FIFTEENTH.
I MET THEM IN THE VERY SAME COFFEE SHOP THE WEEK BEFORE THEY MOVED.
THEY LIVE IN CHICAGO NOW, WITH A BEAUTIFUL TWO-YEAR-OLD SON.
THE BED I SLEEP ON WAS THEIRS, THEY GAVE IT TO ME BEFORE THEY LEFT.
-Avocado
-Lime
NICE, HUH?
AND LING USED TO COME INTO MY SHOP TO HAVE HER HEADSHOTS PRINTED. WE'D SPEND HOURS TALKING ABOUT MOVIES. SHE LIVES IN LOS ANGELES NOW, AND TWO MONTHS AGO SHE LANDED A SMALL ROLE IN A VERY SUCCESSFUL TV SERIES.
I KEEP THE ISSUE OF A MAGAZINE I BOUGHT AT RANDOM, ONE WITH AN ARTICLE ABOUT HER, IN THE BOOKCASE SHE LEFT FOR ME.

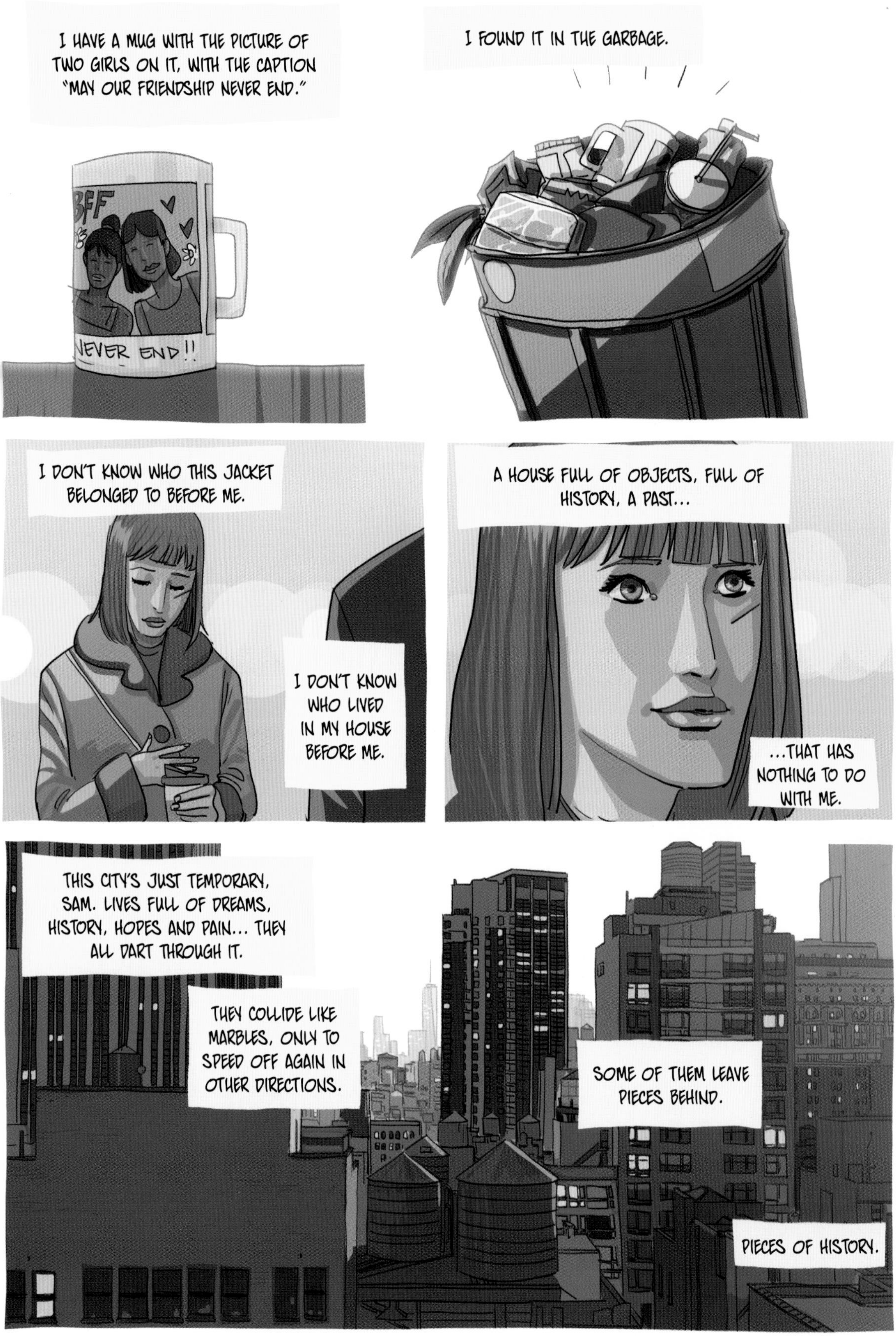
I HAVE A MUG WITH THE PICTURE OF TWO GIRLS ON IT, WITH THE CAPTION "MAY OUR FRIENDSHIP NEVER END."
BFF
NEVER END!!
I FOUND IT IN THE GARBAGE.
I DON'T KNOW WHO THIS JACKET BELONGED TO BEFORE ME.
I DON'T KNOW WHO LIVED IN MY HOUSE BEFORE ME.
A HOUSE FULL OF OBJECTS, FULL OF HISTORY, A PAST...
...THAT HAS NOTHING TO DO WITH ME.
THIS CITY'S JUST TEMPORARY, SAM. LIVES FULL OF DREAMS, HISTORY, HOPES AND PAIN... THEY ALL DART THROUGH IT.
THEY COLLIDE LIKE MARBLES, ONLY TO SPEED OFF AGAIN IN OTHER DIRECTIONS.
SOME OF THEM LEAVE PIECES BEHIND.
PIECES OF HISTORY.

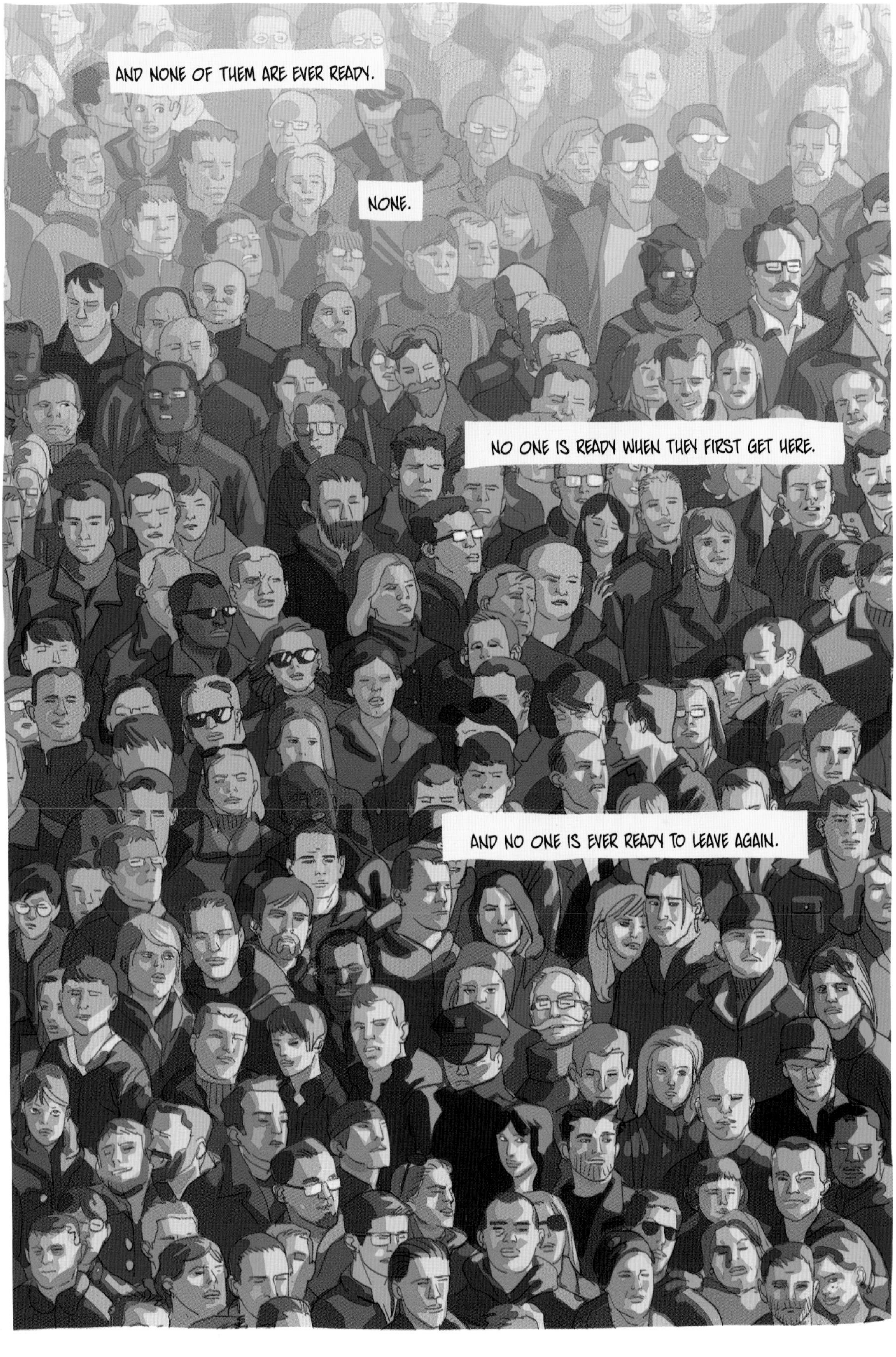
AND NONE OF THEM ARE EVER READY.
NONE.
NO ONE IS READY WHEN THEY FIRST GET HERE.
AND NO ONE IS EVER READY TO LEAVE AGAIN.

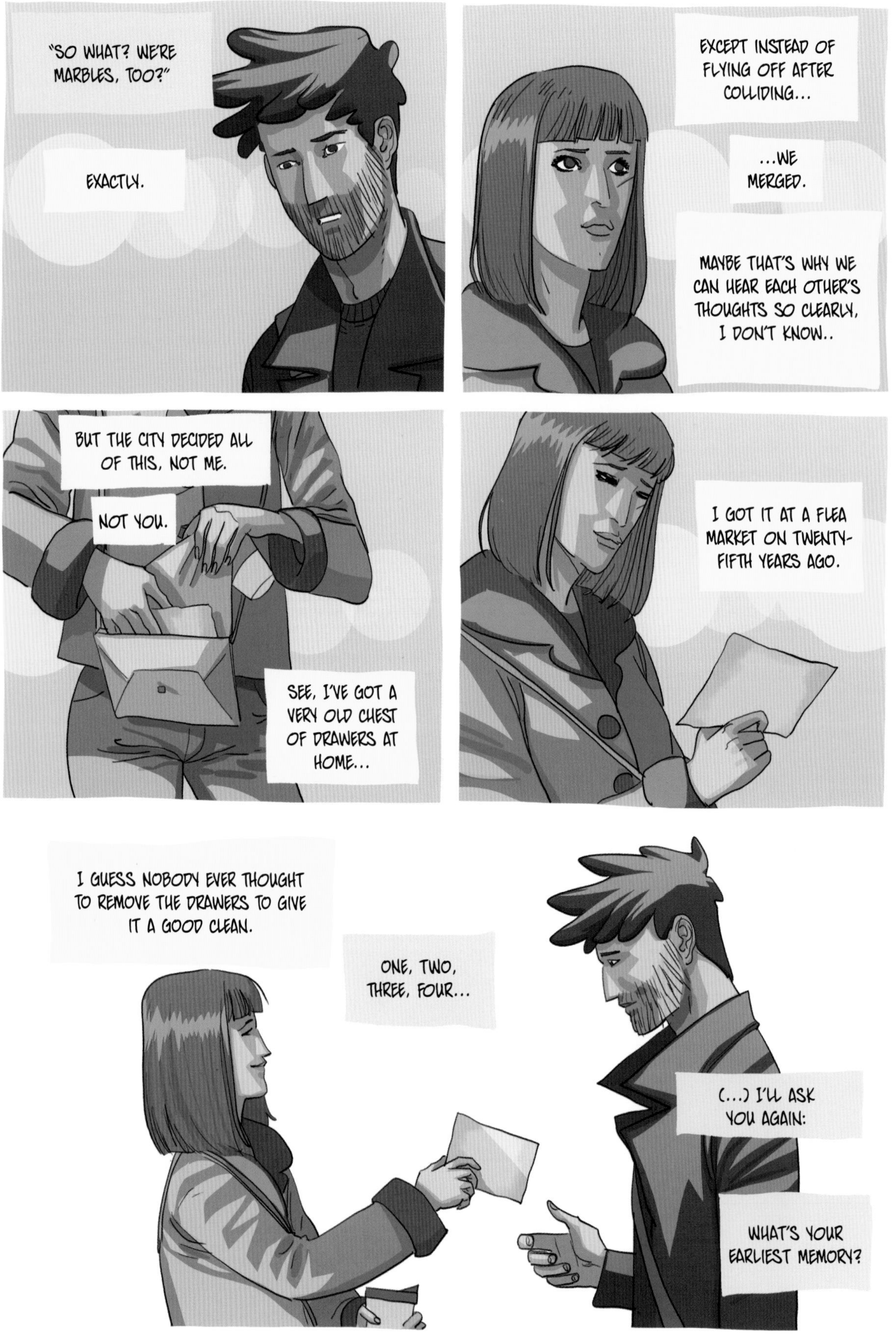
"SO WHAT? WE'RE MARBLES, TOO?"
EXACTLY.
EXCEPT INSTEAD OF FLYING OFF AFTER COLLIDING...
...WE MERGED.
MAYBE THAT'S WHY WE CAN HEAR EACH OTHER'S THOUGHTS SO CLEARLY, I DON'T KNOW..
BUT THE CITY DECIDED ALL OF THIS, NOT ME.
NOT YOU.
SEE, I'VE GOT A VERY OLD CHEST OF DRAWERS AT HOME...
I GOT IT AT A FLEA MARKET ON TWENTY-FIFTH YEARS AGO.
I GUESS NOBODY EVER THOUGHT TO REMOVE THE DRAWERS TO GIVE IT A GOOD CLEAN.
ONE, TWO, THREE, FOUR...
(...) I'LL ASK YOU AGAIN:
WHAT'S YOUR EARLIEST MEMORY?

(...) MY FIRST MEMORY IS A SONG CALLED
"I'VE GROWN ACCUSTOMED TO HER FACE." IT HAS BILL EVANS ON PIANO,
FOLLOWED BY CHET BAKER'S TRUMPET,

PUNCTUATED BY THE HORNS ON FIRST AVENUE,

AND THE SIREN FROM A RANDOM FIRETRUCK.

IT'S THE LOW, DEEP VIBRATIONS OF THE DOUBLE BASS THROUGH THE LOUD-
SPEAKER THAT TICKLE MY HEART, AND MY BACKSIDE.

I COUNT TO FOUR, TO THE BEAT OF THE MUSIC, BECAUSE IT WAS ONE OF THE FIRST
THINGS MY FATHER TAUGHT ME TO DO.

SOME OF YOU MIGHT FIND HAVING A SONG STUCK IN YOUR HEAD,
EVEN FOR JUST A SHORT WHILE, ANNOYING.

BUT FOR ME, AFTER LOSING MY HEARING, I LIVED MY LIFE TO THE SOUND
OF JUST ONE SONG, TRYING NEVER TO FORGET IT.

THE SAME BACKGROUND MUSIC TO EVERY BOOK I READ.

THE SAME SOUNDTRACK TO EVERY MOVIE I EVER SAW.

THE SAME SONG TO STEER ME THROUGH THIS LIFE.

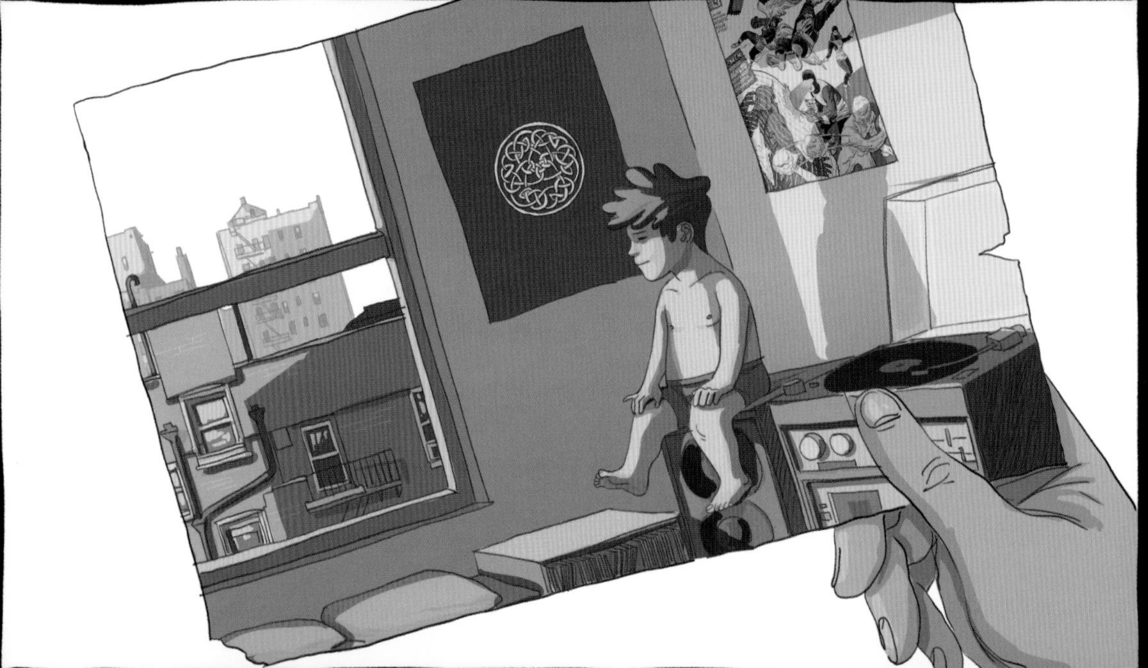

IT WASN'T HER VOICE IN MY HEAD THAT SHOCKED ME, THAT
DAY, IN THE PRINT SHOP. AT LAST, I WAS CERTAIN OF IT.

IT WAS SOMETHING ELSE I HADN'T HEARD IN AGES.

BUT AS I CLUTCHED THAT PHOTOGRAPH,
I COULD HEAR IT AGAIN, SO CLEARLY NOW.

I HEARD THE HORNS, MIXED IN WITH THE PIANO, A SIREN AGAINST
A SOPRANO SAX, THE CITY'S MURMUR GIVING THE DOUBLE BASS ITS BEAT AND
VIBRATING INSIDE MY BODY, FROM THE FEET UP

AND ABOVE ALL OF THIS, I FELT IT, THE BEATING OF A HEART.

A HEART THAT WAS TIMED PERFECTLY TO THE MUSIC.

MUSIC IN PERFECT SYNCHRONIZATION WITH THE HUGE AND HEAVY
MECHANISMS OF AN ENTIRE CITY.

NYC 1983

Samuel Paige 3 y⁰
listening to
Chet Baker

ONE, TWO,
THREE, FOUR...

COUNTING HELPED ME FORGET ABOUT LUCK,
LUCK MADE ME NERVOUS.

LUCK COULD CONFUSE A CHALLENGE WITH A CRY FOR HELP.

BUT IT CAN ALSO TURN THE MECHANISMS OF AN ENTIRE CITY, AND

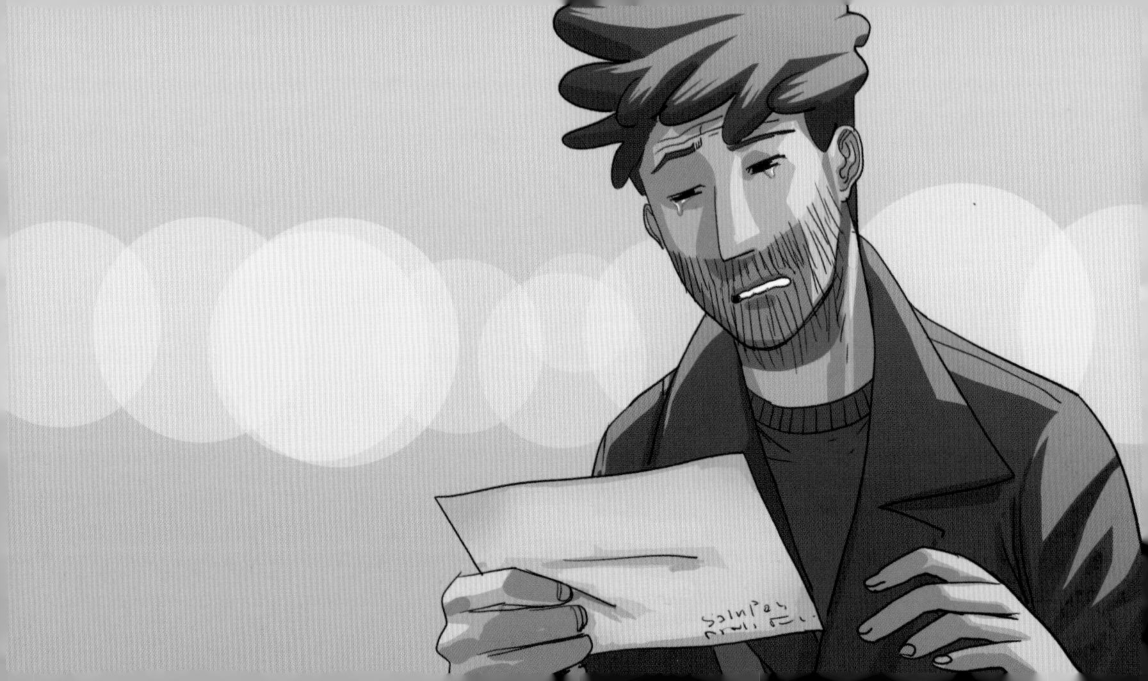

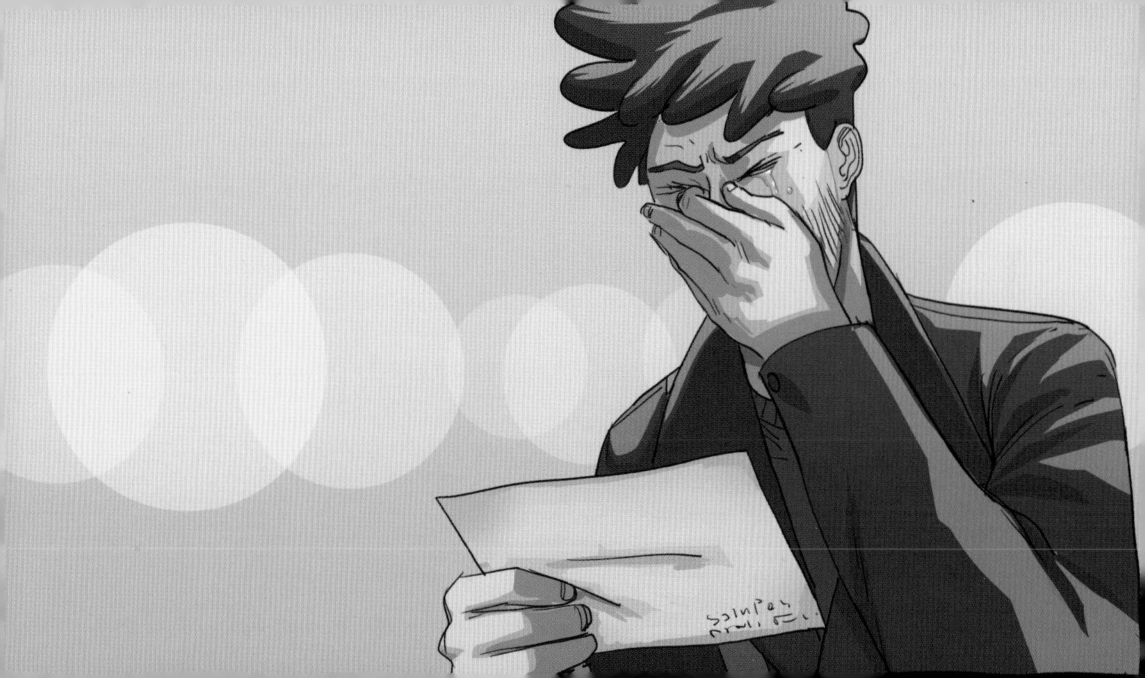

SAM HATED NUMBERS, BUT HE COUNTED EVERYTHING.

COUNTING HELPED HIM FORGET ABOUT LUCK.

LUCK MADE HIM NERVOUS.

HE WAS COUNTING MY HEARTBEATS, FOUR BY FOUR, AS THEY WERE FINELY TIMED TO THE SOUNDS OF HIS WORLD.

AND BECAUSE THEY WERE SO STRONG THAT HE COULD HEAR THEIR VIBRATIONS.

HE COULDN'T AVOID ME ANYMORE.

SO HE CLOSED HIS EYES...

...AND I WAS STILL THERE.

IN FRONT OF HIM.

IN HIS HEAD, TOO.

BECAUSE SOMETIMES, WHEN TWO MARBLES COLLIDE AT GREAT SPEED...

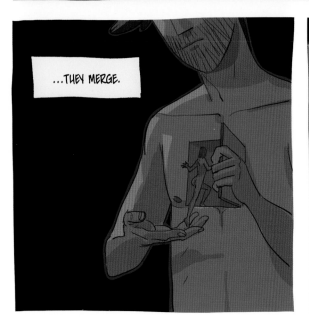

...THEY MERGE.

TO HELP EACH OTHER REDISCOVER A LOVE FOR THE MOMENT AGAIN.

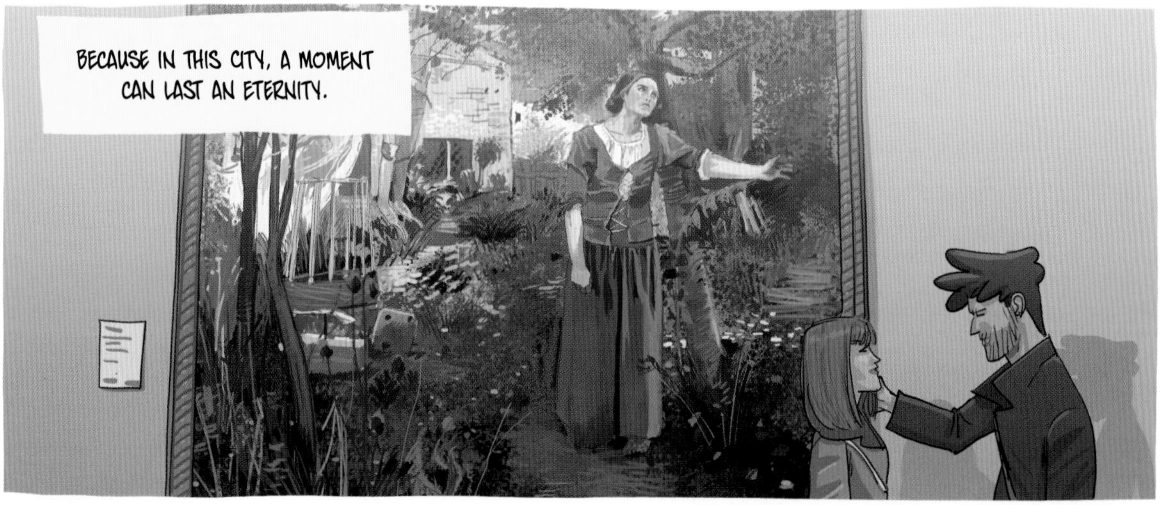
BECAUSE IN THIS CITY, A MOMENT CAN LAST AN ETERNITY.

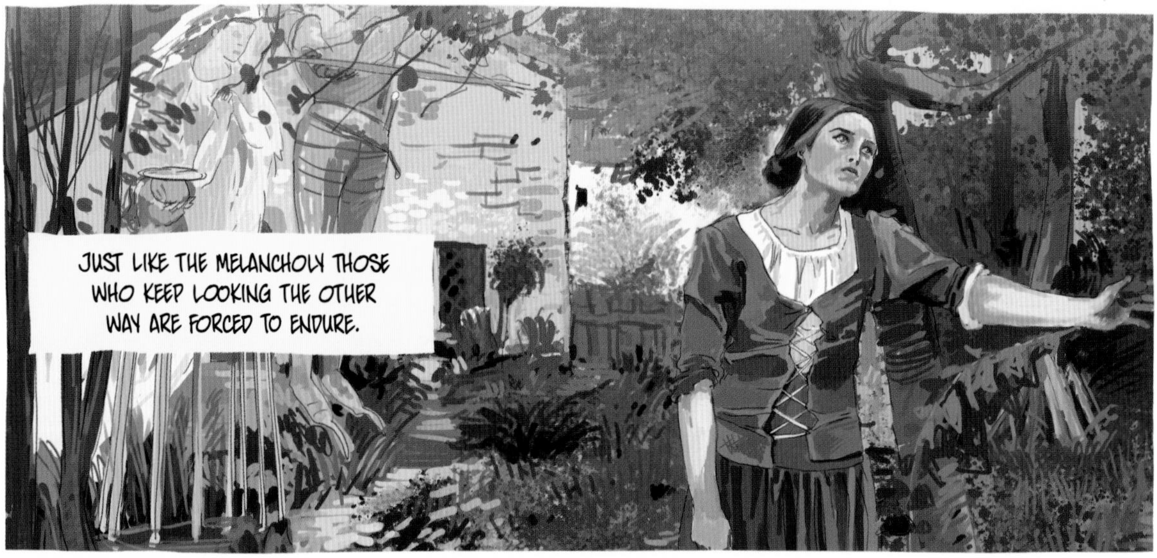
JUST LIKE THE MELANCHOLY THOSE WHO KEEP LOOKING THE OTHER WAY ARE FORCED TO ENDURE.

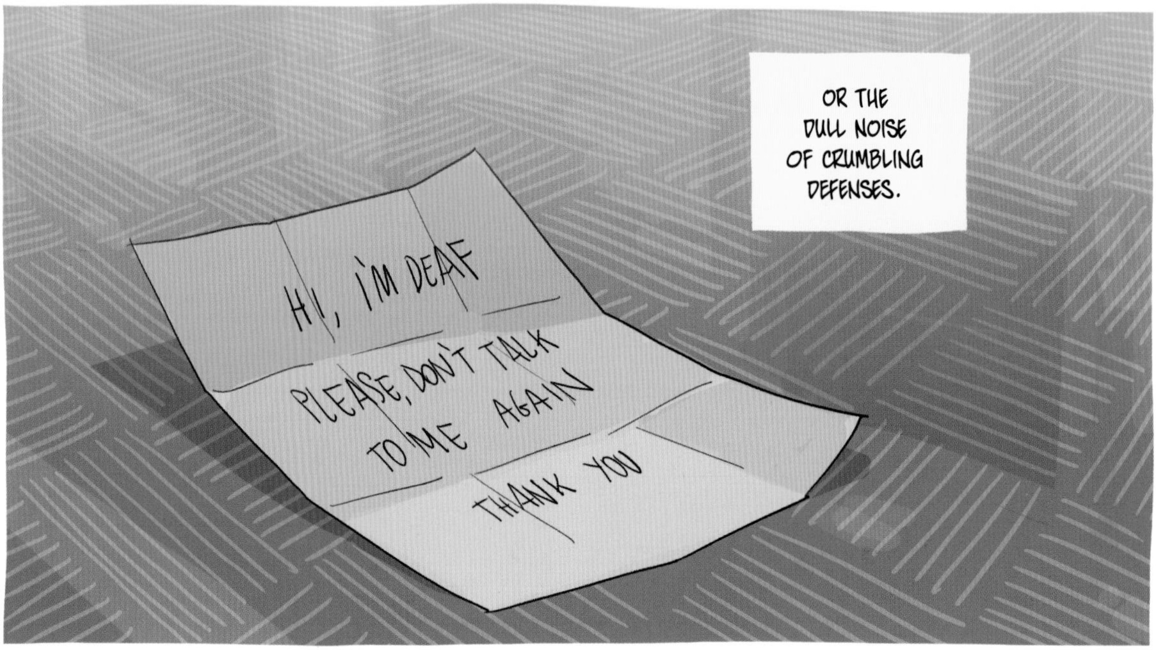
OR THE DULL NOISE OF CRUMBLING DEFENSES.
HI, I'M DEAF
PLEASE, DON'T TALK TO ME AGAIN
THANK YOU

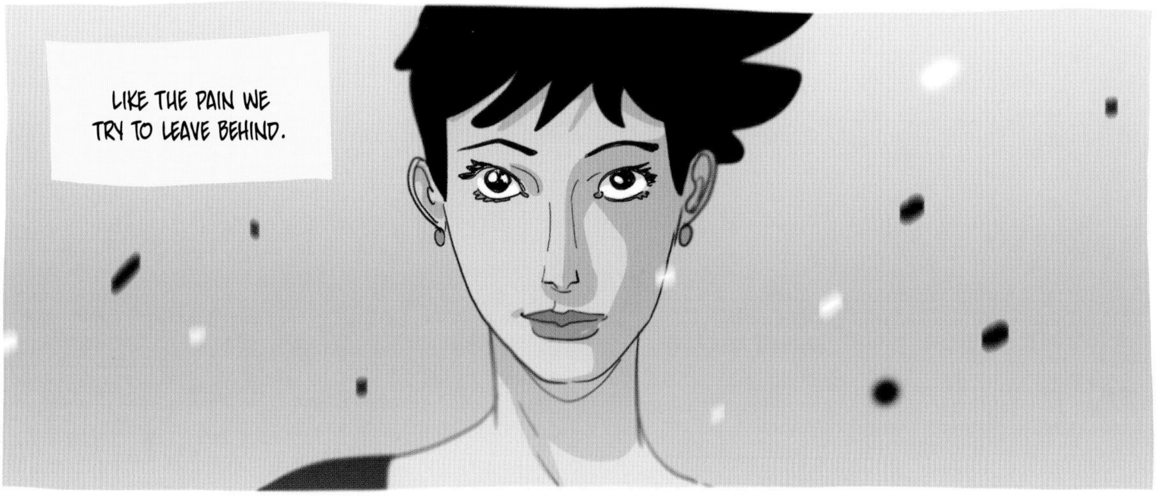
LIKE THE PAIN WE TRY TO LEAVE BEHIND.

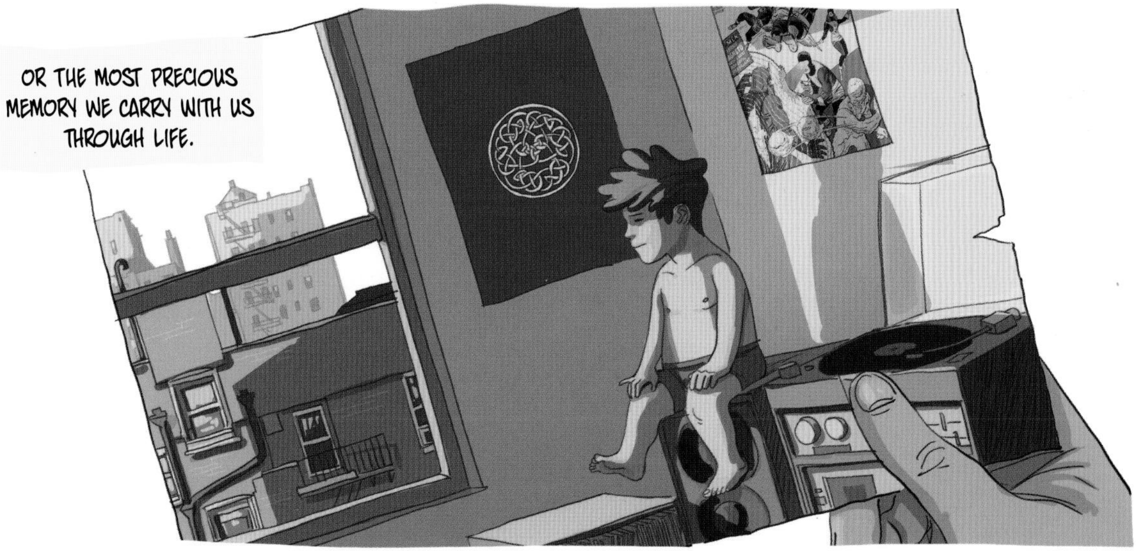
OR THE MOST PRECIOUS MEMORY WE CARRY WITH US THROUGH LIFE.

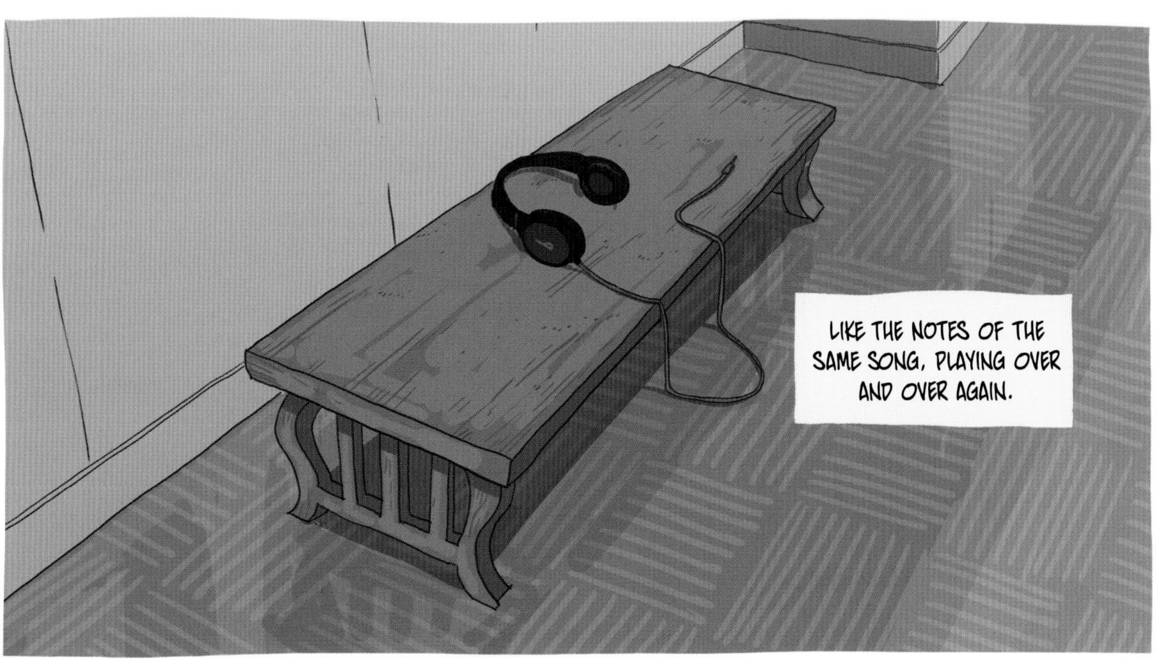
LIKE THE NOTES OF THE SAME SONG, PLAYING OVER AND OVER AGAIN.

OR THE RHYTHMIC AND
CONSTANT SOUND OF
MASSIVE GEARS RUMBLING
BENEATH OUR FEET.

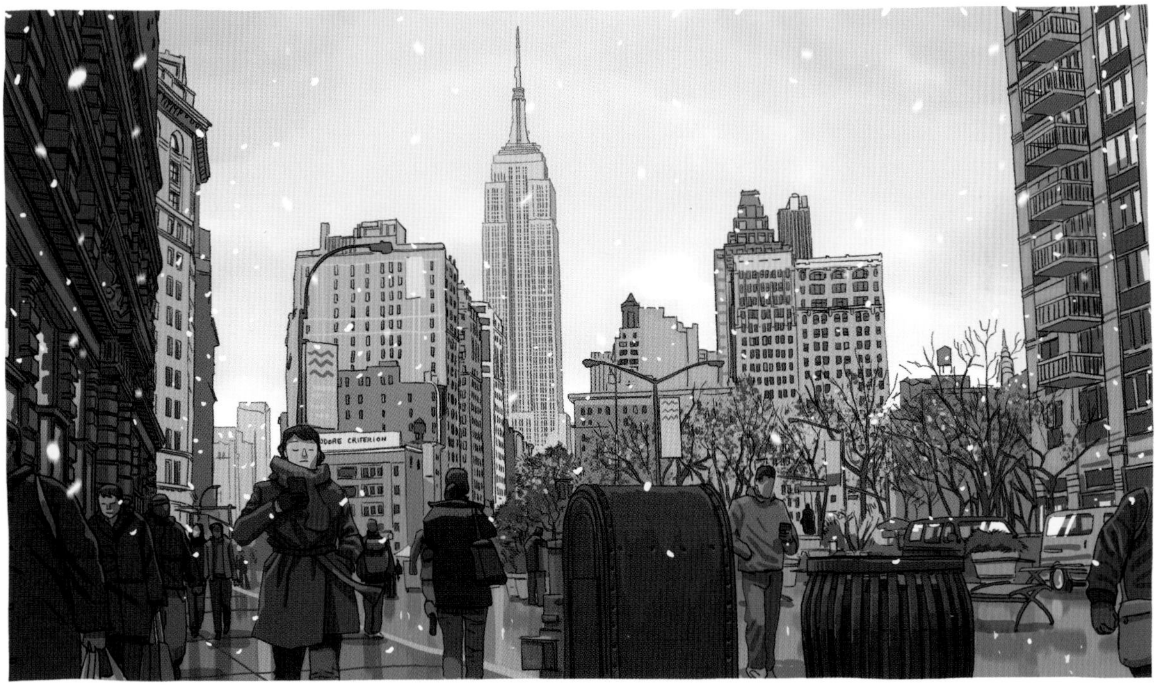
CRITERION

ONE, TWO, THREE, FOUR...

ONE, TWO, THREE, FOUR...

ONE, TWO...

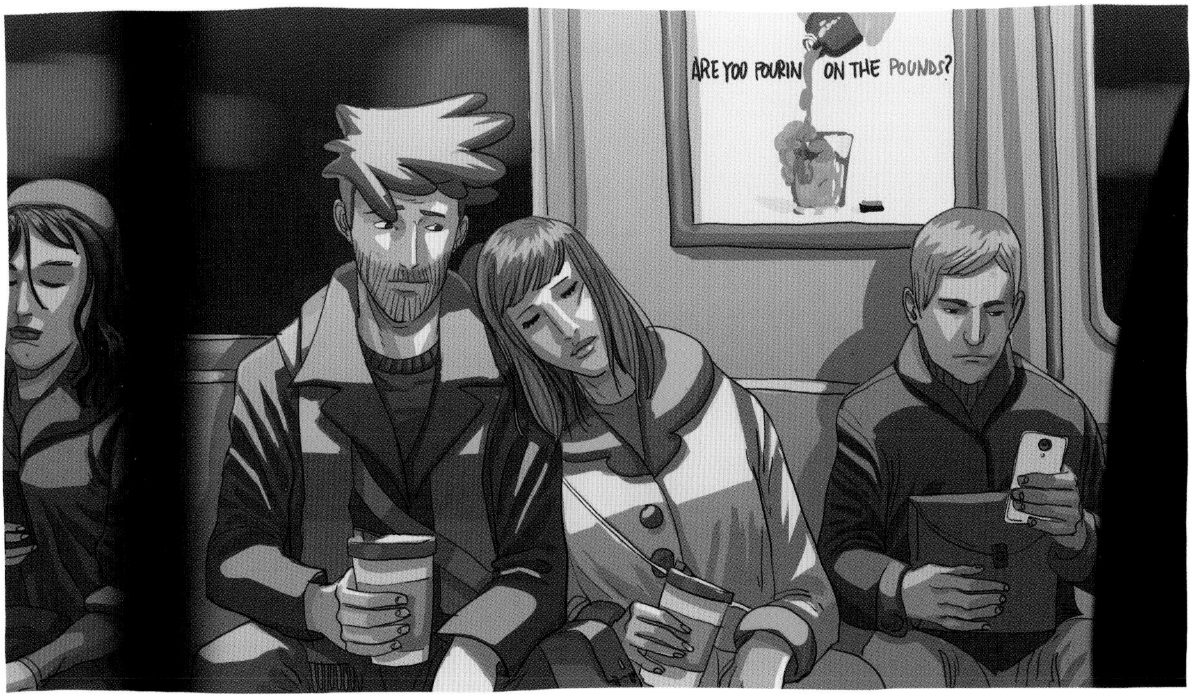
ARE YOU POURIN ON THE POUNDS?

THREE

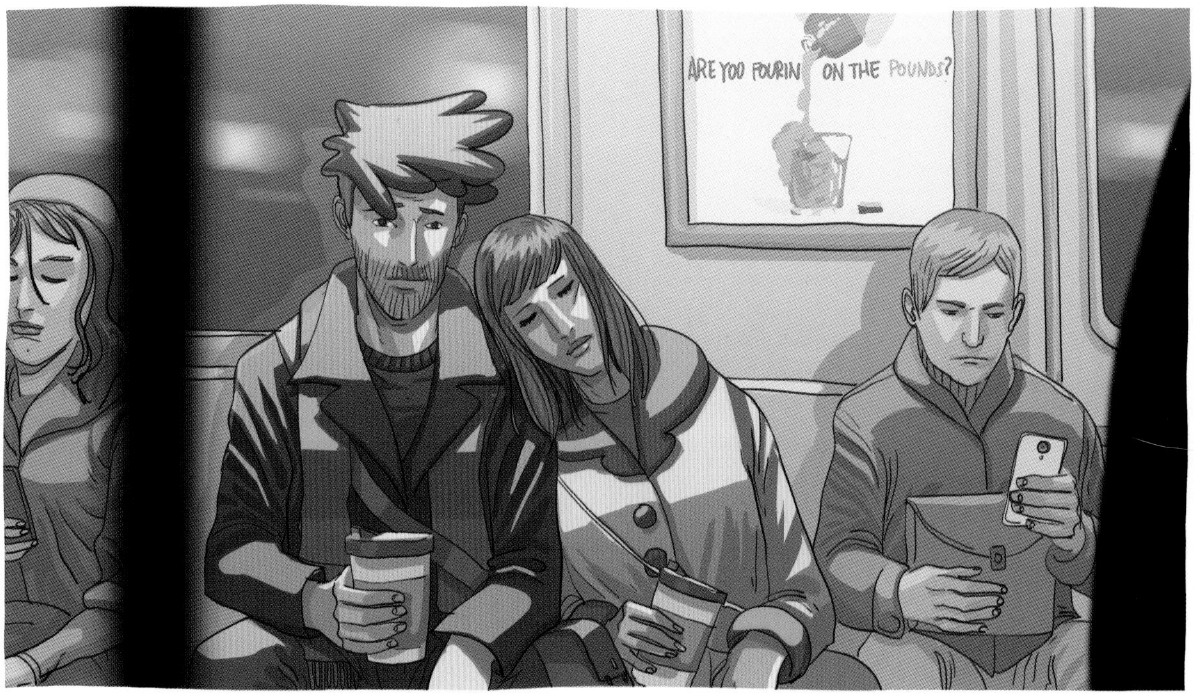
ARE YOU POURIN ON THE POUNDS?

FOUR.